CODES

RANDOM EVOLUTION VS. DIVINE DESIGN

Book 3 of The Machine or Man Apologetics Series
HENRY PATIÑO

Isaiah 44:6 Psalm 24:1
(Gebo Wunjo Othala – Chi Rho Owns Earth)

Areli Media

Codes
Random Evolution vs. Divine Design
Book 3 of The Machine or Man Apologetics Series
Copyright © 2019 by Henry Patiño
Published by Areli Media

Photo credits: PA Images/Alamy Stock Photo (119)

ISBN-10: 0-9962441-6-6
ISBN-13: 978-0-9962441-6-9
eISBN-10: 0-9962441-9-0
eISBN-13: 978-0-9962441-9-0

Special Sales: Most Areli Media titles are available in special quantity
discounts. Custom imprinting or excerpting can also be done to fit special
needs. Contact Areli Media.

TABLE OF CONTENTS

Chapter 1: What Is Life?   1
   Reductionists and Vitalists   5
   Meaning and Self-Awareness   17
   Cause and Effect in a Closed System   30
   The Dysteleological Illusion   40
   Reason or Rationalization   53
   Personhood and Deocentric Valuation   57
   The Myth of Simplicity   60

Chapter 2: Supersymmetry in the Microworld   63
   Amino Acids and Proteins   77
      The Gene Expression System   85
      The Transcription Process   87
      The Translation of Two Separate Codes   91
      The Indispensible Role of Proteins in the Gene
      Expression System   95
      Only 20 Sombreros?   97
   The Universal Riddle of the 20 Amino Acids   99
      The Unfolding Miracle of Folding   103
   The Problem of Sequence Specificity: The Protein Code   107
   The Riddle of the Left-Handed Amino Acids   112

Chapter 3: Codes Are the Product of a Mind   117
   The DNA Language   117
      Breaking the Code   121
      The Translation of the Codes   127
   Who Came First, the Chicken or the Egg?   134
   Chemical Serendipity   142
      The Miracle of Life from Light   144

Chapter 4: Is There a Chance for Chance?   **149**
    The 14 Concessions   160
    Not Enough Time, Not Enough Matter   164
    The Symmetry between the Universe and Life   172

Chapter 5: The Evolutionary Mechanisms Proposed for the
Evolution of the Living Cell   **177**
    Chemical Abiogenesis and Organic Compounds   178
        The Early Atmosphere Was Not a Reducing Atmosphere   181
        Synthesizing Progenitor Aggregates Is Light Years
        from Synthesizing a Living Cell   189
        The Need for a Metabolic Motor   191
    Affinity and Necessity as the Cause for Self-Organization   194
        Evolutionary Biochemical Predestination?   195
        Order Out of Chaos?   209
    The RNA World   214
        The Impotence of RNA   221
        RNA Mutants   226

Chapter 6: Evolution "Proved" by Computers?   **229**
    Ev is not Eve   237
    Avida's Vida Comes from the Intelligence of the Programmers   238

Chapter 7: The Evolution of Irreducible and Complex Organs:
  Darwin's Black Box   **243**
    The Evolutionary Riddle of the Eye   245
    The Irreducible Immune System   256
    The Tyranny of Paradigms   263
    Trash the Space Trash Theory   273
    Junk DNA and Vestigial Organs   279

Chapter 8: A Designer Must Exist   **285**
    Biomimetics and the Argument from Ignorance   296

References   **309**

Index   **313**

CHAPTER 1

●●●

WHAT IS LIFE?

I have stood on a mountaintop and looked as far as the eye could see on every side. Awestruck, with tears in my eyes at the unique beauty surrounding me, I marveled at the snow-capped, piercing ridges from horizon to horizon. It was an ocean of blue, misty mountains spread before me, filled with craggy canyons and towering cliffs.

My breast swelled with wonder at the rocky, jutting, pyramidal peaks enveloped by skirts of wispy white clouds. The cold wind caressed my face, and my skin tingled in the sunlight. The far-off sounds of cowbells wafted in the breeze, rising from the rich green meadows in the Swiss Alpine valleys below.

At first, I sensed a deep solitude, but as my eyes focused beyond the grand scheme, it became apparent that life was all about me. Tall, steep rocky cliffs towered into the clouds and then burst through them higher in the sky. And yet along this sheer granite face, trees clung desperately, rooting into the crags. *In every place we look, life clings tenaciously*, I thought.

High above, two eagles soared effortlessly, gliding on thermal currents and weaving their way across the blue. Their shrieks echoed in the canyons. Beyond the tree line, moss clung to shady crags, and small creatures scurried from boulder to boulder behind me. *Life abounds even in these altitudes,* I thought.

We can also look into the deep forests with their tall canopies that shroud the ground far below. The rains there come in buckets, and the rivers swell to swamp the land during the rainy season. Look under the canopy, and life abounds. Look at the soft loam covered with leaves, and life abounds. Look into the rivers and lagoons, and life abounds.

We can look in the polar regions and see worlds of ice, unrelenting cold, endless snow, frozen seas, bitter winds, and darkness that hides the sun for months. Yet life clings stubbornly there, too. We can look into the deepest oceans, miles below the surface in deep darkness and bone-crushing pressure. We see superheated water rising in smokers like erupting little volcanoes that would boil a lobster in temperatures reaching 700 degrees Fahrenheit. And yet life abounds there, too.

In Yellowstone National Park, we can look inside acid lakes with boiling water made by the brooding fire of the cauldrons hiding beneath the ground. We can look at low places of the Earth like Death Valley, where the temperature soars to a searing 120 degrees Fahrenheit. It matters not where you look—life flourishes on our magnificent blue planet.

We can look across the desert dunes at endless undulating waves of sands like slow-motion snakes, ever shifting with the wind. There is a deep silence in the desert for which words could never hope to give justice. For those raised with the ever ambient clatter of whooshing cars, horns, sirens, and other city sounds, which we often subconsciously ignore, the loudness of the stark silence is beyond measure. But even for those like me who were raised on farms or in the countryside, it is also drastic beyond comparison.

There are no cows mooing in the distance with their bells echoing against the mountains. There are no dogs barking from afar, no roosters crowing, no horses neighing, no tractors plowing, no birds singing in the trees. This all-pervasive surrealistic silence in the desert swallows us whole and forces upon us an appreciation for life in the midst of such challenging conditions.

The temperatures during the day bake you; at night, they freeze you. How can such harshness be filled with such unrelenting beauty? How could life survive in such extremes? And yet, in the vastness of drifting sand, life still thrives. The thought came to me: *What power life has that it can adapt to survive in such demanding extremes. How did this powerful force we call life begin?*

I sat on the sand one night and looked up at the star-filled sky. It is unlike any experience you can imagine—almost spiritual. *So many stars*, I thought. *Stars that cannot be seen by the glare of city lights come out to greet the traveler in the desert.*

We cannot but wonder how unique life is in the midst of so many worlds that inhabit our universe. There are no words that can describe the wonder of so many stars. I thought of those many stars, each an engine of nuclear power unimaginable, billions in every one of the trillions of galaxies. I thought, *What awesome force could have contained all the power of this entire universe in a singularity smaller than the size of an atom?*

In this immense universe, which every second continually expands with mounting acceleration, what are humans but insignificant specks? Are we just the accidental children of stars? Are we simply stardust, as Sagan often said in his *Cosmos* series? Are we alone, hurtling heedlessly through space and time on this spaceship we call our blue planet, the third rock from the sun? How did it all begin?

Life. How marvelous life is! How resilient it is in spite of the adversity of the many harsh conditions that abound on our planet. I marvel at how diverse the life forms are that inhabit the many wide and challenging conditions. How did this universe and life come to be? It occurred to me that the mystery of life is the central mystery of humankind.

What is life? We can observe that some things are alive and others are not. But in spite of all the advancements in biochemistry, we have yet to isolate any chemical reaction or basic chemical compound that can be credited with causing that intrinsic property we recognize as *life*.

Life has shown itself to be stubbornly irreducible to mere chemical reactions. The discovery of DNA and the language of its code, as well as the language of the protein code, have produced even more questions than answers. DNA is the language of the gene-expression system in life, but it is not life itself. Advancements in our technology continue to reveal in ever-increasing magnitude that life is more mysterious and complicated than the modern mind ever imagined.

Nevertheless, some continue to believe that life can be reduced to molecular reactions. Ontological reductionism proposes that life and all other things in this universe can be ultimately reduced to particles and forces. The vast majority of evolutionary-minded biologists are reductionists. The naturalist worldview sees life as simply an evolutionary continuum rising from non-life through random serendipity. Life, in their view, is simply an evolutionary adaptation of lifeless matter. Hence, there is no significant difference in value between the two.

> *Life is only a special and complicated property of matter, and ...* au fond *[basically] there is no difference between a living organism and lifeless matter (Ponnamperuma 337).*

This then is the central question of humankind: Did life happen as a fortuitous accident of the cosmos, or was it designed with purpose and meaning? Is life nothing more than sophisticated lifeless stardust? In one form or another, this question has been asked by people since the very dawn of time.

Reductionists and Vitalists

Since the time of the ancient Greeks, many scientists believed in abiogenesis, or spontaneous generation; that is, life could spontaneously generate from non-living matter. Aristotle was convinced, for example, that aphids arose from the dew that falls on plants and that maggots appeared from rotting flesh.

The influence of the Judeo-Christian worldview in Western culture brought a different perspective. It claimed that life was created by a personal God who exists outside and beyond, unfettered by our space-time continuum. But many in the scientific community still held to the abiogenic synthesis of life. The passage from non-living to living was considered a mystery that would eventually be answered as we grew in knowledge about life and in our ability to use technology. Time would eventually reveal the segue that would explain this transition in naturalistic terms.

In 1665, with the aid of the microscope, Robert Hooke published the first drawings of microorganisms. The microscope opened up the microcosmic world for investigation for the first time in human history. Antonie van Leeuwenhoek followed, describing tiny organisms such as protozoa and bacteria. An entire unseen universe could now be seen with human eyes.

The proponents of spontaneous generation saw this accomplishment as scientific evidence for abiogenesis. Motivated by their presuppositional desire to do away with a Creator who could hold man morally accountable, many sought some natural and purely physical solution to the genesis of life. Peering through the microscope, the pervasive nature of these microorganisms seemed to be the evidence they needed for their preferred theory of abiogenesis.

However, in 1668, Francesco Redi dealt the first blow against their newfound hope. He proved that maggots did not spontaneously arise from rotting meats when flies were physically prevented from laying eggs on the meat.

The proponents of abiogenesis then temporarily acceded that in higher organisms, spontaneous generation may not occur, but they continued to insist that it did occur in microorganisms. Our inability to appreciate the complexity of these microorganisms due to our limited technology fueled the concept that spontaneous generation could easily create simple organisms. The term *simple-celled organism* became an accepted biological description of these tiny living organisms.

In 1768, Lazzaro Spallanzani demonstrated that these tiny microorganisms were also pervasive in the air. But in his experiments, he also proved that they could be killed by boiling. Following in the footsteps of Spallanzani, Louis Pasteur finally put to rest the argument. In his experiments, he showed that microorganisms do not spontaneously arise in sterile, although nutrient-rich media. He said their colonization depended on exterior intrusions and not on some natural form of abiogenesis.

The vitalist argument that life could only come from life seemed to have a momentary victory, but all of that was about to change. In 1828, German chemist Freidrich Wöhler mixed silver isocyanate with ammonium chloride and was completely surprised to find that the yellow substance in his flask was urea.

During that time, scientists who held to the vitalist theory incorrectly claimed that organic substances found in living organisms could not be synthesized outside of living things. Wöhler proved that not all organic substances are made in living things. There are natural processes that can create organic compounds. In fact, not all organic compounds are found in living things. An organic compound is a compound that is made up principally of carbon and may contain other elements such as oxygen, nitrogen, hydrogen, phosphorous, and even other elements. All living things are made of organic compounds, but all organic compounds are not found in living things; hence, there are many organic compounds that have nothing to do with living things.

Nevertheless, the fact that urea, an organic compound, could be synthesized greatly discredited the vitalists and gave fresh wind to the sails of reductionists. If urine could be made in a laboratory, then the idea that all living chemistry could be duplicated by simple chemical processes seemed feasible. The reductionist worldview took hold with great force in the scientific community as a result of this simple discovery. Charles Darwin also provided a great wind for their sails. The Darwinist idea that through small gradual changes non-living matter could form simple organisms became plausible. Our ignorance of the unimaginable complexity of even the smallest single-celled organism helped greatly to convince many.

We must interject here that without any reservation, humankind will, in due time, achieve the goal of reproducing any chemical compound found in living things. Even through recombinant gene splicing, humans may create a new form of life as a hybrid of another living organism. They may create cyborgs, which are living things comprised of some robotic components. They may even forestall death for a limited time with bioengineering. They may, through the science of recombinant gene splicing, even produce chimera— part human, part animal creatures. They may clone human beings, a technology that is almost upon us, although not perfected.

But in spite of our incredibly sophisticated modern technology, we do not have the power to produce a living being from non-living matter. We may be able to grow organs and perhaps one day an entire human body in a laboratory, but we cannot produce the person behind the brain. We cannot, from the impersonal composite of chemicals, arrive at personhood. Moreover, any achievement of this kind could take place only by beginning with already living tissue. No organs have ever been created from non-living matter.

The reductionist claims that personhood is simply an illusion created by the electrical synapses in the brain. Of course, that is not a scientific fact proved by any empirical evidence. It is a subjective belief that stems entirely from an underlying naturalistic presupposition. In other words, it is simply a metaphysical belief.

It may be that some day in the distant future, someone will be able to grow a brain in a laboratory. The brain is like an organic computer. But I do not think that the hardware of that organic computer will be able to produce the software that runs it.

It is the spirit of humankind that gives us our identity, our dignity, our intrinsic rights as an infinitely valuable being created in the image of God. The scriptures tell us that God took the raw elements of this Earth (the hardware) and breathed into it the spirit of life, and humans became living souls. The source of life is God. Life is the fingerprint of God's handiwork. The soul is the persona, while the spirit is the person, the software that commands its host. The body is simply the hardware that houses the software that runs it.

In essence, this is the argument between the vitalists and the naturalists. Vitalists believe that in order to have life, we must first begin with life. It is prophesied in the New Testament that one day, during the darkest night of humankind, people will be able to create a humanoid life form, but it will not be done through a human agency alone (Rev. 13:15). It will be accomplished for the sole purpose of legitimizing the rule of the Antichrist. In that day, the nations will be deceived by the power of sorcery (Rev. 18:23). Humankind will claim to have developed life from the non-living, but it will not be so; that demonic plan will be aided by the supernatural power of demonic spirits.

The purpose of this book is to explore which of these two arguments—vitalism or naturalism—is true. Today, we are just beginning to understand the sheer complexity of the very basic components of the living cell. The multifaceted, multidimensional structure of even the protein is, from an engineering point of view, a miraculous structure of unprecedented complexity. After decades of trying to create a single protein through natural random chemical processes in countless labs around the world, humans have utterly failed. Nevertheless, even if someone were to succeed in creating a protein or even the more complex DNA molecule from non-living material, all it would prove is that without intelligence, it could not have been done.

Random, undirected processes cannot produce that level of specified complexity, as we will see later. Moreover, the enormous gap between synthesizing a protein or the more complex DNA molecule and the act of creating a living cell is many light years removed from one another.

To the reductionist or naturalist, there is no difference between the living and the non-living. To naturalists, life is merely an accident in the cosmos. They reason that since all elements that comprise our bodies are created through the nuclear processes of stars, a person is regarded simply as a child of stardust.

The late Carl Sagan popularized the idea that we are the children of stardust. Holding to his evolutionary and pantheistic worldview, he also popularized the idea that the universe was cyclical and had been created and destroyed many times. During the intermediary process-es between the Big Bang and the Big Crunch, the nuclear processes within various-sized stars were then responsible for the formation of the higher elements seeded throughout the universe by their even-tual explosions. These chemicals, according to the gradualist model, through gravitational attraction, eventually coalesced into planets and, through accidental and random reactions, eventually evolved into human life. And thus Sagan's famous quote, which he used in the introduction to the *Cosmos* series: "We are made of star stuff."

But I think he is way off the mark. To begin with, modern science has learned conclusively that our universe is expanding outward at an increasing rate proportional to the distance from us. This is called the Hubble Constant. There can be no collapse of the universe because it is traveling too fast and too far for gravity to contract it. There simply isn't enough mass in the entire universe to reverse the expansion rate. That was settled with the evidence of the three mapping satellites of the cosmic microwave background radiation. Sagan's idea that the universe underwent a cyclical collapse and explosion has been proven false.

Furthermore, I think the scientific evidence favors the biblical notion that we are, in fact, children of light and not stardust. From the chaos of the Genesis Singularity, the first thing created was a photon, the basic component of all electromagnetic radiation. It is from light that all things in our universe were made.

From the first record we have of our ancestors, light has been a central mystery. What is strange is that the more we learn about light, the more mysterious it becomes. It is an almost otherworldly thing. It does not behave as ordinary matter, and yet without it, we could not exist. Not only do we depend on it to be able to observe the world around us, but it is also through its peculiar property that the chain of life can even exist. It is an exotic element of our universe upon which all visible reality has been built.

> Indeed, as we are about to see, science and the Bible agree that light belongs to an altogether unique category of reality. It is exceedingly exotic and operates on a privileged plane of existence that we ourselves can never experience—at least not in this life (Guillen 71).

The scriptures align with modern science in declaring that radiant energy was, in fact, the first thing formed in our universe, and from it came all others. This remarkable fact shows that the more we learn about our universe, the more science backs up the Genesis creation story. In fact, light in the scriptures is used to symbolize God. And certainly, the properties of light do offer insight into the nature of

God, who is in a timeless state and whose character is invariable and independent of anything within this material universe.

> *This is the message we have heard from Him and announce to you, that God is Light, and in Him there is no darkness at all (I John 1:5 NASB).*

> *I am the LORD, and there is no other;*
> *Besides Me, there is no God.*
> *I will gird you, though you have not known Me;*
> *That men may know from the rising to the setting of the sun*
> *That there is no one besides Me.*
> *I am the LORD, and there is no other,*
> The One forming light and creating darkness,
> *Causing well-being and creating calamity;*
> *I am the Lord who does all these (emphasis added) (Isa. 45: 5–7 NASB).*

> *Then Jesus again spoke to them, saying, "I am the Light of the world; he who follows Me will not walk in the darkness, but will have the Light of life" (John 8:12 NASB).*

It is from God's radiant energy that our universe was created. Light is in a timeless state; the past, present, and future are united in light. Although we may not be able to completely comprehend this, it does not mean that it isn't so. I find it amusing that one of the reasons atheists have rejected God since the time of the Enlightenment was mainly because they thought nothing could exist outside time. In their narrow minds, that was nothing more than mythological superstition.

> *For light itself—which travels at 100 percent the speed of light—time slows to a complete stop. Time*

doesn't flow. Time doesn't exist. Light and light alone inhabits a realm where past, present, and future have no meaning because the three exist all together and at once (Guillen 75).

Neither could the atheists have imagined then that modern physics would verify the Genesis record in declaring that light was the first act of creation and all things after came from that light.

In principle, light can be transformed into ordinary matter—even flesh and blood.

These two possibilities are not merely theoretical. Nowadays, scientists can and do make them happen repeatedly and without much effort. The two processes are called "pair annihilation" and "pair creation."

In pair annihilation, an electron collides head-on with a positron, its antiparticle. Result? The two particles—the two tardyons—annihilate and become light. In pair creation, light collides with light. Result? The light disappears and rematerializes in the form of two tardyons—an electron and positron.

Taken together, the two discoveries science has made about light are truly extraordinary. The first— that light is in a realm by itself—is amazing enough. But the second—that light and ordinary matter are somehow interchangeable—is positively mind-blowing (Guillen 76).

In fact, within our human frame of reference, light, or to be more complete and accurate, electromagnetic energy, is the most accurate entity in our universe that can symbolize God. Not only did all matter come from light, but all living things also cannot survive without light. Yet it is not God. It is, according to scripture, an emanation of His glory. It was the first thing He brought forth into our universe to begin its transformation from a disordered state into a more ordered state.

The naturalist evolutionary model claims that the Genesis Singularity of the Big Bang came from nothing. It just magically appeared from nothing. In other words, the claim is that nothing instantaneously became everything. There is no empirical evidence that can prove that this actually happened. That view is simply a metaphysical choice that stems directly from naturalistic presupposition. It is the same faith-based choice reflected in the idea of abiogenesis. It is, in fact, an irrational faith. If all that existed was nothing, nothing could come of it. There would still be nothing.

The Judeo-Christian cosmological model is, in contrast, rational. It was God's radiant energy at the Alpha Point that was converted into plasma and then into the more complex forms of the elements to bring forth our physical universe. But initially, within the dense plasma cloud, the density of the matter was such that it obscured the light within it. When the expansion of space-time reached a certain point, light escaped. The precise point at which light broke forth from the darkness of matter and separated marked the first period of creation—day one—as recorded in Genesis.

How is it that the Genesis record, written more than 3,000 years ago, stipulates that God separated the light from the darkness, giving us a vivid description of the process modern physics has discovered in the separation of light from the dense plasma state only recently?

It may also surprise you to find out that we are also beings of light. Our bodies radiate photons continuously. The wavelength is too long for us to see because it is in the infrared spectrum, but if you looked through an infrared camera, you would see a person in the blackest of darkness. We literally glow with infrared light. I worked as a firefighter for the city of Miami Beach for almost 30 years, and I often used these infrared cameras. They were quite useful in finding a struggling swimmer in the surf at night. They also helped us find hot spots in the darkness of smoke to prevent rekindling.

It is worth mentioning again that our Judeo-Christian Cosmological Model is not in accordance with the pantheistic model, which suggests that the creation and the deity are one and the same thing. In the Judeo-Christian model, God was before creation, and the creation is not God but merely the clay with God as the potter. God, who is not trapped in space-time, created space-time and all that is contained in it.

Naturalists are prone to prefer very slow, gradual processes, because the longer the time available, the more plausible it becomes for them to imagine small, randomly generated changes accumulating into big changes. But it was not the death of stars that led to the creation of planets and life on Earth through the slow, gradual evolutionary model based on gravity accretion. It was the electromagnetic force that created matter through Birkeland currents. In plasma, Birkeland currents can create matter almost instantaneously.

It was God who formed the Earth through His electromagnetic power. In fact, I suspect that God may also have created DNA through some form of electromagnetic power since its double helix shape is very similar to the shapes of the Birkeland currents. It was not a random accident but an intentional design. We can see the similarities between the spiral DNA and the spiral helixes of filamentary matter created by the Birkeland currents in the cosmos. (See *Supersymmetry or Chaos*, the second book in this series, for a more complete understanding of the role of Birkeland currents in the creation of matter.)

No, we are not the children of the gradualist gravity model of evolving stardust. Do not be deceived by empty words meant to draw us from the Creator. Yes, we were fashioned from clay, but we were molded by God's light and given the *neshama* (spirit) of God that sparked life into us. And for this reason, we are called children of light.

Let no one deceive you with empty words, for because of these things the wrath of God comes upon the sons of disobedience. Therefore do not be partakers with them; for you were formerly darkness, but now you are Light in the Lord; walk as children of Light (Eph. 5:6–8 NASB).

Is life really the product of impersonal forces guided only by random processes? The philosophical implications of reductionism have great consequences in our social interrelationships. Does human life have any higher significance if life is but an accidental progression from non-life?

In opposition to the naturalist claim, the Judeo-Christian Cosmological Model claims that life is more than chemicals. Living things are made of matter, but not just matter. They are imbued with something special that cannot be explained in material terms—a vital force. The Judeo-Christian worldview sees life emanating from the spirit, which God breathed into the body of the first human to make him a living soul. Reductionists have caricatured this as a mystical cop-out since this ethereal vital force at the present time is untestable and defies any scientific definition.

That may be so, but it seems that evolutionists are a bit schizophrenic about their evolutionary doctrines. They tell us that anything untestable is not real, and yet they believe in multiple universes, which they cannot test. Moreover, reductionists have been unable to explain life in chemical terms. They cannot explain a thought in chemical terms, much less life. The fact is that they are completely deficient when it comes to a real explanation for or a definition of life. However, that does not mean that thoughts do not exist or that life does not exist.

At best, evolutionists' crude attempts to define life result only in definitions of the characteristics of life and not life itself. When a biologist describes life, he or she resorts to three main characteristics that are observable in our earthly temporal existence: respiration, metabolism, and replication. But these are merely descriptions of living functions.

Some describe life with as many as six characteristics, but all of them fail to describe life itself. They are merely observed characteristics that evidence life, but they are not intrinsically life itself. The glaring problem for evolutionists is that reductionism has failed to provide a testable chemical equation for life. And for this reason, many biology textbooks do not even attempt to do so anymore.

The irony of it all is that the very definition of biology is "the scientific study of life," and yet under naturalistic presuppositions, there is no clear definition of life itself. How strange it is to establish an entire branch of naturalistic science based on the study of a subject the originators cannot even define.

Some try to escape this conundrum by simply stating that life is the time between birth, or hatching, and death. But, again, this is not a definition of life but rather the measurement of time in which this cryptic process takes place.

The Judeo-Christian worldview maintains that beyond the entity we call *life* is yet another entity called *personhood*. Within each of us, we have millions of living cells, but are we only the sum total of the lives of those cells? The donated eye of a person who dies in an accident is still alive when it is transplanted into a blind person. But there are not two persons looking through that eye, no matter how many movies claim otherwise.

There is no change in the personhood of an individual who has foreign tissue in his or her body. A transplanted heart or liver does not affect the person behind the brain. That person's identity remains the same, even when parts of other human beings are grafted into his or her body.

We are not just the sum total of the living cells within our body. As a matter of fact, our bodies change almost completely several times during our lifetimes. That is, most of the cells in the body will die and be replaced with new ones. We do not change our identity every time most of our cells are replaced. Our "self" is something other than the collective entity of our cells or the processes of mere respiration, metabolism, and replication.

We have been able to keep tissue alive artificially for years. Through respirators, we have even kept human bodies alive after the individual residing within the body seems to have departed. So it is logical to suppose that the characteristics of life are merely external observations displayed by an internal reality, which we cannot reduce to equations.

Our identity is the person behind the brain. The brain is the instrument that allows each person to be expressed. If the instrument is damaged, the person behind the brain may not be able to express, but that does not necessarily preclude the possibility that that person is still there. There are countless examples of individuals being in deep comas for extended periods of time who have become conscious again.

Meaning and Self-Awareness

The problem for evolutionists is that the implications of their presuppositions do not accurately reflect the way humans are. What definition stemming from a naturalistic worldview could be used to separate the worth of a person from the rest of living things? Can we find a higher meaning in a naturalistic reality? The pure reductionists say no, but they cannot live consistently with this view, as we'll see later. Some naturalists shy away from the stark implications of their fundamental worldview and try to build a value system from a void.

Self-awareness, say some, is what gives our lives value. But is it really the act of being conscious that gives us worth? Are humans who are in a coma not endowed with human value and dignity? Just what is self-awareness? Is it the existentialist mantra *I think, therefore I am*?

Usually, the plant kingdom is referred to as unconscious. Is consciousness a state in which living things can sense their environment? Certain flowers sense darkness and close their petals, while others sense darkness and open them to permeate the night air with their delicate perfume. Some plants, like the Venus flytrap, react to touch and close their trapping structures, digesting their insect victims. Others close their leaves when touched. These are automatically triggered responses to certain external stimuli. Are they not sensing? Does not an amoeba sense food when it extends a pseudopod to deliberately surround and engulf its prey?

But we suppose that these living organisms are not capable of "knowing" that they are living things. Does a chimpanzee know it is alive? Does it not seek to preserve its life when threatened? Does a dog know it is alive? It seems to me that self-awareness is too limited a term to explain the human experience. How can we know that animals are not self-aware?

Is consciousness the ability to reason? Reason is the ability to rationally consider one choice over another. Does a mosquito reason when the sun is so hot outside that it should hide under the shade of leaves? Is a mosquito conscious of life? How do we know that a mosquito is not self-aware? Rats certainly seem to be self-aware. They are quite intelligent creatures, able to learn and remember past mistakes. In fact earthworms also learn from previous mistakes. What, then, is the difference between a rat or an earthworm and a human?

And if reasoning is the measure of value, then it stands to reason that those who can reason best are more valuable than those who cannot. Can we differentiate between the intrinsic worth of two humans based on their intelligence (ability to reason)? Certainly this was proposed by the eugenics movement that attempted to integrate the Darwinian worldview with societal standards.

Anyone familiar with the works of Margaret Sanger cannot deny that her greatest motivation was to herald the liberation of women from sexual mores, which she considered regressive and repressive modes of morality built on the mythological belief in God.

> *Most of us know Margaret Sanger as an early champion of birth control, but not everyone knows that she also wrote several books expounding a complete worldview. Sanger was a committed Darwinist, a champion of Social Darwinism and eugenics, which was very much in vogue in the early part of the 20th century. Her goal was to construct a "scientific" approach to sexuality based squarely on Darwinism.*
>
> *Sanger portrayed the drama of history as a struggle to free our bodies and minds from the constraints of morality—what she called the "cruel morality of self-denial and sin." She touted sexual liberation as "the only method" to find "inner peace and security and beauty." She even offered it as the way to overcome social ills: "Remove the constraints and prohibitions which now hinder the release of inner energies [her euphemism for sexual energies], [and] most of the larger evils of society will perish."*
>
> *Finally, Sanger offered this sweeping messianic promise: "Through sex, mankind will attain the great spiritual illumination which will transform the world, and light up the only path to an earthly paradise"* (Pearcey 143).

That Darwinian social liberation has come at a high price. Selfishness always inevitably sheds blood. Since the *Roe v. Wade* decision in 1973, America has aborted about 55 million human beings. And that number reflects only the ones that have been reported. The number of unborn human beings killed by Planned

Parenthood, which Sanger founded, will never be known this side of heaven. But in that well-known *Book of Works* of the celestial kingdom, Sanger will take her place next to Hitler, Genghis Khan, Mao Tse-tung, Muhammad, and Stalin for her complicity in the shedding of innocent blood.

Beyond the chaos created in the family structures affected by this "sexual liberation," there are grave political consequences. The literalists' and fundamentalists' interpretation of the Darwinian ideology of the survival of the fittest led them to suggest that we should give a national IQ test and proposed that those who scored below some subjectively chosen level should be sexually neutered. They intended to give evolution a push by advancing only the genes of the most intelligent members of our species.

You may say, "That will never happen here in America." Guess what? It already has. In *War Against the Weak*, Edwin Black's brilliant history of the American eugenics movement, he documents and chronicles this dark chapter of our American history. By the early 1900s, as a direct result of the rise in popularity of the evolutionary paradigm among educators and philosophers, most members of the American upper class had wholeheartedly embraced the philosophy of eugenics.

Its proponents were well financed by organizations such as the Carnegie Institute, which greatly facilitated the dissemination of their pernicious egalitarian doctrines. Consequently, this pseudo-scientific philosophy was thoroughly popularized throughout all levels of society, but especially the intelligentsia.

> [Black writes,] "They were supported by the best universities in America, endorsed by the brightest thinkers, financed by the richest capitalists."
>
> Instead of focusing primarily on promoting "good" marriages, early eugenicists like Charles Benedict Davenport vigorously promoted "negative eugenics,"

aimed at "redirecting human evolution" by legally preventing—by means of forced sterilizations—the "unfit" from reproducing. Toward this end, Black points out, "esteemed professors, elite universities, industrialists, and government officials," relying on biological rationales, unleashed a sterilization pogrom to cleanse the gene pool of the "feebleminded, the pauper class, the inebriate, criminals of all descriptions, including petty criminals ... epileptics, the insane, the constitutionally weak ... those predisposed to specific diseases, the deformed, and those with defective sense organs, that is, the deaf, blind, and mute."

By 1910, "eugenics was one of the most frequently referenced topics in the Reader's Guide *to* Periodic Literature." *In its boom years in the 1920s, eugenics became a serious, scientifically supported and influential social and political movement. Courses in eugenics were taught in more than 350 American universities and colleges, leading to widespread popular acceptance of its pernicious tenets. It was endorsed by more than 90% of high school biology textbooks. Eugenicist societies formed to promulgate and discuss the theory and academic eugenics journals sprouted. What is more, philanthropic foundations embraced the movement, financing research and policy initiatives. Many of the most notable political, cultural and arts figures of the era believed in it— including Theodore Roosevelt, Winston Churchill, George Bernard Shaw, Clarence Darrow, Helen Keller and Margaret Sanger—and their opinions could only reinforce the movement's popularity.*

Eugenics reached hurricane strength after the U.S. Supreme Court sanctioned forced sterilization as a public good in 1927. About 6,000 eugenic sterilizations took place in the United States between 1907 and 1927. By 1940, the number had climbed to nearly 36,000. By the time the practice ended in this country in the early 1970s, nearly 70,000 of our fellow Americans had undergone the operation, all under the mandate of law (Smith 107).

The mirroring of Hitler's Nazi ideology in America was simply a few years behind Germany. Had it not been for the public reaction to the Holocaust, as it became known after the end of World War II, our nation would have sunk into that mire much deeper and much more quickly. The tide is again turning toward the philosophy of Darwinian egalitarianism. The Progressive ideology is moving in the same direction. When a nation abandons its faith in God, pragmatism becomes its god.

The truth is that Sanger and Hitler were consistent with their underlying worldviews. If there is no God and the rule is the survival of the fittest, then eugenics and Nazi social policies are in line with the fundamental reality of the world. In order for our species to properly evolve, humankind must cull the inferior genes from our collective genetic pool.

Only the Judeo-Christian high view of humans stands against this momentous drive justified by the evolutionary mantra of the survival of the fittest. What definition stemming from a naturalistic worldview could be used to separate the worth of a human being from the rest of living things? Can we find a higher meaning in a naturalist reality?

Is our worth in our ability to communicate? Most animals have a rudimentary form of communication. We find this in animals living on the land and in the sea and air. They have distinct sounds to call their young or sound an alarm. Others show anger, and others show fear and submission. Chimpanzees have been taught to use sign language. Researchers, according to the prestigious journal *Science*, have now discovered that dogs understand human words. In an experiment using brain scans to study the brain activity of dogs, scientists became aware that dogs could actually understand human language.

> *Lead researcher Dr Attila Andics, of Eötvös Loránd University, Budapest, said: "During speech processing, there is a well-known distribution of labour in the human brain.*
>
> *"It is mainly the left hemisphere's job to process word meaning, and the right hemisphere's job to process intonation. The human brain not only separately analyses what we say and how we say it, but also integrates the two types of information, to arrive at a unified meaning.*
>
> *"Our findings suggest that dogs can also do all that, and they use very similar brain mechanisms."*
>
> *During the brain scans, the researchers spoke words like "good boy" and "well done" spoken with a praising intonation, the same words in a neutral voice and also words that were meaningless to them, like "however," in both intonations. The scans showed the dogs left brain tended to be activated when they heard words that were meaningful to them. This did not happen when they heard words they did not understand. The right hemisphere activated when they heard a praising intonation.*
>
> *But the reward centre of their brains—which responds to pleasurable sensations like being petted, having sex and eating nice food—was only activated when they heard praising words spoken in a praising intonation.*

"It shows that for dogs, a nice praise can very well work as a reward, but it works best if both words and intonation match," Dr Andics said.

*"So **dogs** not only tell apart what we say and how we say it, but they can also combine the two, for a correct interpretation of what those words really meant. This is very similar to what human brains do"* (Johnston).

My son Jason had a Red Nose Pit Bull named Jamma that understood at least 40 commands. He was an amazing dog. If Jason said, "Do you want to play?" Jamma would jump up and get one of his toys and wait by the backdoor to the yard. If Jason said, "Do you want to go for a walk?" Jamma would jump up, grab his leash, and wait for us by the front door.

The first time I met Jamma, Jason had him in the backyard. He said, "Sit, Jamma!" Jamma sat down, and Jason took out a toy and showed it to him. He then gave me the toy and said, "Go hide it somewhere in the house."

I went through the entire house trying to find a clever place to hide it. Finally I lifted the cap on the toilet tank in the upstairs bathroom and placed the toy on top of the float mechanism. Then I placed the cap back on. I went downstairs and out to the backyard and said. "Okay, I hid it."

Jason said to Jamma, "Go find the toy." Jamma took off through the house and went into every room smelling, until finally he came to the toilet and began to bark. He pushed up the cap of the tank with his nose and found the toy. I was utterly amazed. There is no doubt in my mind that Jamma understood many of the things we said to him.

It has become more apparent as we learn more about animals that they are capable of communicating in their own rudimentary language, through whatever peculiar noises or body gestures they are capable of producing. They can even understand our language in basic rudimentary commands. And yet they cannot write a book or a poem, or compose a symphony. Nor can they discover the laws that govern our universe. Of all the creatures that inhabit Earth, only humans can appreciate the complexities of nature.

It is unquestionable that the difference between an animal's rudimentary communication and a human's is immense, but does that mean that humans who communicate better than others have greater value? To accept our ability to communicate as the valuation principle means that not only the mute but also those with inferior capacities to communicate are genetic garbage that in a selective environment must be disposed of.

In fact, the naturalist cannot say that anything separates us in value from other animals without using the same criteria to differentiate between humans. The long-cherished ideals of equality and individual rights are contraposed to evolutionary Darwinism. There is no basis from which the naturalist could give all of humanity any meaning beyond that of an accidental biological machine.

There is a higher consciousness in humans, an intrinsic and universal transcendental need. It comes from the fact that humans alone, out of all the creatures in this world, have been created in God's image. People alone have the capacity to understand evil and good, not just dangers to their existence. Only humans have the capacity to use propositional, not emotional, language. Chimpanzee may warn of danger with certain sounds and gestures. They communicate in emotional language. Apes may show anger or fear with other specific noises and gestures, but they cannot fathom their origins or write poems or symphonies, or express their philosophical worldviews.

Humans alone, out of all the creatures in this world, possess a sense of destiny. We think of death and make elaborate plans to bury the body of our loved ones. We contemplate the origin of the universe and seek the face of God. In fact, all humans are inherently aware that there is a marked difference between human life and the rest of the animal kingdom, even when our brains say otherwise. We instinctively know it deep in our hearts. Why is that?

It is not being self-aware but rather possessing a higher consciousness that separates us from all other creatures. That higher consciousness is the expression of personhood. That personhood is the expression of our being made in the image of the person of God. That is why we can love.

Naturalists do not believe in personhood; they claim that personhood is an illusion created by the brain. They believe that the universal transcendent need expressed in humans is simply the result of a massive illusion, a trick of the brain.

They claim that we are nothing more than an advanced form of a primate. With the advancement of genetic technology, evolutionary scientists are keen to point out that primates differ very little from humans in their genetic makeup. And thus, they accentuate this commonality to endorse their evolutionary concept of our common heritage from an ancestral ape. But contrary to their evolutionary assumption, more research has shown that contrary to their initial hopes, the differences between humans and primates are much greater than their evolutionary paradigm had anticipated.

Although 98 percent of the two species' genes have identical gene sequences, they have been found to have surprisingly significant and widespread differences in the proteins produced by their genes. A group of international researchers led by Asao Fujiyama of RIKEN Genomic Sciences Center and the National Institute of Informatics found that the variations in the types of proteins produced by primates and humans are much greater than they had initially expected.

The problem for the evolutionist is that genetic compatibility does not necessarily mean there is a direct ancestral linkage. If that were so, we could see genetic compatibility in a straightforward relationship from the more ancient and simple organisms to the more advanced and developed ones. That is not the case in nature.

For instance, the earthworm and the fruit fly have 68 compatible genes. From an evolutionary standpoint, certainly the fruit fly is not far removed from the earthworm. There are 220 compatible genes between human beings and the earthworm. So according to this presupposition, human beings are actually closer to the earthworm than the fruit fly.

Each of these genes provides a particular function used by the Creator arbitrarily to form whatever organisms He desired. The use of these similar genes to create a desired objective shows that there was a single engineer, not that these organisms developed magically from one another.

Some may object to my use of the word *magically*, but since no mutation has ever been shown to transform one kind of organism into another, I cannot frame the evolutionary hypothesis in any other term and remain accurate.

The same is true for anatomical similarities. We may possess anatomical similarities with apes, but these do not imply a phylogenetic relationship. In other words, these anatomical similarities do not necessitate a familial interrelationship. They simply point to a single architect of life who chose to use these features in the enormous variability of His magnificent creation.

The evolutionist is eager to point out the similarities, but not so much the differences. Research in the anatomy of primates and the organs associated with speech has shown that they are not basically different from ours and that they therefore ought to be able to speak like we do. But they cannot. They can be taught a few commands with sign language, but they cannot speak as humans do. Although the intelligence of a chimpanzee may be comparable to that of a five-year-old human being, the chimpanzee cannot speak.

And the sounding out of words is not the most important issue. When I was younger, I worked at the Parrot Jungle in Miami. I was amazed at the words parrots could be taught. They certainly mimicked the sounds of our words, but they had no idea what those words meant. They simply repeated the sounds.

I can tell you that these parrots all had an individual personality and impressive intelligence, but they could not carry on a conversation about abstract things such as the appearance of the constellations in the stars, the beauty of flowers, or the injustice of bigotry. These are the sole domain of personhood. Only persons—beings made in the image of God—have the ability of propositional speech rich in abstract thinking.

Naturalists assumed that speech was instinctual. They presumed that our brain evolved into such an advanced stage that speech simply was an inevitable by-product of our intelligence. But it is not that we just have a greater capacity to reason that gives us speech. My children and grandchildren were speaking between the ages of two and three, and yet chimpanzees, which, according to naturalists, have the intelligence of a five-year old, cannot speak.

We also have instances of feral children brought up entirely in the wild who have just as much intelligence as other children, and yet they never learned to speak a single word, even when two of them were raised together. Some of them, after receiving intense help, later learned to speak, but always with limitations. It seems that speech is learned from other human beings at the earliest stages of life. How, then, did the first human begin to speak?

I am convinced that Adam learned to speak because he spoke to God in the cool of the garden. The Living Word is the author of propositional language, and the scriptures are a record of that propositional truth.

So we see that at the heart of these questions rages the battle between two competing worldviews: naturalism and Judeo-Christianity. Each worldview provides a model through which our universe and life are explained. An objective analysis of both views must consider how each one measures up against observable, testable reality.

Naturalism claims that everything in the universe has evolved through impersonal, random, undirected, purposeless, chemical serendipity within a closed matrix of chaos. The similarities among all living things are seen as evidence of their common heritage produced by the evolution of the species through natural selection. All operations in the naturalist worldview are ruled strictly by cause and effect, without need for teleology or purpose.

There can be no such thing as transcendental significance in a universe created by impersonal random forces. Reality is simply the sum total of chaotic and meaningless chemical reactions. Beginning with the impersonal, we cannot arrive at anything other than the impersonal.

Reality = chaotic impersonal matter/energy
x space-time x chance.

In a closed system in which there is no God, humans are merely stardust, and there is no valuing framework from which any higher significance can be given to one evolved entity over another. There is basically no difference between the value of an infant of the *Homo sapiens* and a lump of inanimate rock.

There can be no higher meaning in a world created by impersonal forces operating through random, disordered chemical reactions. All things are ultimately sameness if they evolved from a single singularity without purposeful prevision and design. There can be no differentiation between one form of the product of the impersonal forces of evolution and another. With naturalism, we are left with a monism of quite stark social implications.

In such a world, there can be no right or wrong, no good or evil, no just or unjust, no lawful or unlawful, no true or false—all is ultimately sameness. What is, is. What is has come to be through a purposeless, linear cause-and-effect process by which chance becomes the deciding factor of the direction of the evolution of the universe and all it contains.

Cause and Effect in a Closed System

The primary foundational assumption of naturalism is that our universe is, in fact, a closed system in which there can be no external influence from any divine or extraneous source. Therefore, all processes in our entire universe run on random chemical reactions ruled by the principle of linear cause and effect.

This worldview, which has been largely accepted as the operating norm in our Western culture, has its roots in the Enlightenment, when people rejected all religious traditions, myths, or dogmas of any type and chose reason as their guiding force. Faith and reason were seen as antithetical options.

The historical truth is that self-serving papal dogmas and the flagrant corruption of the church-state apparatus filled the known world with myths and useless traditions that marred the cause of truth and filled the coffers in Rome with gold. Reason could bow to no authority other than "facts." Certainly, we can empathize with this logic. I certainly do.

But as is often the case in history, people swing from one side of the pendulum to the other and fall off the opposite cliff. In rejecting all traditions, no matter how venerated, they threw out truth, no matter how rational. By automatically ruling out the existence of the supernatural, they threw out the baby with the bathwater. This choice was without reason. It was a metaphysical choice based on subjective preference and not on rational consideration. It was an attempt to do away altogether with the idea that there are moral imperatives. It was a choice based not on reason but on sheer antagonism toward any moral absolutes.

By automatically dismissing God as the universal that unifies all truth, they removed the very basis that makes reason valid. A universe without God has no foundation for reason to exist, nor can it be a universal from which truths are ascertained. A universe birthed in chaos and guided by randomness cannot bring forth a consistent, rational universal for anything other than chaos.

People were right to choose reason as a guiding light; for that purpose, God created humans who can reason and said, "Come now, and let us reason together" (Isa. 1:18 NASB). Reason leads to truth, and the ultimate truth is not in opposition to reason. Reason is the path that brings us to the door of truth. But reason alone cannot bring us into the lap of truth. People must be willing to receive the truth before obtaining it. In the end, it requires a step of faith. Reason leads to faith in the truth. Reason is not opposed to faith. But faith in reason alone cannot provide us with truth.

Humans, when they tired of the repressive and overly rigid religious structures, sought to do away with all forms of morality. Reason became their god. In fact, they often capitalized the word *reason* to personalize it. We looked at this in more detail in the first book of this series, *Machine or Man?* For this context, suffice it to say that reason alone failed to find a final truth, a universal worldview that could explain all of reality consistently and coherently. The high hopes of the rationalists during the early stages of the Enlightenment were that through reason they could develop a coherent worldview that would emancipate people from the myths and superstitions of the past. Their faith was placed not in divinity but in mathematics and science as the universal paragon of truth.

Mathematics enables us to quantify all of reality and thus arrange it in a relatively comprehensible structure. The geometric spirit of Enlightenment thinkers hoped that through reason they could come to a complete understanding of reality. The Pythagorean understanding of transcendent mathematical forms became the hope for the universe that could explain the particulars in a coherent structure.

Reality was defined as concrete things that could be observed and quantified. But in doing so, the rationalists made a metaphysical choice to reject *a priori* any spiritual component to reality that could not be tested, observed, or quantified with our present technology. In so doing, they backed themselves into a corner, subjectively excluding the possibility of what science and reason had not and has not yet disproved.

Are mathematics and science the universal through reason in which a person's mind can find the ultimate truth? Newton's brilliant work, *Principia Mathematica,* provided for Enlightenment thinkers a comprehensive way to understand our universe as a giant machine that runs through the natural order of things without any need for divine intervention. The planets orbit around the sun, not because the finger of God pushes them along, but because of gravity. This gave birth to our postmodern view of cosmology as absolutely independent of any spiritual dimension (i.e., a closed universe).

In this, the Enlightenment thinkers were partly right. God has instituted a form of independence for our world. He set the laws in motion and ordered the universe. There is an element of autonomy that He has given us. Humans have a free will and can choose what direction they may go. His choices are real, and the consequences are equally real. But neither the universe nor humans can be absolutely independent of God because He is still sovereign. Our free will does not contradict God's sovereignty, because He willed it to be so. He chose for us to have a free will. Therefore, the limited autonomy we have is reflected by the limited autonomy the universe has. This is not in opposition to the Judeo-Christian worldview.

Unlike the pantheists' worldview, the Judeo-Christian worldview understands that the universe is not an extension of God. It is in a very real sense independent of God. God stands outside the universe, but it is not completely independent of God. The naturalist or Darwinist proposition that the material universe is absolutely independent of God is a metaphysical choice not predicated on scientific data, but rather on moral preference.

We will provide here evidence that God not only created the universe but also sustains it by His power. God is not some impersonal cosmic force intrinsic to the universe, and neither is

He an aloof entity completely removed from our universe. He is a person, a being who stands outside, before, and after His creation. In a very real sense, He stands outside of space-time and yet with His power sustains it.

The naturalists were therefore correct to reject the idea that all physical processes are explained through divine intervention. God has given our universe and human beings a certain autonomy that is very real. Our choices are real. God does not choose what color of tie I wear with my shirt. I do. The apple falls to the ground, not by the finger of God but because of gravity, a force that God designed and created.

There is a tension between free will and the sovereignty of God that is written in every aspect of the universe He created. We see this interplay in the subatomic particles that behave as described by the particle theory of quantum physics as though they had free will. That is, they are not bound to Newtonian mechanical physics. And yet, although the microworld is explained by mathematics through measures of uncertainty and probabilities, the macroworld continues to behave in predictable Newtonian fashion.

Similarly, although our mathematics tells us that antimatter and matter exist in equal quantities, the fabric of the universe does not rip apart and annihilate. Only the Judeo-Christian worldview allows for this measure of autonomy within the overall structure maintained by the sovereignty of God. All other models lead to either absolute autonomy and anarchism or fatalism and determinism, the loss of our human autonomy in its proper place.

But our autonomy, although real, is not completely unfettered. Neither is the universe completely autonomous from God. God is not, as the deists claim, an absentee landlord. He did not wind up the clock and step away altogether. As we saw in the second book of this series, *Supersymmetry or Chaos*, He was intimately involved in its creative process, fine-tuning the narrow parameters of our developing universe deliberately so human life could inhabit this blue planet. Furthermore, He is intimately involved in sustaining it, as we will discuss later.

The most powerful explosion in the history of the universe was the Big Bang. And yet the Big Bang was not ruled by chaos. It was somehow ordered in the process of exploding so we ended up with a smooth universe rather than a lumpy one, which would have given us a universe of black holes rather than galaxies. The rapid inflation theory propped up by materialists to explain this phenomenon has now been proved wrong by the findings of the three mapping satellites that measured the cosmic microwave background radiation.

We covered this in the second book of this series, so I will not extrapolate more than to say there are areas of anisotropy that show that the rapid inflationary theory could not have possibly created them (the Gaussian equations of the rapid inflationary theory demand that the entire universe be isotropic). Instead, these areas of anisotropy are, in fact, symmetrically aligned to the eclipse of the rotation of Earth around its sun. Furthermore, they are aligned with the equinoxes. Such precise alignments to our solar system could hardly be expected to be an accident of random forces.

It is the magnificence of this universe that God hopes will cause us to reason and bring us to the understanding that it is His fingerprint, His canvas of love for us and all the creatures He brought forth. For this reason, His creative power magnificently designed and engineered it. And although we have a measure of free will, His majestic sovereignty over all things remains absolute.

Reason is the path that leads us to truth. But the metaphysical choice made by the naturalist to automatically exclude from scientific inquiry any consideration of the invisible spiritual dimension or God because they cannot be substantiated by physical testing is a choice made by our technological ignorance. In their limited view, reality is only what can be physically observed and quantified within our visible space-time dimensions through our present technological prowess.

During the Enlightenment and even for some time after it, our technology was so rudimentary that it never occurred to people that invisible dimensions could actually exist and be measured or predicted by mathematics. The idea that the universe could contain invisible dimensions was flatly rejected as mythological in nature and akin to superstition. And yet today, modern physicists have learned otherwise. The superstring theory, for example, tells us that we have seven parallel invisible dimensions all around us.

So the resulting cosmology of their limited worldview during the Enlightenment became a vast machine-like universe devoid of any spiritual component. Is the universe nothing more than a vast machine and humans the tiny cogs in the wheels of those gears? Cause and effect were therefore limited to what could be physically observed and tested. Nothing exists outside our closed universe, and therefore all processes within this universe must be explained through linear cause-and-effect processes within it. Does naturalism coherently explain the nature of humans and the nature of the universe?

Ironically, the very essence of the occult theology is to free the will from the tyranny of any exterior restraints. The very crux of its doctrine is to elevate the human will to godhood. The quest for absolute moral autonomy is at the heart of the human rebellion toward God in the garden and at the heart of everything evil that transpires on Earth. It is the mother of all sin.

Atheists/naturalists think they are rejecting all mystical notions when they embark on their quest to free the will from all moral restraints. They are unaware that they are precisely following the Luciferian plan. In their final quest for moral autonomy, they will destroy the purpose and beauty of the will, which is to express the humanness of humans and instead make a person an automaton without any transcendental significance.

If there is no God, then humans are but organic machines inside an inorganic machine called the universe. If there is no God, the human will is but a chemical illusion created by the flickering electrical signals in the brain. We are hopelessly and helplessly trapped in an infinite stream of cause-and-effect reactions that are the true choice-makers, and not our will. In his book *Miracles*, C. S. Lewis brilliantly exposed some of the logical implications of holding this naturalistic or materialistic presupposition.

If it is true that we have evolved from stardust and we are merely the sum total of random chemical reactions in a closed system (through proposed mechanisms of natural selection without any divine interference), then it stands to reason that in this closed system, there would be no validity to human thought or the choices we make.

In such a physical system in which all events are results of a prior physical event (a linear cause-and-effect chain reaction), then every event is completely dependent on its previous event, and there can be no event that is original, independent, or meaningful. All events occur only because of their prior conditions. It was determined to occur, whether by lawful or random ordering. Therefore, every thought or emotion is merely the result of brute force (the forced patterns of the brain's atoms). To the reductionist, the human will is but an electrical hologram in the brain.

*

It then follows that in a closed system, every thought is chemically pre-determined, and freedom of choice is merely an illusion. Love or any other emotion is merely a chemical reaction lacking completely in any transcendental significance. Creativity in art can have no transcendental beauty. All expressions in poetry are void of any meaningful connection to the author since his or her will is disconnected from the process.

The individual will, the personhood of a human, the mind behind the brain are absent in such a mechanistic worldview. Our artistic creations cannot be viewed as expressions of beauty unique to the mind of the artist. They become simply the outcome of predetermined impersonal forces, the result of random electrochemical synapses. Our actions are predetermined by our human genome. Our so-called choices are merely illusions fabricated in the brain.

Beauty is therefore an empty and meaningless illusion. Love has no significance other than a reproductive drive to promote the survival of the species. There can be no dignity to the person inside the body if all we are is the body. There can be no real distinction between the inanimate and the animate world.

Concepts such as beauty, integrity, honesty, love, mercy, justice, fidelity, friendship, marital bonds, familial bonds, human ties, equality of worth, and individual rights are all illusionary conventions created in our minds and have no objective or tangible significance. They are upper story subjective preferences that are outside the realm of objective reality (Schaeffer). These are nothing more than ethereal holograms of the human brain, lacking any real substance whatsoever.

*

It is not that cause and effect is an invalid process of coming to truth. Our exploration of the world depends on cause and effect to determine the natural processes. It is that cause and effect cannot be artificially restricted to a closed universe. There is nothing in the cause-and-effect principle that demands a closed universe. In fact, it is the principle of cause and effect that demands a primal cause to our universe and necessitates an open universe since something had to be the first cause in order to bring our universe into existence. "Nothing" cannot be a primal cause. If nothing existed prior to the Big Bang, there would be no Big Bang.

*

The Darwinian paradigm based entirely on the presupposition of cause and effect in a closed universe has consequently produced a divided field of knowledge (as we discussed in detail in *Machine or Man?*). The material universe is viewed as the objective exterior reality and recognized as factual, while notions of the supernatural are considered non-factual preferences that are dogmatically labeled as purely subjective.

Schaeffer pictured this divided field of knowledge as a two-story house without stairs to connect them. The upper story is thus the realm of metaphysics and is recognized in this Platonic, dualistic divided field of knowledge as the private, subjective, and relativistic arena where no concrete truths can be found. It is the realm of the unquantifiable, the untestable, the unobservable, and therefore the mythological and the relativistic. The lower story is thus the objective and factual realm of science.

*

In antithesis to the Judeo-Christian worldview, our postmodern culture has adopted this dualistic, divided field of knowledge that considers the matters of the heart and the matters of the mind to be completely separate. Science is relegated to the realm of objective, neutral knowledge detached from subjective opinions, and religion is relegated to the realm of subjective hopes, wishes, and superstitions detached from objective facts. This dualism has its roots in Platonic thought. It has fractured postmodern man into a schizophrenic reality.

In the upper story, they have placed religion and any metaphysical ideology as subjective, irrational, and non-cognitive faith.

Metaphysical Realm – irrational, subjective, non-cognitive faith

Physical Realm – science, objective, rational, cognitive data

The illusion created by this dualistic worldview is that Darwinism or naturalism is squarely in the lower story of objective reality, while theism or religion is placed exclusively in the upper story of subjective and irrational knowledge.

*

Postmodern cosmology is, then, of an exterior universe that is absolutely disconnected from our inner being. But this mechanistic implication runs completely opposite to the way people think of themselves naturally, which is evidence that this worldview does not meet the litmus test of reality. It does not conform to the way people are.

It robs humans of their humanness. It divorces the inner from the outer. It leaves humankind in a schizophrenic understanding of reality. People's inner longings are incongruent with their cosmological worldviews. The Great Divorce is not between science and religion; it is between a human's inner longings as a human and the cognitive rationalizations of cosmology in order to find autonomy from God. Postmodernists live in a self-imposed, incoherent reality that can only lead to a profound disenchantment with meaning and purpose in life. A person becomes nothing more than an organic machine.

*

We can accept with our minds that the Darwinian, naturalistic worldview is true, but we cannot live consistently with that model. We can smash a rock with a hammer, but we cannot smash the head of a six-month-old baby of the human species with the same callousness. Something intuitive in us recognizes that life, especially human life, has transcendental significance. The naturalistic paradigm fails to account for the nature of humans and is therefore not consistent with reality. In fact, their assumption that the universe is a closed system is a metaphysical doctrine and belongs not in the lower story but in the upper story of their divided field of knowledge. It is not the result of empirical data but an *a priori* metaphysical choice.

The third major metaphysical doctrinal position for the Darwinists is the assumption of dysteleology. Because the naturalist philosophical worldview stipulates that all things are strictly run by a purposeless cause-and-effect process in a closed universe, teleological explanations of anything in our universe are considered heretical to Darwinists. But can we actually explain reality without teleology?

The Dysteleological Illusion

The next dogma of critical importance to the naturalist is the assertion that the universe is purposeless. In other words, the universe is described in *dysteleological* terms. (I know ... they like to use these fancy terms that makes them feel educated and elite. Dysteleology just means purposeless. Teleology means the opposite—purposeful.) The *American Heritage Dictionary of the English Language* (1973) defines teleology as follows:

> Teleology – The philosophical study of manifestations of design or purpose in natural processes or occurrences, under the belief that natural processes are not determined by mechanism but rather by their utility in an overall natural design.

Dysteleology is another major unsubstantiated metaphysical presupposition of the Darwinian model that stipulates that cause and effect are completely independent of any purpose. The Judeo-Christian worldview stands in opposition. Because God created the universe with a purpose, it has a design. That design is evident for all who care to look. The antithesis of teleology is dysteleology. The *American Heritage Dictionary of the English Language* (1973) defines it as follows:

> Dysteleology – 1. The doctrine of purposelessness in nature. 2. Purposelessness in natural structures, as manifested by the vestigial or nonfunctional organs or parts.

The dysteleological dogma of naturalists is simply the by-product of their fundamental metaphysical assumption that our universe is in a closed system (i.e., there is no God). Evolution is consequently described as a purposeless and random progression that needs no guiding hand from any divine source. But can it pass the litmus test of reality?

If our universe was formed and now runs fundamentally purposeless, then its components could not be anything but intrinsically purposeless. All of existence is then dysteleological. But is all of reality really purposeless?

Can the naturalist describe a human organ without describing its purpose? A naturalist can describe the anatomical components of the heart—the type of tissue, the names of the arteries that feed the muscle, the size of the right ventricle as opposed to the left ventricle, the sino-atrial node and the atrio-ventricular node of the electrical system, and the Purkinje fibers that run through the ventricles in great detail, but can we truly understand a heart without knowing its purpose?

Can we truly understand the myocardium without knowing that it was designed to beat continually, unlike all the other muscles in the body? Can we understand why the left ventricle is so much larger than the right ventricle without knowing that its purpose is to pump blood to the entire body once it has been oxygenated, while the much smaller right ventricle pumps deoxygenated blood only through the lungs and back to the heart?

Can we truly understand the sino-atrial node without knowing that its purpose is to initiate and send the electrical impulse that causes the atria to contract and dump the blood into the ventricles? It is the pacemaker of the heart that can speed up when we exert ourselves and slow down when we rest.

Can we understand the AV (atrio-ventricular) node without knowing that its purpose is to withhold the electrical signal given by the sino-atrial node for 0.12 seconds before firing into the ventricle and causing it to contract? The AV node is like an electrical capacitor that holds an electrical charge for a specified moment in order to give time for the ventricles to fill with blood from the atria above. Without that time delay, the ventricles would not have time to fill with the blood emptied from the atria above them, and the heart could not function with any efficacy. The purpose for that 0.12-second delay speaks not of random ordering but of intelligent design.

But what of the inanimate world? Does lifeless matter have purposefulness? Can we adequately describe an electron without teleology? Can we describe the electron shells in which the electrons reside without explaining that the purpose of this precise configuration is to allow atoms to merge with other atoms and create compounds? Were it not for the unique design of these electron shells in concentric circles of probabilities around the nucleus, atoms could not form molecules.

An examination of the atom evidences the ingenious design that allows the basic elements to compound in more complicated structures that are necessary for life to exist. Life could not exist in a monist universe of floating atoms that could not merge with other atoms. And yet, in the first moments of the Big Bang, all was sameness. All that existed was radiant energy. If we began in a monist singularity, what caused us to differentiate into a more ordered state when the second law of thermodynamics would predict the opposite?

Purposefulness is intrinsic to understanding any part of our universe. Even if we were to think of our universe in naturalists' terms as a vast and impersonal machine, it still bears purposefulness. Can we truly understand a machine by simply studying its component parts? We can know all about the chemical compounds that make up the corresponding parts such as the gears, pulleys, capacitors, resistors, and microchips of a machine, but if we do not know its purpose, we remain ignorant of the true nature of the device. Can you name one machine ever created without a purpose? Even machines have purpose.

Unlike conscious, living organisms, that purpose is not internal to the machine. It is a reflection or product of the intelligence that designed it. Even the Newtonian idea that the universe is but a giant self-regulating machine does not negate the need for the divine. No machine has ever been built without intelligence as a cause and without intelligence to maintain it.

To blindly believe that a machine such as this universe, which is so complicated and filled with symmetry, is the product of unintelligent, purposeless, random ordering is to disavow all observable data and choose a naturalistic metaphysical model out of sheer antagonism for the divine. That choice has nothing to do with real science and everything to do with psychological preferences, which I call deophobia.

Modern minds often state that they are not prone to be partial to faith. We often hear them say, "I am a skeptic. I wish I had your faith." There is no such thing as a total skeptic about ultimate beliefs since no belief can be doubted except on the basis of another conflicting belief.

The skeptic is also a believer; that is, he or she has made a metaphysical choice and placed his or her faith in that model. To deny the existence of intelligent design in our universe is a metaphysical choice and not a scientific statement. The question that needs to be considered is this: "Which choice is rational and most consistent with the empirical data observed, and which choice is not?"

If we consider naturalists' mechanistic view of the universe, we cannot account for the ordering of the machine without intelligence. There are no known random processes that can bring forth the enormous symmetry and universal laws that govern our universe. Hence, theirs is the irrational faith. In fact, the mechanistic Newtonian view of the universe is not accurate with reality.

Darwinism and reductionism are archaic concepts that were grounded in Newtonian physics, although not as Newton intended, for he was a devout Christian. The universe was viewed by the naturalist as a self-regulating machine that was running from eternity past and that stretched in space into eternity. All components of this universe were seen as three-dimensional solid "things" that had run like clockwork from infinity and shall continue so throughout infinity. Reality was confined to the observable and testable visible dimensions. The idea that life is but a chemical machine is a relic of this simplistic, static, Newtonian ideology, and it has been shown to be not only ignorantly simplistic but untrue mathematically.

Albert Einstein taught us through his brilliant equations that our universe is neither infinite in size nor has it existed for infinity. The universe is not static; it is dynamic. It began a finite time ago, and it stretches a finite time or distance from the space-time origin of the Big Bang. We live in a dynamic, multidimensional universe and not in the static machine-like universe originally envisioned by the naturalists, as they erroneously extrapolated from Newton's mathematics. The essence of matter is no longer understood as solid grains of stuff that run in machine-like fashion.

> *The universe as modern physics understands it is neither infinite nor eternal. It has a calculable age and, according to the Second Law of Thermodynamics, is moving inexorably toward total entropy, in which nothing that could be called matter will exist. Space and time are no longer two different forms of infinity, but space-time is a single finite entity—liable to "warping," having a beginning at a calculable time-distance from the present, and having also a limit at which it ceases to exist. At this limit, the so-called singularity, space-time no longer exists, and the laws of physics no longer operate. Moreover, there is no "point of absolute rest" from which the universe could be surveyed. All points are relative to all others, and there is only one absolute, namely, the speed of light. Furthermore, the work done on the fundamental*

structure of matter has led into a world where entities that can hardly be called "things" in any ordinary sense operate according to principles that cannot be described in mechanical terms. There is no way in which the fundamental elements in the structure of the atom as modern physics understands it can be visualized. Leptons and quarks, muons and photons are not pieces of matter in any imaginable sense. Nor is it possible to form any visual image of anti-matter. "Matter is an affair of changing relationships between non-material entities" *[Thorpe 111]. Neither the organic images of ancient Greek science nor the mechanical models of Newtonian science have any further validity* (emphasis added) (Newbigin 68–69).

Beyond the brilliant observations of Leslie Newbigin, there are the supposed discoveries of dark matter and dark energy that materialists now claim compose 96 percent of our physical universe. Furthermore, the mathematical stipulations of the M-theory now tell us there are seven invisible dimensions to our universe. It seems, according to the vast majority of naturalist scientists, that 96 percent of our universe is actually invisible. Perhaps this dark matter may even inhabit the seven invisible dimensions mathematically derived from the M-theory. The old Newtonian and Enlightenment ideology, that only what can be visibly or sensibly observed and tested can be scientifically considered real, is now absolutely shown to be nothing more than scientific ignorance of our true physical reality.

Moreover, the M-theory suggests that even the surreal tiny quarks that compose atomic particles are not the fundamental particles of matter. Matter is fundamentally composed of even smaller vibrating strands of energy or membranes. The pitch of the vibration determines the essence of the material it expresses.

The archaic notion that living things are merely machine-like structures rooted in the naïve misapplication of Newtonian physics is simply not in touch with the understanding of reality expressed by the advancements in physics in our modern day. W. H. Thorpe's deep observation, "Matter is an affair of changing relationships between non-material entities," ought to bring enlightenment to those who still insist that life is but a cold, souless machine. Even matter is more than a machine. It is borne from the changing relationships between non-material entities.

> In the eighteenth century, Hume and Kant systemati-
> cally refuted the traditional philosophical arguments
> for God's existence, pointing out the unwarrantability
> of using causal reasoning to move from the sensible
> to the supersensible. Only the realm of possible expe-
> riences, of concrete particulars registered in sensa-
> tion, offered any ground for philosophical conclusions
> (Tarnas 309).

The entire premise of the Enlightenment, denial of the super-natural, was based on the illusion that the concrete forms of the sensible world are radically different from the supersensible forms of the Judeo-Christian worldview, which they declared as simple superstitions. Specifically, they dogmatically insisted that science and faith have no interconnection. That fundamental Enlighten-ment misconception has been proved utterly false.

The old ideas that reality is composed of concrete forms that are observable and quantifiable are no longer supported by our sci-entific discoveries. Even the supposedly solid structures of matter are now known to be composed of mostly space. Reality is not as simplistic as we once thought in blissful ignorance. It seems that the concrete "stuff" of the sensible is composed of supersensible "stuff."

The Enlightenment ideology, which stipulated that reason, through an exclusively horizontal cause-and-effect system by mathematics and science could lead us to universal truth, has also been found wanting. Mathematics has shown us that it could not be the universal from which all things are measured.

> And not even mathematics can provide us with an absolutely secure mental framework any longer, for—according to the famous Gödelian theorems that have never been disproved—within any rigidly logical mathematical system there are propositions (or questions) that cannot be proved or disproved on the basis of the axioms within that system, and consequently it is uncertain that the basic axioms of arithmetic will not give rise to contradictions (Newbigin 69).

Logician Kurt Gödel, in his *On Formally Undecidable Propositions of Principia Mathematica and Related Systems* published in 1931, brought the Enlightenment ideology in regard to mathematics to an abrupt end. His two incompleteness theorems mathematically established the limitations of all but the most trivial of axiomatic arithmetic systems. The first theorem stated that no consistent system of axioms is capable of proving all truths about the relations of natural numbers. The second theorem stated that such a system cannot demonstrate its own consistency.

In other words:

> Any effectively generated theory capable of expressing elementary arithmetic cannot be both consistent and complete. In particular, for any consistent, effectively generated formal theory that proves certain basic arithmetic truths, there is an arithmetical statement that is true but not provable in a system (Kleene 250).

Thus, mathematics cannot be the universal with which to measure all things. No axiom can be absolutely proved through only the language of arithmetic. And yet we know that it speaks truth. We know that this mathematical truth exists, but it cannot be proved strictly by mathematics.

Every day, engineers use these mathematical equations to calculate stress and design bridges and skyscrapers. We use them to send satellites into deep space to explore the planets. We use them in perfect confidence that they are functionally true. Humankind functions as if they are true in all its endeavors. And yet the particular of mathematics has failed to become the universal. Nevertheless, the particular is true because it aligns with the real Universal. It points to something higher than mathematics that designed it thus, as the only paragon from which universals can be attained.

Modern science has come to understand that in the singularity of the Big Bang and in the heart of black holes, the laws of science break down. In other words, science is also finite, even within the very finite spectrum of our universe. In other words, there was a space-time moment at the beginning of our universe when the laws of physics, chemistry, and mathematics did not exist; they could not work. Nothing within the finite realm of this universe can be the fulcrum of universal truths.

Therefore, science cannot be used as a universal for truth because the universe was birthed before the laws of science existed. Moreover, the universe began. That means that something other than the universe and science began it. At this point, naturalists go counter to their fundamental cause-and-effect ideology. They avoid the first cause without any rational reason other than to avoid the supernatural. The choice is a psychologically induced choice and not one demanded by any empirical data.

Something caused the singularity to exist. It is irrational to think it could magically appear from nothingness. Naturalists cannot even remain consistent in their view. They take an irrational leap of faith and believe against their cause-and-effect ideology that there was no primal cause. They rationalize this by saying that because science did not exist at that point, it cannot be rationally discussed.

I'm very familiar with this two-step shuffle. I have seen it danced in Washington, D.C. by many politicians who refuse to face the truth and for personal reasons flower their words with rationalizations that can dizzy the mind. The fact remains: Something cannot come from nothing. Not discussing it changes nothing. Rationalizations are not reasons. They are attempts to legitimize a previous presupposition and have nothing to do with empirical science.

Moreover, since the universe did not exist at this point before the singularity, reason then dictates that something higher than science and mathematics exists outside our universe, which we have not even begun to fathom.

It is not that science and mathematics do not lead us to truth. It is that they cannot be the universal from which truth emanates. Truth and reality must have come from something else. But do not hold your breath; the priests of scientism will not easily abandon their clerical gowns. The dogma of the religion of scientism is as entrenched as that of the formalistic and overly rigid medieval religion that the Enlightenment rejected.

All reality points to supersymmetry from the most fundamental particle upward, as we covered in *Supersymmetry or Chaos*. Suffice it to say for now that all reality points to a purposefully designed universe that can inhabit life, which was chosen from the first microsecond of the existence of the Genesis Singularity before science existed.

Their fundamental insistence in a dysteleological origin (randomly ordered purposelessness genesis) is refuted by the purposeful design that proceeded from the first instant our universe materialized all the way to the present form of our magnificently structured universe. Furthermore, all of humanity engages in purposeful activity in every aspect of their lives. Teleology is inescapable in our world. In fact we judge others and ourselves on whether or not we achieve those purposes. Even the scientist in setting up any kind of experiment has a purpose which that experiment is designed to accomplish. A scientist cannot practice science divorced from teleology.

When we build homes, we do so with the purpose of sheltering ourselves from the elements. When we make appliances, we do so with a specific purpose in mind to make things easier for us. When we get married, we do so with the purpose of living with the one we love and perhaps even establishing a family. We could go on ad infinitum with examples from every aspect of our human existence. Purpose is the central core of that human existence and our activity. A life without purpose is hopeless and adrift.

Purposefulness is intrinsic to our very being. It is part of that aspect of humanity that Schaeffer calls the "mannishness of man." To reject this reality in order to stay consistent with the metaphysical creed of dysteleology is simply sheer irrationalism of the first order. It is a subjective denial of reality that can be labeled nothing less than self-deception. Reason must guide the true seeker of knowledge to the truth.

Our real and palpable observations of human nature obviates that a human being is not a simple organic machine devoid of purpose. Humans are more than the sum total of their mechanical components. Everything they do is filled and guided by purpose, which by their will they choose. The fact that humans are completely dependent on purpose to have any meaning in their lives infers that they were designed with that purpose—to have a measure of autonomy—so their choices are real. How then could a purposeless genesis of our universe produce humans, whose survival is dependent on the purposefulness of their actions? How is this absurd disconnection with reality rational?

The natural antipathy to teleology rabidly insisted upon by Darwinists is simply predicated on the reality that it implies with certainty that intelligence had a hand in our creation. But like it or not, our universe displays purposefulness in every aspect of reality. In fact, science could not exist without it. What can we know in biology that is meaningful without knowing purpose? The naïve Laplacean ideology, which stipulates that by gaining a complete knowledge of the elemental components we can know everything about it, is absurd and impractical as a scientific methodology.

The knowledge of true reality cannot be gained without asking five important questions: *what, where, when, how,* and most importantly, *why.* Undoubtedly, *what, where, when,* and *how* are important, but they are woefully incomplete without answering *why.* The *why* question is implicitly the teleological query. The science of biology would be truncated without it.

When we study animals, we consistently ask all five of these questions in order to fully know that animal. If we study only the *what, when, where,* and *how* questions of a lion's powerful muscles, their specially designed retractable claws, and incredible canines, we do not come to a complete knowledge of that lion without knowing that the purpose for these components is to capture prey.

In accepting the reductionist dysteleological model for reality, Darwinists are incapable of coming to the light of complete knowledge. They are doomed to the darkness of self-imposed partial knowledge and an incomplete view of reality because they have deliberately, from the onset, excluded the possibility that a real aspect of our universe may be the spiritual dimension. It is the reality of the spiritual dimension that brings meaning to our existence.

The naturalist worldview is thus not based on pure reason. Naturalists must by faith accept the negative metaphysical choice that the supernatural does not exist while ignoring the fact that all reality is pervasively teleological. So instead of reasoning, they are rationalizing by ignoring the obvious. This purposefulness imprinted into the universe is, in fact, the telltale evidence of intelligent design. They must ignore a huge part of reality to make this leap of faith into their negative metaphysical choice, which is, quite frankly, based on their psychological predilection to avoid the moral mandates of a Creator.

Ironically, reductionists may intellectually insist that our universe is purposeless, but they cannot function in the real world without acknowledging the intrinsic teleological aspect of reality. The reductionist cannot say, "I know my wife" by knowing the chemistry of her biological functions or the physics behind her anatomical capabilities. He may know that her brain functions through 10 billion electrical circuits passed on by chemicals with electric charges between their synapses in the cerebral cortex, but if he does not understand the longings and dreams that give her purpose in life, he knows nothing of the person behind the brain. He simply does not know his wife if he does not know the purpose for her choices, predilections, and actions.

*

Since every machine humans have encountered has been designed by intelligence, it is simply intellectually absurd to stipulate as the foundational framework of reality that our universe is a machine constructed by nobody for no purpose. It is not only intellectually absurd, it is also scientifically unsubstantiated by the observation of our universe. The idea that the whole universe, the entire observable reality, can be truly understood only through linear cause and effect, excluding purpose, is the abandonment of reason and can be adhered to only through a blind leap of faith into the irrational.

*

The dysteleological model is an absurd creed believed blindly by those who wish to blot out the sun with their thumb. It is nothing more than a vain attempt to deny the reality of the Creator. Knowing the chemistry and physics of that machine gives us only a partial understanding of it. Even in this physical realm, we remain in darkness if we do not understand the purpose for which that particular machine was designed.

Reason or Rationalization

The whole enterprise of scientific methodology rests on the belief that the universe is rational. The philosophical imperative that reason must connect the universals with the particulars is absolutely necessary in a rational universe. If the particulars were not connected rationally to the universals, we would be in an irrational universe. Science without a universal paragon cannot exist.

> *If every instrument reading in a laboratory were simply an isolated happening that could not be connected in an intelligible way with other readings, the whole enterprise would be futile. But, in fact, a scientist faced with an apparent irrationality does not accept it as final, nor does he take refuge in the idea of arbitrary divine intervention. He goes on struggling to find some rational way in which the facts can be related to each other, some formula or mathematical equation that will tie them logically together. This struggle is a deeply passionate one, sustained by the faith that there must be a solution even though no one can yet say what it is. Without that passionate faith in the ultimate rationality of the world, science would falter, stagnate, and die—as has happened before. Thus science is sustained in its search for an understanding of what it sees by faith in what is unseen. The formula credo ut intelligam is fundamental to science (Newbigin 70–71).*

Here is the big disconnect with scientism or Darwinism and reality: This faith in the rationality of the universe cannot be derived from a dysteleological foundation where randomness and chaos rule. One cannot arrive at reason without purpose. A purposeless accidental universe is a universe in which there is no rational constraint. Reason is an ordering of facts into a congruent and logical system. What axiom of order and logic can come from chaos and disorder as the matrix of reality? There is, therefore, an irrational inconsistency in the minds of scientists who believe in reason and logic without reason to do so.

They have borrowed or, more properly, stolen from the Judeo-Christian worldview the very foundation of their enterprise. It is because God, a rational being, created the universe with intelligence and congruence that a human, another rational being, can come to understand it through reason and logic. This is the true foundation of the scientific methodology. There is no way to engineer a rational congruence between all natural processes in a closed universe ruled by purposeless chaos. To believe so, as scientism does, is an irrational leap of faith unsubstantiated by reality and even by the presuppositions they naïvely maintain.

How do we test our scientific models? We test them by observation and predictions. What predictions would be expected if our universe were dysteleological in origin? If, in fact, our universe was created by their imagined dysteleological model, the particulars could not be correlated to a universal. The universe would not be fundamentally rational or ordered in any logical fashion. Chaos and randomness are the antithesis of logical order and reason.

We would expect there to be an infinite number of randomly produced atoms that did not work, each portraying different charge values for their subatomic components. We would expect there to be an infinite number of failed organs of every type before hitting fortunately upon the one that works with accidental purpose. We would expect to find humans with an enormous variability to their forms such as having two hearts and some perhaps with three, or perhaps an eye in the back of their heads to stop danger from behind. That would definitely have a superior survival advantage. Why such homogeneity?

We would expect to find numerous structures that function as DNA in order to pass on genetic information. In other words, we would expect to find an infinite variety of gene expression systems. Why just one for all living things? If randomness is the operative principle, then randomness should be pervasive in all physical forms.

Is it? Does observation support the reductionist foundational presupposition? Is the universe filled with countless random variations of all elemental things? Is the universe rational?

And these supposedly measly few vestigial organs that they very loudly use to prop up their dysteleological model—they are regarded as such merely because of medical ignorance, as we will see later. In fact, vestigial organs are reductionists' teleological attempt to disprove teleology. In other words, their premeditated purpose is to disprove that organs have a purpose.

The dysteleological model is merely an artificial theoretical illusion that cannot be followed consistently in real life, not in their labs, and not in their private sphere. Darwinists cannot remain consistent with their philosophical presuppositions. They cannot explain the obvious design and purpose found in every corner of our material universe as rising from a dysteleological genesis.

They cannot explain the nature of humans in simply a linear, cause-and-effect chain reaction. Such one-dimensional thinking is incapable of accounting for human's deepest transcendental needs of love, music, poetry, art, family, friendships, and so on. Our notion of the equality of humankind (regardless of intelligence, color of skin, wealth, stature, looks, abilities, or any other superficial trappings) comes solely from the Judeo-Christian higher view of humans' value. We are hardwired to sense these things because we are created in the image of God. These are universal longings expressed by all human beings on the planet and throughout human history. Yet by the naturalist's account, these things can only be the products of an illusion in our brains. But if they are only illusions in our brains, then natural selection is an absurd proposition that cannot account for the universality of these illusions.

One way of stating the absurdity is as follows: however we may explain our mental states, we know that we have them. I think that I exist. If this idea is only a series of electrical pulses in my brain, the capacity of the brain to produce these pulses must be the result of evolution by natural selection. But since the idea that I can by my will affect the operation of these pulses is an illusion, the existence of this idea can have no effect upon what happens in the world of physical and chemical change. Therefore, it can have no bearing on natural selection. Therefore, the existence of this illusion is an unexplained mystery since it cannot have arisen from natural selection. The "explanation" fails to explain (Newbigin 74).

How then can naturalists explain this persistent and fundamental illusion of personhood experienced by every human being arising from an impersonal reality? They must willfully blind themselves to most of reality in order to remain consistent with their chosen dysteleological metaphysical worldview.

A note of warning is appropriate here. These universal higher aspirations of humankind are also the object of loathing, despised by tyrants of every form from the beginning of time. And it should give us pause to consider the consequences of ignoring them. They are just as much a part of reality as our material existence. The danger of denying the reality of these human concepts as rooted in absolute terms because we were created in God's image then leads to the devaluation of human rights and the suppression of the masses by the strong, the elite, and the powerful.

Those intuitive longings intrinsic to all humankind are the characteristic elements of personhood. They are the natural outworking of our personhood. It is what separates us from the rest of creation. It is the evidence of our purposeful, divine origins.

*

The spirit of a human did not ascend from apes. Humans descended from the heavens. No, we are not gods, but we came from God.

*

We are, in a very literal sense, His children. Though we inhabit this earthly tabernacle that will perish and rot away, our being is eternal because it comes from the eternal One.

Personhood and Deocentric Valuation

It cannot be denied or ignored that the common trait of every culture throughout history in every corner of the world is precisely that people has regarded human life as having some transcendental value. How could that universal notion of transcendental significance have evolved from an impersonal genesis? The Judeo-Christian worldview maintains that our physical similarities or differences with other animals have nothing to do with our higher significance. Our transcendental worth stems from the single fact that we have been created in the image of God. Outside of that reality, there is no foundation for personal rights and liberty.

Moreover, the commonalities among species may be explained as something other than evolution, for all life is the work of a single Creator who chose to use a successful design in forming our structures many times over. We would not expect Detroit to start from scratch and throw away all the equipment in its factories every time a new car was designed.

In light of the fact that there is not an endless variety of specimens between man and ape that can evidence this supposed evolution, we must conclude that our similarities in function end just there. In fact the unified structure of efficiency found throughout nature points not to random ordering but to intelligent design.

But the Judeo-Christian worldview does not regard the rest of creation as valueless. There is great value to all life forms, and we must never become calloused and insensitive to the wonderful gift of life that God has given us in order to protect and care for them. All living things are precious. In fact, all material things on our planet are precious. He made us the caretakers of this wonderful planet. The planet does not belong to humans. It belongs to God. We are simply the caretakers of His world. Although unfortunately, we have historically behaved as greedy, abusive exploiters of God's domain.

Nevertheless, intrinsically most of us are aware that there is a great deal of difference between the value of a dog and the value of a human life. Of all living things, people are most aware of death and its deep chasm. We bury our kin and make elaborate provisions to honor lives that are lost. But if, as naturalists claim, we are simply evolved beings, then there is no difference between the value of a dog, a rat, an amoeba, or a child.

*

The only plausible reason that can substantiate a real qualitative difference in the intrinsic worth of a person compared to all other living things is the Judeo-Christian position, which separates human beings from the rest of creation because they were created in God's image.

*

This unique position found exclusively in the Judeo-Christian worldview reflects God's intent to endow humans with this special significance by creating them as beings who can make moral decisions. And for this specific reason, humans are thus endowed with infinite value based on the value framework dictated by the Creator. This is not an anthropocentric view, as evolutionists are prone to say. We are not the center of valuation—God is. Therefore, this high view of human life is an expression of deocentric valuation.

Without a God as an ultimate paragon, all nature, including humans, is simply the product of an impersonal chemical process, and no real qualitative distinction in worth can be made between any of the chemical products of a randomly generated evolution in this regard. The naturalistic position as well as the pantheistic position cannot even differentiate between the value of a human being and inanimate matter. As we said previously, the breaking of a rock with a hammer is, in essence, morally equal to the breaking of a human head with a hammer within the framework of a worldview where morals are relative.

In a naturalistic system, the value of humans is reduced to that of all other evolved things. This is also true of pantheism, which regards all living things and matter as sameness. The sad situation is that by taking this position, they do not elevate the value of other living things or even matter. On the contrary, they, like naturalists, simply lower the value of human life. The naturalist lowers it to the level of a fortuitous chemical accident. Humans are nothing more than simply the accidental product of stardust. Pantheists lower the value of humans to an insignificant cell in the cosmic organism of the universe.

In the final analysis, the naturalistic system cannot explain what life is. All they are left with is the description of the process of life and the description of the functions of the organism that life exhibits. Outside of the Judeo-Christian proposition that humans are endowed with infinite worth because they have been created in the image of God, there is no way to validate human life with any greater significance than any other thing that exists in the universe. Naturalism has no way to provide or explain any transcendental meaning to the human experience in its totality. It fails to describe all of reality consistently and rationally. It flies against our very basic instincts and intuitions. For this reason, a great disenchantment has grown in our modern culture.

Postmodernists cannot reconcile their deepest inner longings with their exterior cosmology and cognitive reality. Humanity has been fractured into a schizophrenic worldview where the deepest human longings are considered holograms of the brain, illusions of neurochemical signals in a deterministic and mechanistic universe.

Humans, no longer persons, are therefore not unique individuals with transcendental value. Personhood is considered nothing more than an illusion created by the internal programming of the organic computer called the brain. People are nothing more than organic machines. But the failure of naturalism does not end with the deep disconnect with "man's mannishness." It fails to explain the very origin of life itself.

The Myth of Simplicity

The Darwinian abiogenic myth that small, gradual changes in non-living matter could gradually evolve into a living organism was originally thought possible because of our ignorance of the complexity of life even at the basic unicellular level, and because at that time, scientists believed the universe was eternal in existence. A universe with infinite time to undergo the evolutionary process would make this fantastical claim that simple life forms could accidentally form more plausible. But we now know the universe is finite in time and space.

But even more glaring is the fact that our ability to peer deeper into the cellular structure has revealed an unbelievably complex system that is anything but simple. In spite of our advances in technology, there is a grave misconception in regard to the complexity of life, propagated by evolutionary biologists. Predisposed to create an illusion of an evolutionary process in the formation of life, they often use the term "simple life forms" to describe species they may consider more archaic in their imagined evolutionary ladder.

*

There is no such thing as simple life. This term is an oxymoron of the highest order.

*

Biologists who use this term are either naïve or intentionally deceptive, for even the "simplest" of organisms is infinitely complex. One may well say that they are less complex than other forms, but they are certainly not simple by any stretch of the imagination.

As we will see, our Master Designer has arrayed this magnificent universe that we inhabit with an intrinsic design and complexity that could only have been formed through careful planning and meticulous forethought in design. From the design of the basic components of matter to the design of living organisms, every aspect is fraught with intricate checks and balances that could not, in an eternity of time, have risen by random chemical processes.

The universe is filled with symmetry from the atomic level to the macroworld of stars and galaxies. Could that pervasive symmetry arise naturally through random processes without purpose? As we begin the next chapter, we will consider this question. (For a more thorough discussion on the origin of the universe, see the second book of this series, *Supersymmetry or Chaos*)

Our purpose in this third book of the series is to consider and rationally compare the answers given by naturalism in contrast to the Judeo-Christian Cosmological Model regarding the central mystery of humankind: Where did life come from?

To obtain life, we must first obtain a universe that life can inhabit. Hence, our quest must begin at the foundational level. Is there a symmetry exhibited by this universe that allows for life to exist? Does the universe exhibit the evidence that supports the naturalistic model, which stipulates that all things have evolved through random processes, or does it exhibit prevision and design?

If the naturalistic model is correct, then all things developed from chaos, and supersymmetry in the universe would not be expected to evolve through random processes. If, on the other hand, the universe was designed by intelligence, then we would expect to find supersymmetry interlaced throughout all of reality. Let us briefly consider the nature of our material universe before discussing life.

CHAPTER 2

●●●

SUPERSYMMETRY IN THE MICROWORLD

To begin to appreciate the functional design of the incredible living cell, one must understand the enormous complexity of the design of its basic components. Hence, the discussion of life must begin at the level of the atom.

At one time, most scientists believed in Aristotle's concept of continuous matter. That is, one could divide matter infinitely and still have the same intrinsic properties of the element when one began. Some, such as Democritus, held that matter was intrinsically grainy. These grains, which he called atoms (*indivisible* in Greek) combined with other atoms of different kinds to form all matter.

In 1803, British chemist John Dalton came up with the idea that chemical compounds always combined in precise proportions. This, he theorized, could be explained by the grouping together of atoms to create molecules. The combination of different kinds of atoms then produces what we refer to as compounds. It is true that all the atoms of an element display a singular and distinctly unique atom as its base component, but we have since found that these atoms are composed of even smaller particles.

The argument between the two schools of thought was finally settled in the early twentieth century. A contributing factor was Einstein's paper on Brownian motion that explained the irregular and random motion of small particles of dust suspended in a liquid. This was explained as the effect of atoms colliding with one another.

Today, we have the electron microscope that allows us to see the atom, and we have been taught that the atom is composed of a nucleus containing protons (positively charged particles) and neutrons (neutral particles), and surrounding the nucleus are electrons (negatively charged particles). The intricacy and complexity of these particles and their interactions with valence electrons is what governs chemical reactions and the existence of compounds made of specific and precise combinations of elements.

The incredible intricacy of the atom was not fathomed when Darwin proposed the theory of evolution by natural selection. Science had no idea of the incredible intricacy and design of the microworld. It wasn't until the 1960s that scientists discovered that protons, electrons, and neutrons were not, in fact, the elementary particles of the atom. Experiments using rapid accelerators colliding protons with other protons or electrons with other electrons showed that they were actually composed of even smaller particles. These particles were called *quarks* by Murray Gell-Mann of Caltech. This discovery earned him the Nobel Prize in Physics in 1969.

It appears that there are six varieties of these super tiny quarks, which are grouped in three distinct families. These three families are labeled red, green, and blue. Physicists have categorized the six varieties of quarks with these exclusive distinctions: (1) up, (2) down, (3) strange, (4) charmed, (5) bottom, and (6) top.

Stephen Hawking in describing these quarks referred to them as flavors:

> *The first three flavors had been known since the 1960s but the charmed quark was discovered only in 1974, the bottom in 1977, and the top in 1995. Each flavor comes in three "colors," red, green, and blue. (It should be emphasized that these terms are just labels; quarks are much smaller than the wavelength of visible light and so do not have any color in the normal sense. It is just that modern physicists seem to have more imaginative ways of naming new particles and phenomena—they no longer restrict themselves to the Greek!). A proton or neutron is made up of three quarks, one of each color. A proton contains two up quarks and one down quark; a neutron contains two down and one up. We can create particles made up of the other quarks (strange, charmed, bottom, and top), but these all have a much greater mass and decay very rapidly into protons and neutrons (67).*

The basic structure of matter is based in a three-quark code, and strangely enough, the basic building blocks of life are based on three families of macromolecules: (1) the nucleotides of the DNA (which also come in triplets called codons), (2) the proteins, and (3) fatty acids. Life is described by three characteristics: (1) respiration, (2) metabolism, and (3) replication. Matter is divided into three visible spatial dimensions, which are in a time continuum. That is also not coincidental, since life as we know it could not function in a universe with less than three spatial dimensions.

> *Many authors have drawn attention to the fact that the properties of wave equations are very strongly*

dependent upon the spatial dimension. Three-dimensional worlds appear to possess a unique combination of properties which enable information processing and signal transmission to occur via electromagnetic wave phenomena. Since our universe appears governed by the propagation of classical and quantum waves it is interesting to elucidate this nature of the connection with dimensionality and living systems.... If living systems require high-fidelity wave propagation for their existence to be possible, then we could not expect to observe the world to possess other than three spatial dimensions (emphasis added) *(Barrow and Tipler 266, 269).*

There is a sort of three-in-one system, which is reflected in wide and divergent fields throughout our material existence. There are three visible spatial dimensions, but perhaps if the M-theory is correct (and it is looking very much like it is), then there may be seven other invisible spatial dimensions, all of them existing in the dimension of time and therefore intertwined into time. Einstein taught us that time is inseparable from space; they are a continuum, and the reality of our visible universe is best explained as a three-in-one, space-time continuum. Time itself is divided into (1) past, (2) present, and (3) future; yet they are also in a continuum. The past, present, and future are connected. We cannot truly define the division between past and future since the present is always moving and can be infinitely divided into smaller and smaller increments of past and future. Therefore, the past, present, and future of time is also one continuum.

What is the likelihood that a purely random ordering would end up with this repeating pattern design of three? Isn't it more rational to assume in the face of such ordering that it is not purely coincidental? This order in the observable universe is the fingerprint of God that provides for the seeker of truth the evidence of His existence.

It is therefore not coincidental that God describes himself as triune (Father, Son, and Holy Spirit). Humans are also described as triune (body, soul, and spirit). Matter, space, time, life, God, and humans are designed by a component of three, but more accurately, a triune component. The number three happens to be the symbolic number of Christ in the scriptures.

The number four pertains to Earth. The symbol for Earth is a cross (+) since it marks the four quadrants (north, south, east, west) and the equinoxes (spring equinox, summer solstice, autumn equinox, and winter solstice). (For more information on numerology, see my upcoming book *A Witness in the Sky*). Christ's ministry lasted three years. It started on His thirtieth birthday and ended on His thirty-third. He died and resurrected on the third day, exactly thirty-three hours after He died on the cross at Calvary. Isn't the random process of evolution marvelous?

The atom is composed of three particles: (1) protons, (2) neutrons, and (3) electrons. But the components of these basic elementary particles of the atom are quarks, which are also divided into three family groups. Brian Greene, in his book *The Elegant Universe*, probes this same fascinating conundrum that mystifies the naturalist:

> *Why are there so many fundamental particles, especially when it seems that the great majority of things in the world around us need only electrons, up-quarks, and down-quarks? Why are there three families? Why not one family or four families or any other number?* (emphasis added) *(9)*.

Each of these three families is further broken down into four members, so the symmetry is even more astounding since it also includes the number four, pertaining to Earth:

First Family

1   the electron with a mass of .00054
2   the electron-neutrino with a mass of $< 10^{-18}$
3   the up-quark with a mass of .0047
4   the down-quark with a mass of .0074

Second Family

1   the muon with a mass of 1.1
2   the muon-neutrino with a mass of <.0003
3   the charm-quark with a mass of 1.6
4   the strange-quark with a mass of .16

Third Family

1   the tau with a mass of 1.9
2   the tau-neutrino with a mass of <.033
3   the top-quark with a mass of 189
4   the bottom-quark with a mass of 5.2

How does chaos produce three families with four members each? Why not three components in one and 10 in the second or 20 in the third? How does chaos produce such supersymmetry?

But the order and symmetry of the elemental particles does not end there. According to the string theory and the most advanced of them called the M Theory, there are even more elemental entities than the quarks. These are thought to be composed of vibrating tiny strings or membranes whose vibrating pitch determines their essence. These are tiny vibrating strands of energy. Each vibrating strand of energy produces the observed properties of the particle by the string's intrinsic oscillatory pattern.

In other words, the atom is composed of three fundamental components: (1) vibrating strings or membranes, (2) quarks, and

(3) the fundamental particles of the atom: (1) proton, (2) neutron, and (3) electron. In other words, these fundamental particles of the atom are themselves broken down into three stages: (1) the particle, (2) the quarks that compose the particle, and (3) the vibrating strings that compose the quarks. I just do not have enough blind faith to believe that random ordering could create such symmetry. Call me a skeptic, if you will.

It is obvious to the casual observer that the harmony created in the vibrating matrix of our universe that produces our reality is an expression of God's symphony during the creative process when He spoke it into being. The very essence of matter is the vibrating voice of God. We are literally His song of love. The elegance of the design of our universe in symmetry and beauty unequivocally demands an intelligent designer.

The fundamental elements that comprise our material universe are God's alphabet through which the words of His song were made. If we were to consider the atoms of the elements as letters in an alphabet, we could see that the combination of those letters making a distinct word would be synonymous with atoms creating molecules that are exhibited in the form of a given compound. But the letters are the smallest divisible entities that, when mixed in specific variations, can create the different compounds.

Therefore, in our illustration, each letter is as an element in the Periodic Table of Elements. But after closer inspection, we find that each letter is composed of lines that are either curved or straight. These are the electrons, neutrons, and protons of the atom. But an even closer inspection shows that these lines are composed of many dots that create the illusion of lines. They are the quarks that create the electrons, protons, and neutrons.

Now we go one step further and find that these quarks are created by tiny small filaments or membranes of vibrating energy that, depending on the pitch of their vibrations, can create the observed properties of each of these quarks. This complexity and symmetry cannot possibly arise from chaos without some form of directed energy to accomplish it. To believe that such symmetry could be borne out of purposeless chaos is irrational.

In addition to the complexity of this design, the precise properties of each of these individual subcomponents must be within a very narrow parameter in order for the chain of these larger components to have the necessary charges and properties necessary to create stable elements so life can exist. The resonant properties of these vibrations must be in precise patterns in order for matter to have the necessary stable characteristics that allow, for example, for stars to be formed and burn at rates that will allow a stable environment for life and chemical processes to occur.

Moreover, it is the distinct, intrinsic vibrating properties of these strings or membranes that create the exact properties of the four fundamental forces of nature and the constituents of these forces: (1) electromagnetism (photons); (2) strong nuclear force (gluons); (3) weak nuclear force (weak gauge bosons); (4) gravity (gravitons). These elemental constituents of the four elemental forces provide the very mechanism for transmitting the forces they respectively constitute.

1. The photon is a sort of messenger carrier that, when interacting with particles of like poles, carries this message: repel, or move apart. For particles of opposite charge, it carries this message: move together, or attract.

2. Gluons perform the same function for the strong nuclear force.

3. Weak gauge bosons are correspondingly the messengers for the weak nuclear force.

4. Gravitons work with the force of gravity. It is now also assumed by many that the graviton is the messenger for gravitational force.

But the delicate interplay, not only between the different forces but also with all of matter, is by necessity limited within a very precise, narrow parameter. As we saw in *Supersymmetry or Chaos*, any small change in these elemental forces would spell disaster for the universe as we know it.

The exactness in the essential values of these elemental charges forces upon us the only logical and legitimate conclusion. It must have been designed. The idea that all of this was orchestrated by mere serendipity from the first microsecond of the Big Bang is at best naïve. With certainty, the decision to subjectively dismiss the possibility of premeditated design, as materialists insist, is the very evidence of a closed mind when one is faced with such overwhelming symmetry.

We can begin to appreciate the absolute importance of these narrow parameters in the resulting forces and particles created by these vibrating strands of energy. Here, the ridiculous assertion that all of this could have developed without prevision and design must be viewed as self-deception of the utmost magnitude. The symmetry of the universe reflecting an obvious pattern created by design and the universality of the existing triads, which reflect the triune structure of the Godhead, cannot be ignored by anyone who claims to have an open mind.

All four forces of nature have very widely differing strengths, but as it turns out, that variation must be exactly what it is in order for matter to exist in our universe. What would be the statistics of evolving from chaos into a universe with such symmetry and complexity through random chance processes? Even the four elemental forces are united with symmetry in such a way that it would be utterly impossible for them to have developed by pure random processes. The interconnection between the magnitude of the precise powers each possesses cannot be a random accident since that precise interconnection is the only possible one for our particular universe to exist as it does in order to inhabit life.

The similarity with the strong, weak, and electro-magnetic forces is that they too are all connected with enforcing symmetries, albeit ones that are significantly more abstract than the one associated with gravity...

This realization shows that, although the gravi-tational force and the strong force have vastly dif-ferent properties (recall, for example that gravity is far feebler than the strong force and operates over enormously larger distances), they do have a some-what similar heritage: they are each required in or-der that the universe embody particular symmetries. Moreover, a similar discussion applies to the weak and electromagnetic forces, showing that their exis-tence, too, is bound up with yet other gauge symme-tries—the so-called weak and electromagnetic gauge symmetries. And hence, all four forces are directly associated with principles of symmetry (emphasis added) *(Greene 125, 126).*

Stars can shine because of the delicate interplay between gravity and the strong nuclear force. Our sun is a nuclear furnace, which is continually converting hydrogen into helium through the process we call nuclear fusion. The outward force of this nuclear blast is resisted by gravity so it does not explode into space. That fine interplay is what allows our sun to burn in the consistent manner that allows for life on Earth.

Too much force in gravity would cause the sun to implode. Too little force in gravity, and the sun would blow up. If the strong nuclear force were too weak, the sun would implode. If the strong nuclear force were too strong, it would explode.

It is the interaction between the positive charge of the protons and the negative charge of the electrons that gives the atoms their stability. If the electromagnetic force were too weak, atoms would fly apart and not be stable enough to create compounds. If the electromagnetic force were too strong, the atoms would not be able to combine with others, and again, no compounds would be formed.

How can one even consider that these wonderfully complex elemental particles and the complementary forces among them, as well as the exact interplay of our four fundamental forces of nature, were all miraculously engineered by randomly generated blind chance to reflect a system that is so carefully calibrated?

How could that "code of three" extend to the basic entities of all reality (atoms, quarks, visible spatial dimensions, etc.) through the medium of an undirected explosion? What are the odds of this happening from mere random processes? The pervasive synchronicity observed throughout our entire universe cannot rationally be the product of random serendipity.

I am a skeptic at heart, and I simply don't have that much faith. I cannot take the blind leap of faith required to plunge into the infinitely more speculative naturalistic framework or worldview. The symmetry evidenced in our universe extends from the subatomic world to the macroworld. The genius necessary to create a material system that maintains a harmonious balance, even in the microworld, is unfathomable by our puny human brains.

All the data that have been collected establish that there is a symmetry among the quarks in the sense that the interaction between any two like-colored quarks (red with red, green with green, or blue with blue) are all identical, and similarly, the interaction between any two unlike-colored quarks (red with green, green with blue, or blue with red) are also identical. In fact, the data support something even more striking. If the three colors—the three different strong charges—that a quark can carry were all shifted in a particular manner (roughly speaking, in our fanciful chromatic language, if red, green, and blue were shifted, for instance, to yellow, indigo, and violet), and even if the details of this shift were to change from moment to moment or from place to place, the interactions between the quarks would be, again, completely unchanged (Greene 125).

The very nature of the interplay between these subatomic particles is what allows the formation of either a proton, a neutron, or an electron. The number of protons within an atom is what determines elements to be of one essence or another, giving rise to all the elements in our Periodic Table of the Elements. These elements then combine to produce compounds based on the interplay of the electrochemical dynamics inherent to each atom. That ability to combine different elements to form compounds would not exist without the elegant symmetry that rules the forces and particles in our universe.

In addition, to this electromagnetic symmetry, there is another miraculously engineered structure in the way electrons fly around the nucleus, which is universal to all atoms. The electrons of every atom in the universe are spaced within specific and precise concentric spheres of probability, around the nucleus of the atom, in a specific and prescribed order that is ingenious. These electron shells, as chemists call them, only allow a specific number of electrons within their corresponding territories or shells.

The lower shell always fills up first, and then the next shell is filled. These are named *s*, *p*, *d*, and *f*. For example, the atom for hydrogen has only one electron, so it resides in the *s* shell, the closest to the nucleus. The heliuim atom has two electrons. Both reside in the *s* shell, filling this first shell up, for the *s* shell only allows two electrons. The next shell outward from the nucleus is the *p* shell, which can hold eight electrons. The oxygen atom has eight electrons, two in the s shell and six in the p shell, leaving the p shell two short of completion.

When there are electrons missing to complete that outer shell, the atom tries to acquire the electrons it needs to fill that shell. Sometimes, the atom with the incomplete shell joins with another atom to share the electrons in the outer shell so the shell becomes full. Because oxygen has two openings for electrons in the p shell (the outer shell of oxygen), acquiring two hydrogen atoms with one electron each in their outer shells quite easily completes it, and thus we have H2O—water. That creates what is known as a covalent bond.

If it were not for the specific capacity of the carbon and oxygen atoms to make these bonds, life as we know it could not exist. For example, the hemoglobin protein found in our red blood cells that transports oxygen to the cells of the body to allow for metabolism to take place, is made up of four polypeptide chains that are held together by covalent bonds. So without the ability to bond with other atoms, the oxygen we breathe would not be transported to the cells for metabolism, and we would not have life.

*

It is now becoming perfectly clear to scientists that the design of this intricate little fellow we call the atom is not the simplistic grain of matter that Lucretius, Darwin, and the early evolutionists had assumed.

*

How did these quarks design themselves into this elaborate mechanism in order to formulate the different particles of the atom? Of course, these combine in different ways to form all the elements in our universe. Is it really feasible to imagine that all this order could, by random chance, organize itself into these complicated, specific patterns without some mechanism for directing energy?

The symmetry of our reality is universally pervasive and reflected in matter as well as the four forces of the universe due to its symmetry to the commonality of its previsioned design and origin.

> *Through their Nobel Prize–winning work, Sheldon Glashow, Abdus Salam, and Steven Weinberg showed that the weak and electromagnetic forces are naturally* united *by their quantum field–theoretic description even though their manifestations seem to be utterly distinct in the world around us. After all, weak force fields diminish to almost vanishing strength on all but subatomic distance scales, whereas electromagnetic fields—visible light, radio and TV signals, X-rays—have an indisputable macroscopic presence. Nevertheless Glashow, Salam, and Weinberg showed, in essence, that a high enough energy and temperature—such as occurred a mere fraction of a second after the big bang—electromagnetic and weak force fields* dissolve *into one another, take on indistinguishable characteristics, and are more accurately called* electroweak *fields. When the temperature drops, as it has done steadily since the big bang, the electromagnetic and weak forces* crystallize *out in a different manner from their common high-temperature form—through a process known as* symmetry breaking *(Greene 122–123).*

If the naturalist model is correct, why did the forces break in symmetry in a randomly directed universe in such a precise balance so as to allow the formation of atoms and compounds? How does chaos engineer supersymmetry?

If, in fact, random processes ruled the universe during the process of creation, we would expect other failed attempts in creating these subatomic structures. Where are they? There should be an infinite number of failed attempts before hitting upon the successful framework. Where are the intermediates that failed? Am I to believe, against all reason, that nature guided by no purpose randomly got it right on the first try in a thousand different but interconnected parameters that rule our universe?

Evolutionists recognize the high improbability of such a "miracle" and therefore propose that these failed attempts took place in other universes. Ours is the lucky one, where everything "cooked" correctly. But what scientific evidence can there be for other universes, which are untestable from our universe and should, under their closed universe theory, not be a scientific consideration? Is it not the untestability of God their major argument for dismissing from scientific consideration the possibility that our universe was intelligently designed?

So, then, it is legitimate for us to also say that this is not a scientific proposition. It is a metaphysical proposition lacking any scientific empirical data. In fact, what they are doing is nothing more than a subtle avoidance technique called displacement, which cleverly sidesteps the embarrassing data and simply shifts it out of sight. A careful study of the evolutionary paradigm reveals the great popularity enjoyed by the displacement technique, especially in the field of microbiology that deals with the origin-of-life science, as we shall soon see.

The choices are crystal clear. Either we accept the reality of a designed universe created by a supreme designer or we escape from reason to hold tenaciously to a chance-directed evolution that, with the magic wand of random ordering, created miracles greater than the immaculate conception.

Amino Acids and Proteins

Now that we have discussed the obvious discordance of the emergence of our physical universe by pure chance with the symmetry we observe in our actual universe, there is yet an even larger series of steps in the ladder of evolution to humankind that must be taken. These chemical compounds must now become organized into complex, carbon-based molecules we call proteins. Without proteins, even single-celled organisms could not exist.

First, they must form basic chemical building blocks called amino acids. Then, the amino acids must unite in specific patterns to form proteins, without which neither the structure nor the metabolic machinery of the cell could exist.

Hence, the naturalist is confronted with yet another nagging riddle. It is the mechanism for the evolutionary development from already complex, non-living chemical matter to an even more complex molecule that can be used as the building blocks for an organism that displays the unique properties we recognize as life.

The smallest possible living entity is a unicellular (single-cell) organism of which there are basically two types: (1) the prokaryotes, which contain no nucleus and (2) the eukaryotes, which have a nucleus. The prokaryotes are therefore assumed to be less complex than the eukaryotes. The truth is that although they are different, the prokaryotes are not less complex. Even the mycoplasma, which has been heralded by evolutionists as the simplest form of life, has been found to be incredibly complex and sophisticated.

In 1979, evolutionist Thomas Brock wrote in his book *Biology of Microorganisms* that mycoplasma are of particular importance to evolutionists because of their extremely simple-cell structures (723).

This supposed simplicity, they posit, attempts to give credence to the process of evolution, which is the imagined progression from a simpler organism to a more complex organism. But after decades of research, armed with our powerful new weapons of science, the supposedly simple mycoplasma has been found to be extremely complex, beyond anything that could have been fathomed in Darwin's day.

These are the empirical facts: For years, naturalists believed in the concept of spontaneous generation, or abiogenesis (the idea that life could spontaneously arise from non-life), until Louis Pasteur proved otherwise. After all, the cell seemed to be only a blob of protoplasm, a bit of "jello" confined by a cell wall.

Even as late as 1859, Ernst Haeckel, a great admirer of Darwin and one of his chief proponents, held this naïve view of the origin of life. Haeckel, using the primitive microscopes of the nineteenth century, saw the living cell as a simple lump of "albuminous combination of carbon" (Haeckel 418).

In 1859 when the *Origin of the Species* was published, an exploratory vessel, HMS *Cyclops*, dredged up mud samples from the sea floor, which appeared to Haeckel to resemble the structure of the cell that he had observed under microscopes. After bringing this to the attention of another of Darwin's greatest proponents, Thomas Henry Huxley, they became convinced that the mud samples were actually protoplasm. So convinced were they that this mud was, in fact, the precursor material of the living cell that they named it Bathybius haeckelli.

In 1868, Haeckel classified these organisms as Monera and wrote in *The History of Creation, Volume 1*:

> These very simplest of organisms yet known, and which, at the same time are the simplest imaginable organisms, are the Monera living in water; they are very small living corpuscles, which strictly speaking, do not at all deserve the name of organism. For the designation "organism," applied to living creatures, rests upon the idea that every living natural body is composed of organs, of various parts, which fit into one another and work together (as do the different parts of an artificial machine), in order to produce the action of the whole. But of late years we have become acquainted with Monera, organisms which are, in fact, not composed of any organs at all, but consist entirely of shapeless, simple, homogeneous matter. The entire body of one of these Monera, during life, is nothing more than a shapeless, mobile, little lump

of mucus or slime, consisting of an albuminous combination of carbon.... Simpler or more imperfect organisms we cannot possibly conceive (188–189).

For seven years, the scientific community believed they had found the missing link between non-life and life. Then they discovered that these corpuscles were, in fact, just the product of chemical precipitation. The "scientific facts" of that day provided what seemed at that time a plausible scaffolding for the Darwinian idea that life could progress from simple forms to more complicated forms through simple adaptive steps due to selective pressures. The true scientific reality is that these once seemingly simple-celled organisms do have organs of extremely complicated nature, and their metabolic functions are composed of "organs, of various parts, which fit into one another and work together (as do the different parts of the artificial machine)" (Haeckel 184).

It is obvious by this statement that Haeckel understood the necessity of a living organism functioning with coherence with all the interdependent organs in order for the whole to be alive. Little did Haeckel, Darwin, and Huxley imagine that the simple living cell did, in fact, contain this interdependent and coherent system of organelles, without which the cell cannot live.

Moreover, the sheer complexity and engineering masterpiece that has been discovered with our modern technology evidences clearly that there can be no gradual, simple steps of growing complexity in the creation of the "simple" living cell. Their entire theory was based wholly on our ignorance of the true nature of the supposedly "simple" living cell.

Haeckel was the same culprit, who, through the falsification of his drawings, originated and popularized the incorrect idea that the embryos of mammals had gill slits, because in his evolutionary imagination they had evolved from fish. The true scientific fact is that these embryonic tissues that supposedly resembled gill slits have nothing to do with the respiratory system. In fact, they develop into parts of the face bones and endocrine gland.

But in spite of the unquestionable scientific data, which is irrefutable today, they are still touted in some evolution-based textbooks as ontological proof of evolution. It was Haeckel who falsified the drawings of the embryos to promote the Darwinian model as he popularized his famous phrase, "Ontogeny recapitulates phylogeny." Haeckel insisted that through the embryonic stages, all animals maintain the memory of their evolutionary path. By fudging on the drawings, Haeckel deceitfully and falsely represented the true shapes of embryos to bolster his audacious claim. It gained him great notoriety as a bulwark of Darwinism and provided the "scientific evidence" that convinced many. But the supposed "scientific evidence" was utterly false.

Although in scientific circles, the concept of spontaneous generation has been thoroughly discredited since the work of Pasteur, in reality, today it is being pawned on us in a slightly modified form as the theory of abiogenic chemical synthesis. There is only one component that Darwin changed from the original failed theory: the component of time. The ridiculously impossible has been pawned as plausible through the magical mechanism of eons of time. But Einstein showed us that evolution no longer has an eternity to accomplish the seemingly impossible.

The complexity and efficiency of even a single cell is only now being appreciated through the use of the scanning-tunneling electron microscope and modern technological advances in chemistry and crystallography. As we are able to peer deeper into the structures, we are finding that the intricate functions of these so-called simple organisms are incredibly complex and surprisingly elaborate. Some biologists are honest enough to admit the obvious:

> *Mycoplasma can no longer be thought of as a simple organism (Dybvig and Voelker 48).*

*Other aspects of origin-of-life research have con-
tributed to my growing uneasiness about the theory of
chemical evolution. One of these is the enormous gap
between the most complex "protocell" model systems
produced in the laboratory and the simplest living cells.
Anyone familiar with the ultrastructural and biochemical complexity of the genus Mycoplasma, for example,
should have serious doubts about the relevance of any
of the various laboratory "protocells" to the actual
historical origin of cells. In my view, the possibility of
closing this gap by laboratory simulation of chemical
events likely to have occurred on the primitive earth is
extremely remote (Dean Kenyon in Thaxton et al. vi).*

This "ultrastructural and biochemical complexity" of the least
complex single-celled organism is so far removed from "the laboratory simulation of chemical events" created by Darwinists to explain
the evolution of life that Kenyon doubts this chasm could ever be
crossed.

First, a cell membrane must be created in order to contain this
metabolic machinery, protect it from the environment, and yet be
selectively semi-permeable. Chemicals, which are needed, can thus
go through the membrane, while unwanted ones are kept out. In
addition, the needed chemicals and compounds inside must be kept
from leaking out and, at the same time, be able to remove waste
products. That is no small order.

A membrane that accomplishes only a few of these things is
useless. It must accomplish all these things, even in the "simplest"
unicellular life form. The simplest cell membrane is a protein and
phospholipid "sandwich" called a bi-lipid membrane, which is an
extremely complicated and elaborate design.

Although all membrane proteins are located in the membrane,
they have a wide range of structures and functions. Some are bound

to the surface. Others have one region buried within the membrane and domains on one or both sides of the membrane.

Protein domains found on the outside of the membrane surface are, for the most part, involved with processes such as cell-to-cell signaling or interactions. Domains within the membrane, especially those that form channels and pores, are transporters that move only selected molecules across the membrane.

Other domains lying across the systolic face of the membrane display a wide variety of functions that range from the anchoring of cytoskeletal proteins on the membrane to triggering signaling pathways between cells.

These membrane proteins are classified into two broad categories with a wide range of functions. Those membrane proteins that have one or more segments embedded in the phospholipid bi-layer of the membrane are called integral or intrinsic proteins. These mostly span the entire phospholipid bi-layer and therefore are also referred to as transmembrane proteins.

The other broad category is the peripheral or extrinsic proteins. These unique proteins are usually bound to the membrane indirectly by chemical interactions with the intrinsic or integral membrane proteins of the inner layer.

Porins are a particular type of transmembrane protein whose structure differs radically from other integral or intrinsic proteins. The unique barrel shape of these magnificent proteins allow for one side of the protein to control the passage of certain chemicals through both layers of the membrane, while the other side allows a different type of chemical to exit the cell. The utter complexity of this supposed simple membrane is absolutely staggering.

Driving from Zurich, Switzerland, through the majestic and breathtaking Alps on the way to Merano, Italy, my wife and I boarded a train that carried our rental car and made its way through a 20-minute dark tunnel cut through the heart of the mountains to come out on the other side near the border of Italy. I thought of the great convenience of this tunnel, and it struck me that it was also much like the pores and transporters inside the cell. It was a magnificent pathway through an enormous barrier.

But unlike the living cell, this train indiscriminately accepted all types of vehicles, while the pores are quite finicky and only accept those molecules required by the cell to enter. Moreover, these pores equally control which atoms can exit the cell. In this way, the cell accepts the molecules necessary for metabolic processes and equally rids the cell of unwanted waste within it.

The marvelous engineering necessary to dig through the belly of a mountain and end up at the right spot on the other side is quite impressive. But no less impressive are the barrel-shaped porins that have chemical security guards equipped with sensitive scanners at each end of the cell layer to make sure the right things come in and the right things go out. The idea that this unique tubular design with its dual chemical functions at each end developed without pre-visioned design is hard to swallow.

This is becoming quite obvious in many biological functions as our technology progresses. Often, several distinct and carefully designated steps are required to formulate the following four vital groups of macromolecules necessary for cell function (notice the number four again): (1) nucleic acids, (2) proteins, (3) glucose, and (4) lipids. The ingenious methods by which these highly complex molecules are produced to tailor-made designs are incredibly amazing and filled with uniquely specified engineering masterpieces of nanotechnology. As we shall see, all these things must evolve simultaneously in order for a single cell to function as a living organism.

*

Without these vital functions existing fully operational and working in unison, there can be no living cell. What possible selective pressure could become the mechanism that could engineer the development of all these complicated biochemical processes that must evolve simultaneously in order for a cell to function? Each one alone is unworkable, and the cell cannot function without all of them harmoniously networking as a totality.

*

Yet these basic components of the cell do not make a cell any more than a pile of wires and transistors make a computer. Not a single scientist in this world could look me straight in the eye and tell me with all sincerity that jumbling a box of wires and transistors for 15 billion years could create a computer.

The components of the cell must be organized in precise functional organelles within the cell, all working as a unit, to carry on the process of replication, respiration, and other vital metabolic processes such as energy production and maintenance within the living cell. Perhaps the most important system in order for evolution to take place is the ability to replicate and pass information along. The origin of the gene expression system of the cell is therefore the most fundamental aspect of the metabolism of the cell that evolutionary scientists must explain.

As we will see now, that daunting task has become ever more impossible the more we learn about the elaborate and multifaceted metabolic processes of the simple cell. After all, there can be no natural selection if the characteristics cannot be passed down to the offspring. The idea that random chemical reactions could create such specificity and complexity is an absolutely irrational proposition, as we shall now see.

The Gene Expression System

Is it possible to believe that a hurricane going through a trash dump could produce a functional city? For a moment, let's oversimplify the cell in order to get a general idea of the overall function of its building blocks and imagine that the structure of a city is akin to a living cell. The building blocks can be thought of as proteins. Imagine thousands of these proteins specifically serving a precise function of the whole. The specific designs of the building blocks determine the nature of the building they create. Some form outer defense walls around the city with gates that have selective guards to allow the right people in and the right people out. These also create special radar antennae for communicating with other cities.

These outer defense walls have many entry points that select what raw materials need to come in for their factories to work and that dispose of the waste material inside that the cell has used. There are buildings for architectural planning that form a library (DNA) of all the templates of every single one of the other buildings that need to be made in order for the city to function. These are in the downtown district of the cell called the nucleus.

Other building blocks (proteins) are used to make machine shops (ribosomes). These are the shops where they make the many types of building blocks necessary in order for the city to function. The ribosomes reside in the factory district of the city (cell). Others form another specified small suburb of buildings, the power plant district (mitochondria). These not only create but also distribute the fuel necessary for all these processes to have the necessary energy within the city called a cell. This power plant not only synthesizes the fuel (ATP) but also sends it through the "city" as we send "fuel trucks" to power all the needed processes that make a city viable.

Yet other proteins are a unique group of traveling structures that have the electrical power to weld certain buildings and parts of buildings together to make distinctly unique structures that serve very specific purposes in the overall economy. These are specialized proteins called enzymes.

These traveling building blocks also perform as a network of communication throughout the entire city (regulatory protein-enzymes). They may be equipped with retractable arms and special identity tags that detect other specified structures. Moreover, they must also have the ability to move and carry other building blocks from one place to another to form a specified requirement or structure in order for the city to function.

In the "downtown" (nucleus) section of the city, there is a special area that houses the planning and architectural design complex. This is a very specialized structure that is able to provide the master plan for the shape, size, and sequential structures of every building block in the city, including its own.

But this architectural design is not in an architectural drawing. It is in a coded message that is somewhere in the archives of the master code in the library. This master template (DNA) that is written in a four-digit secret code has all the information about every building, street, and object in that city in two single strands of molecules that are entwined into the shape of a double helix. In other words, all the architectural and engineering plans are contained in one long, continuous book. But it is written in a specific language. For the sake of our illustration, let's say it is English.

The Transcription Process

Every time a new building is needed, a special mobile building block known as RNA polymerase (we will call it "Polly") comes near the architectural building and attaches to the long strand of the double helix DNA. Polly is a huge molecule of incredible complexity and sophistication. It basically envelops the two wound threads so that the DNA thread comes in at one end of the enormous molecule and then comes out at the far end of Polly.

Polly contains a special building block (protein) that is kind of a librarian that can find the specifically intended code in the enormous repository where all the information for every nail and screw is kept for the city we call the cell. It also helps open the doors of the architectural building so that together, they can search for the specific book or code they need for the building they are planning to make.

In other words, Polly has a special protein attached to it that opens the library doors to expose the books inside by unwinding the double helix of the DNA. It also has a piggyback building block with special searchlights that allows it to find the right book, or the spot to begin the copying of the code it was instructed to duplicate.

As it runs up this long DNA strand, it has a special protein that looks inside its central library, reading the codes until it finds the exact particular gene sequence called for in order to build the intended protein it has been instructed to fabricate.

Polly then breaks the bond between the matching nucleotides from the parallel threads of the DNA double helix and begins to unwind the two long nucleotide chords from their helix structure, exposing the thread it intends to copy.

Both DNA and RNA are made from nucleotides. There are four nucleotides in the DNA thread: adenosine, guanine, cytosine, and thymine. We will use the first letters of these nucleotides—A, G, C, and T—to symbolize these nucleotides. It is the specific sequencing of these nucleotides that provide the specified information necessary to build every single thing inside a cell. For our illustration, we will say that the four-letter language of the nucleotides is English.

We can say, then, that the RNA molecules also speak English since they are composed of the same nucleotides, except thymine, which is replaced with uracil.

While the double helix of the DNA is still bound together, there is always a correlation between the nucleotides in one thread and the opposite or parallel nucleotide thread. A in one thread of the DNA always matches T on the other thread of the DNA double helix. Likewise, G always matches C on the opposite thread of the DNA. In other words, the counterpart for A is always T, and the counterpart for G is always C in every DNA strand throughout the entire spectra of living organisms.

The Double Helix DNA Strands

DNA   Parallel DNA
A---------------T
G--------------C
T---------------A
C--------------G

It is the specified order of the nucleotides in the DNA thread that holds the secret code for the specified information or building instructions for every component of the cell. Once Polly's searchlights spot the right sequence or book they are looking for in the library, Polly begins to unwind the double helix DNA and separate the thread it intends to copy.

Now, there is a specific entrance port in Polly's side that allows RNA molecules to enter and proceed to the assembly area inside, where the RNA nucleotides are matched by their counterpart nucleotides on the DNA thread that was unwound and sequestered by Polly. The order of the DNA then determines the counterpart order of the RNA built by Polly.

For example, if the DNA thread were read in the order ATGC, the RNA molecules would be assembled by Polly in the matching counter-partners UACG.

1. U from RNA would bond with the DNA thread A.
2. Polly would then bond the RNA, A with T, in the DNA thread.
3. It would then bond the RNA, C with G, in the DNA thread.
4. Finally, it would bond the RNA, G with C, in the DNA thread.

Nucleotide Counter-Partners

DNA   RNA
A--------U
T--------A
G--------C
C--------G

After sequestering the RNA molecules one-by-one entering through this special entry port, Polly matches them with their counterparts in the DNA thread at precisely the point in the sequence it was ordered to duplicate. Once the nucleotides from the RNA are all matched to the corresponding nucleotides of the original DNA sequence, Polly then begins to polymerize, or link together a new chain made by the newly sequenced RNA nucleotides, which now holds the original DNA code in an RNA mirror form from the original thread. Polly can do that because it brings with her the battery power called ATP that allows her to join the new RNA thread being copied from the original DNA.

Section by section, this process is repeated over and over again. This RNA thread then stretches outward at 180 degrees from the direction of the DNA thread and begins to grow in length until Polly finds the very last sequence of nucleotides from the DNA chain it needed to copy and places a marker that says end of sequence.

As Polly moved along, copying the original DNA code, she was also rewinding the two DNA threads behind her since she was done copying that section. Once copied by Polly, the two original DNA strands are reunited and twisted into their original double helix form.

The new chain made from the RNA is called a messenger RNA, or mRNA. It is like a negative filmstrip of the original DNA code (English) it copied. We will call this mRNA "Homer" because his job is to take this English message home to the industrial district of the cell where the machine shop (ribosome) fabricates all the different proteins needed for the cell. Homer is basically a traveling scribe. But even after the mRNA strand is complete, Homer is not completely ready to take the message home to the ribosomes (machine shop).

*

"Not so fast!" say the inspectors as they arrive at the scene just when mRNA is completed. "Before you can leave, we must edit your message."

*

Homer has no choice but to accede. If you think trying to get a building inspection in your city is a hassle, try having not one but some 20 inspectors that must approve your plan. That is what Homer has to deal with before he can head home to the ribosome.

Just in the nick of time, this group of fastidious building blocks (protein enzymes) arrive, every one of them with an attitude.

*

"Our job is to inspect the work of the scribes," says the lead inspector.

"Well, get on with it already" says Homer. "I need to get these plans home pronto, and you are going to make me late."

*

These building inspectors (about 20 or so proteins) hate copying errors. They take out their faithful scissors and snip the roll of negative film into smaller chunks. They throw out the picture negatives not relevant to the task at hand, reshuffle the order, and link the pictures again into another long filament. Homer is now void of any extraneous coding that did not pertain to the exact instructions necessary for the particular protein the ribosome needs to make.

"Now you are free to go," say the inspectors to Homer the scribe.

At this point, transcription is complete, and the mRNA has to travel to the ribosome for translation from the four-letter code language of the DNA and RNA (English) to the 20-letter code language of the proteins (Spanish). Homer (mRNA) takes off, swimming in the cytoplasm like a winding snake with the complete filmstrip in the correct English message, except as a mirror image or negative of the original instructions found in the library.

The Translation of Two Separate Codes

Because transcription has been completed, Homer the scribe is now free to carry his message. He swims off, carrying the precious cargo of instructions through the salty liquid of the cytoplasm, and leaves the downtown section, heading toward the suburbs. After swimming for a while, he approaches and then enters the factory district where the machine shop (ribosomes) is waiting. There are millions of ribosomes in every cell.

There, he finds the mega-machine shop (ribosome) that has been eagerly waiting for the building plans to arrive. The ribosome machine shop is composed of one small sub-unit at the bottom and one large sub-unit at the top. Homer (mRNA) docks to the small sub-unit and is held fast. The small sub-unit positions Homer so his message can be read in groups of three codons. At the very beginning of Homer's message, the three codons have the initiator code, which is the nucleotide triplet AUG. It is this code that alerts the ribosome to begin its work.

Homer has a lot of first cousins called tRNA who work in the ribosome factory. His cousin Starter has the job of beginning the translation process. But Homer has other cousins who will help translate the English message into Spanish. The moment the AUG initiator codons at the head of Homer's message bind with the corresponding cousin Starter (tRNA), the signal is given that causes the second and larger sub-unit of the ribosome to close down like a vice over the mRNA (Homer) chain attached to the lower sub-unit. This action brings Homer's cousins tRNA into a position that allows them access to Homer.

*

"What's up, cuz? asks Homer's first cousin. "You got the goods from the big library?"

"Hey!" responds Homer. "Got it right here, but they are backward."

"Yeah, no problem. You always bring them backward. We can handle it."

"Thanks, cuz, catch you on the next run."

*

There are three work locations inside the ribosome machine shop. The first location is the A-site. Here, Homer's tRNA cousins arrive through a special port entrance to the machine shop. In this work location, the ribosome tests all the entering tRNAs (Homer's cousins) in order to properly match them with the message Homer brought. Homer's message is in triplets of the four-letter language of the DNA (English) but in negative form. His cousins tRNA also have triplets at the bottom end, but in the counter-matching order called anticodons. The anticodons revert the negative of the mRNA into the positive of the original message in the DNA.

If Homer's message reads UCC, for example, then the ribosome has to find a cousin whose anticodons are counter-matching. That would be AGG, because A is the counter to U, and G is the counter to C. In this way, Homer's cousin reverts the negative image that Homer brought in the mRNA back to the positive message of the original DNA that was in the library downtown.

But Homer's first cousins also have a special sombrero on top of their heads. The sombrero is an amino acid that corresponds specifically to the anticodon code they carry below (for our example, that would be the amino acid GLY). In other words, Homer's cousins are bilingual. They speak English in the bottom of their structure but translate it into Spanish, or the 20-letter code of proteins, in the sombrero on their heads.

Once the A site in the ribosome has found the right cousin to match Homer's triplets, it shifts to the P site of the ribosome. In this second work location, it is matched and connected to Homer below. At this point, a protein enzyme called peptidyl transferace (Homer calls him Pepi the welder) comes to help. Homer whistles for Pepi the welder for help.

*

"Hola, Pepi! Bring your torch. Pronto!"
"Don't rush me. I was on my break."

"You're lucky you have a job. Quit stalling!"

"Watch it! Don't look at that flame. If you stare at the flame, you won't be able to see things, even backward, anymore."

*

First, Pepi the welder separates the sombreros (amino acids) from the heads of Homer's tRNA cousins. Second, he welds the amino acid sombreros together.

Once Pepi removes the sombreros (amino acids) from the tRNA cousins, they are disconnected to Homer and shifted to the E site where they are evacuated from the ribosome to be recycled. The E site is the third work location that evacuates the sombrero-less tRNAs back into the cytoplasm of the cell.

*

"Adios, Primo, thanks for helping translate my message," yells Homer as his cousin floats away.

"Sure, cuz," says his first cousin tRNA, waving back. "Just going to get another sombrero."

*

As each of Homer's cousins is brought down to match with the mRNA instructions carried in the four-letter code, Homer brought from the DNA the amino acid chain elongates. Little by little, Pepi the welder continues to make the amino acid chain bigger as the ribosome physically ratchets Homer's long message through its system. Triplet by triplet, the mRNA nucleotides are matched with the anticodons of his cousins, creating a long chain of sombreros with the 20-letter language of the proteins.

Once the ribosome reaches the end-of-message signal, Pepi the welder cuts the long polypeptide chain made by the amino acids and signals that the chain has been completed and must now be folded by the packaging department.

*

"Send the sombreros to packaging," says Pepi as he finishes the last weld. "Going back to my coffee. Call me when you return, Homer. Hasta la vista, cuz."

"It won't be long, so don't take a siesta."

"Ahh, don't worry. This coffee puts a zing in my step."

✳

The message that began in English in the DNA (the four-letter code) has now been translated into Spanish (the 20-letter code) used by proteins. Once the chain has been terminated, this long polypeptide chain now folds into a precise form that determines the exact function of the building block (protein) they were originally instructed to build. It cannot be folded any old way; there is a special purpose for each folding technique to create a shape that allows that protein to function as the library downtown specified.

The new protein building block is then released into the city to perform whatever task was originally dictated by the architectural plans in the DNA. Finally, the Spanish cousins in the ribosome pull out some cigars and celebrate another completed building block.

The Indispensible Role of Proteins in the Gene Expression System

In each step of the translation process, proteins with specialized skills were used. There are 20 specific enzymes (proteins) that help the initial coupling of the amino acids to their specific tRNA partners. There is one particular enzyme for each of the 20 amino acids. Without these enzymes, Homer's cousins (tRNA) would not have the bilingual ability to enable the translation of the message brought from the DNA. These enzymes are the ones that allow them to have the right sombrero.

All the buildings (proteins) that the ribosomes produce are Spanish-speakers (20-letter code), although it was first directed by the master plan of the DNA in English (four-letter code).

There are several major problems for evolutionists in their gradualist model:

- The cellular gene-expression system uses two separate codes (English and Spanish in our illustration) and a messenger that transcribes the original master plan from the DNA in order to carry the code to the ribosome (shop). There, the translator of the code reads it in the DNA language and translates it to the 20-letter protein language to build that specific protein.

- Each of the components of the protein is built in accordance with the original design template found in the DNA (four-letter) code. And yet they are able to translate it from a four-code (nucleic acids) language to the 20-code (amino acids) language that all proteins use.

- Codes require a mind to conceive them. Nature has not shown the capacity to form codes through random chemical reactions. Dead molecules do not create codes.

- There is no step-by-step gradual scenario that can, through random ordering, create this elaborate and multifaceted system containing two secret codes and a translator. To believe in fairy dust is more logical.

- On top of that miraculously engineered feat, all along the process, specialized proteins called enzymes are essential in the translating and transcription process, so DNA alone cannot carry out the translation system without the help of proteins. Proteins need DNA, and DNA needs proteins. How can gradualism explain the origins of the gene expression system when both proteins and DNA must begin together in order for it to work?

I hope by now you are beginning to grasp the overall picture of the integrated complexity and the sophisticated network inside the cell, without which life cannot exist. But the intricacy and complexity of this supposedly simple cell is much more intense then what we have covered to this point. We will now expand on these four main points.

Only 20 Sombreros?

The thousands of specialized building blocks (proteins) are made up of thousands of bricks (amino acids, or "sombreros"). These bricks are not just any old bricks. They are exclusively the amino acids of which only 20 of the thousands that exist comprise the specific language code of proteins.

Imagine a giant square in the town with thousands of sombreros, but only 20 of these sombreros can actually work in the gene expression system. Only 20 specially shaped sombreros can be used by living organisms; all the others are unusable. How does random chance pick the exact 20 out of the thousands by sheer luck? This exclusivity poses a problem for random evolutionary processes. It points to a choice being made by the designer and not a random system.

These bricks are made up of thousands of particles of sand, clumped together also in a specific design that determines the shape of the bricks and consequently allows their specific functions to operate. These sand particles are the organic compounds carbon, nitrogen, oxygen, and hydrogen, which form the molecules and, in turn, form amino acids.

But far from being simple bricks, these amino acids are highly ordered, structured molecules whose chemical function is specifically determined, first by the arrangement of their composition and second by their specific three-dimensional shapes. By having certain physical shapes, they can help dock with other amino acids whose shapes are designed to match. This is also controlled by the chemical/electrical charges in these areas, which prohibit certain unions and favor others.

After duly analyzing this complex organic city we call the living cell with all the interdependent structures, can anyone with an ounce of sense really find it credible that it could have evolved by blind chance? Can we rationally accept as credible the proposition that after millions of sand particles were shuffled and reshuffled incessantly in a giant box, this organic city we call the cell somehow evolved? The plain truth is that random chaotic processes could never create a structure of this intricate and interdependently complex nature. That claim is pure fantasy in whatever scientific jargon it is presented.

Even if random ordering could have created the basic amino acid components, it would be impossible for them to randomly fall into the shape of a protein. The creation of one protein is hard enough, but to believe that random ordering could have created the many varied forms of proteins that are necessary in order for the cell to live is absolutely irrational. Moreover, without an architectural plan to provide the specified code for its complex structure, there would be no enzymes and other specialized proteins that are absolutely necessary in order for a single cell to live and for the gene expression system to work. Without the numerous and specialized proteins involved in the ribosome factory, there would also not be any proteins manufactured.

Without the gene expression system, there can be no natural selection, which is the principal dogma of the evolutionary theory. Selection can only take place if there is a reproducible outcome that can compete for a favorable selection. Therefore, not only does the DNA double helix structure have to exist at the same time as the ribosome machine shop that creates proteins, but the process of mitosis where the DNA structure duplicates must also exist at the same time. Both the nucleic acids and the proteins need each other to work simultaneously in order for the cell to pass on any information after it dies. How, then, can they both evolve simultaneously?

Furthermore, the sequence of the amino acids must also be exact, or they will not produce a protein. The sequencing specificity is the secret code that cannot be invented by random ordering. How does random ordering create the 20-letter code of the proteins? But this is just the beginning of the enormous credibility problem for evolutionists.

The Universal Riddle of the 20 Amino Acids

Imagine a brickyard containing thousands of different-shaped and different-sized bricks. In this illustration, let us imagine that a brick represents an amino acid. There are thousands of amino acids, but for this illustration, we will limit them to only 2,000 to give random ordering a better chance. To give random ordering an even greater chance, we will make 100 sets of these in order to make them more abundant. Let's say that we numbered them one through 2,000 in big red letters on each side of the bricks. Now, after numbering 100 sets of these 2,000 bricks, we dump them into a lake. One hundred sets of the 2,000 bricks give us a total of 200,000 bricks. Imagine that these 200,000 bricks are suspended in a lake filled with some viscous fluid and that the bricks are therefore moving about haphazardly in a continuous current. At the shore of this lake we have cranes scooping into the viscous fluid and randomly extracting one brick at a time. Remember, our bricks are symbols for amino acids.

Our goal is to build with each crane a protein building that, for the sake of the argument, we will make ridiculously simple with only 50 bricks. However, of the 2,000 types of bricks floating in the lake, we have selected only 20 lucky numbers that can be allowed to form proteins. We now arbitrarily choose 7, 14, 21, 28, 35, 42, 49, 56, 63, 70, 77, 84, 91, 98, 105, 112, 119, 126, 133, and 140 as the only numbers that can produce our intended product—the protein building. We will call these the "Chosen Few." All the other numbers between 1 and 2,000 are incapable of making this protein. Only a combination exclusively of the 20 numbers we have labeled as the Chosen Few can make a viable protein.

We have 100 cranes around this imaginary lake, and they are grabbing bricks and throwing them into piles of 50. Each time a pile of 50 is completed, we look to see if the entire pile is composed of only the "Chosen Few." If not, it is discarded. Beyond the cranes are piles of these bricks that did not contain 50 bricks of only the numbers of the Chosen Few. How confident would you be that one of those cranes could form a small 50-amino-acid protein with only the 20 Chosen Few of the 200,000 bricks floating on the lake?

Of all the potential bricks available, when we analyze this building (protein), we find that it is composed of only 20 specified bricks, the Chosen Few. All the other bricks (amino acids) were equal in abundance, but none of them were chosen. There are no chemical reasons for this to have taken place. There are no special advantages to choosing one amino acid over another. The choice seems to be completely arbitrary.

If all the different kind of bricks were equally available, we would expect that random ordering would have used all of them in the reshuffling. How could natural forces have selected only these 20 types of amino acids when there are no chemical reasons to choose one over the other? That arbitrary choice points to a designer.

In describing the protein molecule, Francis Crick, winner of the Nobel Prize in Physiology and co-discoverer of the double helix structure of the DNA and its code, wrote:

> Much of the structure and the metabolic machinery of the cell are based on one family of molecules, the proteins. A protein molecule is a macromolecule, running to thousands of atoms. Each protein is precisely made, with every atom in its correct place. Each type of protein forms an intricate three-dimensional structure, peculiar to itself, which allows it to carry out its catalytic or structural function. This three-dimensional structure is formed

by folding up an underlying one-dimensional one, based on one or more polypeptide chains, as they are called. The sequence of atoms along this backbone consists of a pattern of six atoms, repeated over and over again. Variety is provided by the very small side-chains which stick out from the backbone, one at every repeat. A typical backbone has some hundreds of them.

Not surprisingly, the synthetic machinery of the cell constructs these polypeptide chains by joining together, end to end, a particular set of small molecules, the amino acids. These are all alike at one end—the part which will form the repeating backbone—but different at the other end, the part which forms the small side-chains. What is surprising is that there are just twenty kinds of them used to make proteins, and this set of twenty is exactly the same throughout nature. Yet other kinds of amino acids exist and several of them can be found within a cell. Nevertheless, only this particular set of twenty is used for proteins.

A protein is like a paragraph written in a twenty-letter language, the exact nature of the protein being determined by the exact order of the letters. With one trivial exception, this script never varies. Animals, plants, microorganisms and viruses all use the same set of twenty letters although, as far as we can tell, other similar letters could easily have been employed, just as other symbols could have been used to construct our own alphabet. Some of these chemical letters are obvious choices, since they are small and easily available. Others are less obvious (emphasis added) *(Crick 44–45).*

There are simply no chemical reasons or clear explanations by evolutionary biologists that can give any justifiable reason for the universal riddle of the 20 amino acids. If the origin of life has evolved through random processes, then one should expect that the structures of proteins would have been made from all the available amino acids present in nature.

A randomly generated chemical process with all the amino acids present could not have arbitrarily selected only 20 specified amino acids. That implies a willful, selective choice by a designer that wished to alert us of this specified choice. Otherwise, the thousands of amino acids in nature would have been part of the accidental, random shuffling and reshuffling in the production of proteins. The process would have surely mixed all possible numbers of combinations in the mechanism of natural selection. It is not that the amino acids were not available, for we even find some of the other amino acids within the very structure of the cell.

The choice is absolutely arbitrary. And as Crick pointed out, it surely points to unity in origin, but the fact that no natural chemical explanations can account for this phenomenon and that it seems to be an arbitrary choice more accurately points to an intelligent designer (the "chooser") as the true origin of this unity.

Mere random, chance combinations cannot account for this arbitrary choice. Why didn't another set of amino acids evolve into a protein simultaneously, or even several sets into several different types of proteins? Surely, if mere chance combinations of chemicals produced proteins, there would be other types of proteins using the other available amino acids. Yet all living things are made of proteins exclusively from these Chosen Few, the 20 specific amino acids.

Crick, after exclaiming his curiosity at this phenomenon, goes on to theorize that this shows, what he calls the common heritage of all life. I quite agree with Crick, for there truly is a common heritage, but not from an evolutionary standpoint. The common heritage is evident because of a common design from a singular designer. Pure chemical necessity or even some form of selective pressure cannot explain the commonality, as Crick admits. There is no natural way of explaining why only 20 kinds are arbitrarily elected to create proteins. Perhaps it is time for rational people to realize that this is not due to natural selection but rather supernatural election, which ought to point the seeking mind to the Designer.

The Unfolding Miracle of Folding

But the evidence left by the Master Designer that refutes the Darwinist theology of random ordering with resounding force does not end there. Our ability to observe this unicellular world through modern technology is unfolding the miracle of the magnificent process of protein folding. The very process of the formation of the proteins as they undergo a complex series of folds until they reach a stable, three-dimensional form is in itself a paradox from an evolutionary standpoint. There are thousands of ways the protein can be bent from the long polypeptide chain that is constructed by the tRNA when it is formed in the ribosome. Yet only one specifically ordered folding pattern out of thousands can produce the correct three-dimensional shape that is necessary in order for that protein to fulfill its designed purpose. Once again, we find a predetermined choice for a particularly specified result out of thousands of possibilities that allows the protein to function as pre-designed.

What selective pressure could cause the delicate folding miracle that gives this molecule its ability to function in a particularly pre-designed way? The end result of this miraculous folding is a three-dimensional form that cannot be easily discerned by viewing the long polypeptide chain as the tRNA in the ribosome is constructing it. How did the tRNA know it would fold it in just the exact sequence to make it have the function that this specific protein is supposed to have?

If it is truly a random search for a stable structural integrity, how is it that instead of taking thousands of years to go through all the numerical folding possibilities, as blind random ordering would suggest, the folding is instead miraculously done in seconds? Evolutionists insist that randomness allows the protein, by trial and error, to find intermediate three-dimensional configurations before ending at the specified shape it was designed to have from the beginning when its blueprints were copied in the DNA library. The truth is that if trial and error were part of the folding process, it would take thousands of years to go through all the numerical possibilities. But most evolutionists won't tell you that. The problem is called Levinthal's paradox.

Each polypeptide (amino acid chain) then detaches from the ribosome and folds into either a structural protein, i.e. muscle or skin, or a functional protein, such as an enzyme. It generally takes only a few seconds, but the potential number of combinations of folds is astronomical.

> "This method of folding sounds very simple; it is not. Although proteins do have machinery to help them fold, proteins must fold through a random search for stable intermediates. Therefore, the protein does not fold all at once. By trial and error the protein finds the most stable intermediates until the final three-dimensional protein configuration is energetically very stable in its environment. With this configuration the protein can maintain its function and structural integrity.
>
> Although the substructures within the protein fold spontaneously, there are so many possible conformations that a protein can adopt that it would take thousands of years for it to assume its proper structure. Yet actual protein folding times are on the order of seconds. The difference between the actual and theoretical times of protein folding is called Levinthal's Paradox (emphasis added) (Bendewald 60).

What selective pressure could induce such radical efficiency through a completely undirected medium? It is not just the cell as a whole; every aspect of the design of the basic structures that compose the cell evidences the fingerprint of a master architect of unfathomable genius. The idea that a single cell is just some simple blob of protoplasm, as Darwinists first believed, is as accurate as a flat Earth.

Initially, evolutionists expected the protein molecule to be regularly structured like a crystal. Such a shape could be expected if natural forces created the formation of the protein. Information scientists call this redundant order. Another example of ordered redundancy would be "123, 123, 123, 123." Crystals form this kind of repetitive structure due to their specific chemical bonds. We can find in nature many such repeating structures made by natural processes due to wind, waves, and so on. This is called simple complexity. Nature can create simple complexity. But nature cannot create such asymmetrical and specified complexity as found in the protein as well as the DNA through random processes. Not one test can be shown to empirically create specified complexity through a purely random process—not one.

These initial expecta-
tions were proved wrong by
John Kendrew's research.
Kendrew found that the
complex, three-dimension-
al structure of the protein
myoglobin was extraordi-
narily complex and irregular (Kendrew 662–666). It

Myoglobin*

* Irving Geis. Rights owned by Howard Hughes Medical Institute. Not to be reproduced without permission. First appeared in *Scientific American*, December, 1961, in the article by John Kendrew: *"The Three Dimensional Structure of a Protein Molecule."*

was such an oddly shaped, tangled, twisting, turning chain of amino acids that it boggled the mind. Yet that shape had enormous specificity. It was that exact, specific shape that gave the protein its specified electrochemical properties. It is that specific shape that gives it the hand-in-glove fit to bond with other chemicals by providing access to the active sites in precisely the right places where the peptide bonding can take place (Meyer 95).

In the 1930s, J. D. Bernal, Dorothy Hodgkin, and Max Perutz performed the earliest crystallographic studies of proteins at Cambridge's Cavendish Laboratory; however, the intricacies of three-dimensional structure of proteins were too complex for analysis by conventional X-ray crystallography, and the process of calculating the structure factors by slide-rules and electric calculators was far too slow.

It was not until the late 1940s, when Kendrew joined the Cavendish Laboratory as a graduate student, that new and more sophisticated tools emerged that could be used to attack the problem. The first of these tools was the technique of isomorphous replacement, developed by Perutz during his own researches on hemoglobin, in which certain atoms in a protein molecule are replaced with heavy atoms. When these modified molecules are subjected to X-ray analysis, the heavy atoms provide a frame of reference for comparing diffraction patterns. The second tool was the electronic computer, which Kendrew introduced to computational biology in 1951. At the time, Cambridge University was one of only three or four places in the world with a high-speed stored-program electronic computer, and Kendrew took full advantage of the speed of Cambridge's EDSAC computer, and its more powerful successors, to execute the complex mathematical calculations required to solve the structure of myoglobin.

Nevertheless, even with the EDSAC computer performing the calculations, the research progressed remarkably slowly. Only by the summer of 1957 did Kendrew and his team succeed in creating a three-dimensional map of myoglobin at a resolution the so-called "low resolution" of 6 angstroms; thus myoglobin became "the first protein to be solved" (Judson 538).

The 6-angstrom resolution was too low to show the molecule's finer features, but by 1960, Kendrew and his team were able to obtain a map of the molecule at 2-angstrom resolution (Norman).

The Problem of Sequence Specificity: The Protein Code

As we have previously stated, there are thousands of proteins that serve numerous jobs, but all proteins are made of only 20 amino acids. These 20 amino acids form the alphabet of the protein language. However, the problem for the evolutionists relying on random processes is even deeper than accounting for the selected Chosen Few.

There are countless variations of those 20 amino acids that form polypeptide molecules, which are not proteins. Only specified variations can become a protein. It is the specified sequence in these proteins that gives them the information that causes them to be functional. So the selective mystery is even deeper. Not just any mixture of these 20 amino acids can produce a protein.

*Consider another example of how the specific shape of proteins allows them to perform specific functions. The eukaryotic cell has an uncanny way of storing the information in DNA in a highly compact way. (*Eukaryotes *are cells that contain a nucleus and other membrane-bound organelles;* prokaryotic *cells lack these features.) Strands of DNA are wrapped around spool-like structures called nucleosomes. These nucleosomes are made of proteins called histones. And again it is the specific shape of the histone proteins that enables them to do their job. Histones 3 and 4, for example, fold into well-defined three-dimensional shapes with a precise distribution of positive electrical charges around their exteriors. This precise shape and charge distribution enables DNA* *strands to coil efficiently around the nucleosome spools and store an immense amount of information in a very small space. Thanks in part to nucleosome spooling, the information storage density of DNA is many times that of our most advanced silicon chips....*

But proteins have a second type of specificity—one that helps to explain the first. Proteins do not just display a specificity of shape; they also display a specificity of arrangement. *Whereas proteins are built from rather simple amino-acid "building blocks," their various functions depend crucially on the specific arrangement of those building blocks. The specific sequence of amino acids in a chain and the resulting chemical interactions between amino acids largely determine the specific three-dimensional structure that the chain as a whole will adopt. Those structures and shapes determine what function, if any, the amino-acid chain can perform in the cell—whether as an enzyme, structural component, or a machine for processing information....*

As the amino acids "snap" together, the resulting chains are called polypeptides. *If one of these polypeptide chains folds into a specific shape that enables it to perform tasks within the cell, it is called a* protein.

But that, it turns out, is a big "if." Only if amino acids are arranged in very specific ways will the chain fold into useful shapes or conformations.... *Most amino-acid arrangements, however, produce chains that do not fold into stable structures at all. Other arrangements generate stable structures, but do not perform a function. Relatively few sequences will produce functional structures (Meyer 96–99).*

The protein molecule, as it turns out, has what biologists refer to as sequence specificity. The sequence of those amino acids determines its specific function. If the function of the system as a whole depends critically upon the specific arrangement of the parts, then it is a code. Languages have this same property.

*

So does a computer program. The sentence "My name is Henry" is written in the English language. Each of the letters in that sentence have specific information that, when placed together, performs a function. The code allows the reader, who must also know that code, to decipher the meaning.

If the reader understands the code that interprets each letter, he or she is able to understand the sentence. That is viewed as specified complexity because it transfers functional information in asymmetrical codes. It is not the simple complexity of repetitive symmetrical patterns created by nature.

The numerical sequence 100 1101 101 1001 100 1110 100 0001 100 1101 100 0101 100 1001 101 0011 100 1000 100 0101 100 1110 101 0010 101 1001 says the same thing. It says, "My name is Henry" in the American Standard Code for Information Interchange (ASCII). This is the binary code that my computer is using to store the data I input when I am writing.

Both these have complexity and specific information. The sentence "Xt morh br kturs" has the same number of letters as "My name is Henry." It has irregular, unrepeatable complexity, and it is also asymmetrical, but it has no specific information because it does not have a code. That exhibits what information scientists call "mere complexity" as opposed to "specified complexity."

Codes that exhibit specified complexity (i.e., they carry functional information) are not found anywhere in the natural world outside of living things. Specified complexity cannot appear through random chaotic processes. They must be input by a mind that understands the symbols and the code.

The existence of a code automatically presupposes two minds, but at minimum, one mind. The mind of the message giver is the essential component, and the mind of the message receiver is the secondary component.

In 1977, space scientists sent *Voyager 1* into deep space with many coded messages on a golden plate. They did so with the hope that the second mind would see those codes and infer that intelligence exists on planet Earth. Why? Because random ordering does not create codes; codes provide to anyone who might come upon them the evidence of intelligence existing on our planet. It was basically our note in a bottle thrown into the cosmic ocean.

Included in the many images portrayed in that golden disk is the image of DNA. On the back of the golden record are symbols that instruct the receiver how to use the record player with the stylus in the right position at the exterior of the record. Beyond that, even the numbers 1, 2, and 3 are noted in the code of binary numbers. There are coded instructions on how to read the pictures, and so forth. Our astrophysicists understood that such specific information conveyed in codes would be understood as a sign of intelligence by any "alien" that would happen upon our little satellite.

In 1990, *Voyager 1* passed the orbit of Pluto. Today, it is passing the heliosheath, the region beyond the termination shock (where the solar wind is slowed by pressure from interstellar gases and becomes denser and hotter). Traveling at 38,000 miles per hour, it will take 40,000 years to come within 1.7 light years of a star.

Nevertheless, the fundamental presupposition of this secondary mission of *Voyager 1* is that any alien that by chance comes upon it would assume that random ordering could not have created such specified complexity. The coded symbols prove that a conscious mind sent the message. Whether or not a conscious mind will receive the message is another story. But the point is that a code automatically presupposes a code inventor and message giver. In this, we are in complete agreement with the astrophysicists who designed and engineered the coded message on this gold disk sent on *Voyager 1.*

The complexity of the hardware of *Voyager 1* and the specified complexity of the coded messages inscribed on its golden plate proves to any alien that might happen upon it that an intelligent mind sent it. In exactly the same way, the gene-expression system in the cell is the "Voyager" sent by God to humankind that proves to us that intelligence designed life. The cell is our golden record engineered by the Creator for those with eyes to see and ears to hear.

> *Apart from the molecules comprising the gene-expression system and machinery of the cell, sequences or structures exhibiting such specified complexity or specified information are not found anywhere in the natural—that is, the nonhuman—world. Sequences and structures exhibiting either redundant order or mere complexity are common in the chemical substrate of nature. But structures exhibiting specified complexity are completely unknown there apart from DNA, RNA, and proteins. As the origin-of-life biochemist Leslie Orgel observes, "Living organisms are distinguished by their specified complexity. Crystals ... fail to qualify as living because they lack complexity; mixtures of random polymers fail to qualify because they lack specificity" (Meyer 110).*

Polypeptide chains that do not become proteins exhibit mere complexity, but not specified complexity. They are like "Xt morh br kturs." From the thousands of possible combinations of amino acids, few can carry specific information in the form of proteins. Both the proteins and nucleotides exhibit specified complexity. Moreover, they have a code that is mutually compatible and allows them to function together, for they are both mutually interdependent. The secret of their intercommunication is a marvel to understand.

The language of DNA would be meaningless if it could not interface with the language of proteins. So if random processes were responsible for their origin, they would have to evolve simultaneously. How did random chaotic processes manage that miracle of the first magnitude? What selective pressure could carry out such a feat?

It seems infinitely more plausible to account for this unique phenomenon as an exhibited common design by a common Designer, leaving His fingerprint in the evidence of His previsioned design. Here is yet another vital thread in the intricate tapestry of life that bears witness to His genius design of our creation and specifically of life itself.

As we shall see, the insurmountable problem for the evolutionist is that there is a mutual interdependence that exists between the basic molecules and components of the cell, which would require evolution to develop each of them simultaneously in order for them to function, as they are all needed in the cell at the same time.

Before we examine that, let's look at another one of these arbitrary chemical choices left to force upon the thinking, honest person the evidence that leads us to acknowledge the reality of the Master Designer.

The Riddle of the Left-Handed Amino Acids

To recap, there are many thousands of types of proteins designed to function in thousands of different ways. Some are structural proteins. Others are enzymes or regulatory proteins that catalyze vital metabolic processes. Others are specialized hormones, and so on. Yet all these proteins are formed from 20 basic amino acids in countless variations. However, not all the variations of these 20 amino acids can make a protein. To make a protein, a special further specificity is required in the ordering sequence. That specificity evidences a designed intent by a biological engineer, and not random happenstance.

The precise shape of the molecule, combined with its electrical and chemical properties, is produced by the exact order of these amino acids in the chain. This, in turn, is what determines the specified shape and specific job of that particular protein that was created in the cell's machine shop, which we call the ribosome.

These amino acids are highly ordered and intricately arrayed molecules. Each amino acid has a common "backbone" consisting of two carbon atoms and one nitrogen atom. It is the side group (also called the R-group) that attaches to this backbone that differentiates it between one type of amino acid and another. So even the fundamental composition of amino acids points to a common designer.

But there is still another nagging riddle that confronts the already beleaguered evolutionist. The position of this side group (that ranges from one to 18 atoms) determines the active side of the amino acid. Some are located on the right side of the backbone, and some are located on the left side of the backbone. If the side group is on the right side (right-handed), it is an exact duplicate but a mirror image of the left-handed amino acids.

Both left-handed and right-handed amino acids are equally plentiful in nature. But oddly enough, proteins are exclusively formed only from left-handed amino acids. This is another evolutionary riddle of the first magnitude. It is another arbitrarily selected exclusion that counters a randomly generated genesis.

If the formation of proteins evolved through random processes, and both left-handed and right-handed amino acids were equally plentiful in nature, and if there was no chemical reason to select one antipode over another, we would expect proteins in equal quantities, created from both left-handed and right-handed amino acids. But this is not what we find. All proteins are made exclusively from left-handed amino acids.

This mystery perplexes the evolutionary biologist, as Oparin confessed:

> *The probability of the formation of one antipode or the other is therefore the same. As the law of averages applies to chemical reactions the appearance of an excess of one antipode is very improbable, and, in fact, we never encounter it under the conditions of non-living nature and in laboratory syntheses (Oparin 80).*

Yet this is precisely what one encounters in all living systems. Oparin cheats a little in watering down the true state of the matter through the choice of his language. He claims it is a lopsided selection and an "appearance of an excess of one antipode" over another. But this is a misrepresentation of the true facts.

What is really reflected here is neither an excess nor a lopsidedness but rather an exclusive selection, which is infinitely more improbable. It isn't that 60 percent are left-handed amino acids and 40 percent are right-handed. It is that 100 percent are left-handed and 0 percent are right-handed. How do random natural forces accomplish such a miracle of the first order?

Taking into account the naturalistic principle of random chance as the guiding force in the chemical evolution of proteins, it is impossible that such an exclusive selection should evolve. This is especially so when no natural selective advantage is offered by this arbitrary choice of forming proteins exclusively from left-handed amino acids. The mathematical odds of this phenomenon occurring by purely random coincidence are unfathomable.

There is absolutely no reason to account for this bizarre fact from a chemical point of view. But the fact still remains—all living things are comprised of only left-handed amino acids. In a purely accidental or random chemical genesis, this would be a purely statistical impossibility. Oparin openly admits that "in fact, we never encounter it under the conditions of non-living nature and in laboratory syntheses." Therefore, for all practical purposes, it should be disregarded as a valid mechanism for its formation. Again, we are faced with the evidence of a specific and arbitrary choice made by a master designer.

Reality again points to an intelligent designer leaving his fingerprint for those who are seeking to find truth—not those who blink at the truth to legitimize their moral choices. Here is another vital thread in the magnificently designed tapestry of life that bears the fingerprint of the Supreme Designer.

To believe that random chemical processes miraculously developed this unique and specific choice is simply a leap of faith based entirely on speculation derived from their underlying antipathy toward the notion of a master designer. To believe that randomness could achieve such specificity is a leap of faith of astronomical proportions and has nothing to do with empirical data and everything to do with an underlying metaphysical deophobia.

CHAPTER 3

●●●

CODES ARE THE PRODUCT OF A MIND

The DNA Language

The reader must keep in mind that the unbelievable complexity of the cell as a whole is much more intricate than the complexity of its individual components. For a cell to live, all the functional components must operate cohesively, because they are all interdependent. The malfunction of any of the organelles spells disaster for the living cell in the same way that the failure of any of our organs spells disaster for the human body.

The magnificent thing about a living cell is that it carries an instruction manual within the DNA called the gene expression system. Let's think about that word *instruction* and what it necessarily implies.

When I was younger and bought Christmas gifts for my children that needed to be assembled, I sometimes relied too much on my own knowledge and experience, thinking I could accomplish it faster if I just started putting them together. Like most men, I did not read the instructions. Sometimes it took me a lot longer in the end to go back, read the instructions, and find out why or where I had made a mistake.

I learned the importance of instructions. Without a well-thought-out instruction, the proper assembly cannot be completed correctly. Instructions require an intelligently ordered process. No non-living process can create an intelligent instruction manual. We can create computer programs that can create instructions, but without the initial input of human intelligence, first in the creation of the instructions and then in the programming of the software to reproduce those instructions, there will be no instructions.

To believe that non-living chemicals could create magnificently complex instructions for every single element that comprises all the components of the cell to function coherently and interdependently for each of their particular and varied functions requires an irrational leap of faith that is in contradiction to all known empirical facts regarding the construction of instructions. No evolutionist can point to a randomly generated set of instruction that is as multifaceted and complex as the living cell.

The metaphysical choice made by materialists that chance chemical processes could create the specified complexity found in the gene expression system is an irrational step of faith that goes counter to all known experiences in our universe. The enormous leap of blind faith they make evidences that they are, indeed, priests of the religion of scientism that excels in faith beyond Christian or Jewish beliefs. It has nothing to do with empirical science.

The magnificent structure and function of the gene expression system is made possible by the ingenious language of the nucleic acids. Yes, DNA has a language. Let's talk a bit more about the word *language*. Can inanimate matter create a language? Can a language exist without a mind to speak it and interpret it? If we are to be objective thinkers, we must consider that without a mind, there can

Francis Crick, co-discoverer of the double helix structure of the DNA and its code

be no language since language is the expression of thoughts, and thoughts cannot exist in inanimate matter. Language is the product of a mind. That is an empirical reality.

Now, let's examine these macromolecules called nucleic acids. We will not just consider the mechanical complexity of these structures; we will look at the complexity of the language they use.

Francis Crick explains the functions of these wonderfully ordered giant molecules.

> Nature employs a second, very different chemical language which is also fairly uniform. The genetic information for any organism is carried in one of the two closely related families of giant chain molecules, the nucleic acids, DNA and RNA.... Each molecule has an immensely long backbone with a regular, repeating structure. Again, a side-group is attached at regular intervals but in this case there are only four types; the genetic language has only four letters. A typical small virus, such as the polio virus, is about five thousand letters long. The genetic message in a

bacterial cell usually has a few million letters; man's has several billion, packed in the center of each of our many cells. (Crick 45–46).

His choice of words belies the obvious underlying reality that this must have been a conscious choice. For he speaks of nature, which by his own naturalistic definition is completely void of personhood, as a person who chooses to create a second chemical language. As Crick wrote, "Nature employs a second, very different chemical language which is also fairly uniform."

So not only is there now a second language being chosen, but the language is incredibly consistent. How does random ordering out of chaos accomplish this miracle of the first order? But lest you think this is some simple form of language, let's examine what a language consists of. In human beings, language consists of a text of characters that provide a symbol for a specified sound that can be assembled in groups whose collective sound then expresses a word, which is symbolic of a thought in a mind. By grouping these characters into a series of words, we create a sentence that puts together a specified set of words that represent a specified set of thoughts, and a message is conveyed.

Nucleic acids form the instruction manual of every component within a living cell. The DNA of each cell in our body creates a sentence that is several billion words long, "packed in the center of each of our many cells."

These four letters that Crick refers to are called bases and are grouped in groups of three, called codons. These bases produce 64 possible codons, 61 of which determine the type of amino acid being replicated. The other three codons signal the end of the chain, or the end of the message.

In other words, not only is this text written with a specified complex message, but the message contains an ending code that allows the reader to know the message is complete. How does random ordering accomplish this feat?

Now the complexity of this system cannot really be appreciated until we realize the sheer volume of information encoded and the unrivaled precision in which each cell replicates this enormous amount of information.

The human DNA, composed of forty-six chromosomes and found in almost every cell of a person's body, dictates the exact uniqueness of that individual among every other human being ever to have been born on the planet. Each DNA is composed of a strand of nucleotides so tightly coiled that when stretched end to end would extend about the length of a six-foot person. If all the DNA in the body of an average person were to be placed end to end, it would stretch from here to the moon more than 500,000 times.

The reason this immensely long filament fits inside the tiny space within a cell is that it is incredibly thin in design. In fact, the chain is so thin that if you were to enlarge the DNA to extend from New York to Los Angeles, the molecule would be no wider than the width of an average pencil. And yet inside this marvelous piece of biological engineering, there are more than 6 billion nucleotides.

Perhaps this number does not impress you. But imagine that each of these nucleotides is a letter within a word, and the number of letters found within each of these cells is 55,360,716 times as many letters as are contained in this entire book. In other words, if you were to have a library containing 55,360,716 books of comparable size to this book, it would then contain the amount of information found in the DNA of one single human cell.

How many libraries do you know that contain more than 55 million books? There is not a chip made in the world that can rival the amount of information stored in a single cell. And there is no computer made that can rival the accuracy of the replicating system of the cell.

Breaking the Code

DNA is written in a particular alphabet composed of the four bases (A, G, T, C). A person's DNA, for example, is a mega-book containing explicit instructions about every aspect of your body written in this four-letter code. But writing this book word by word is a multifaceted, complex procedure requiring several intricate and complex steps in order to be successful.

The DNA molecule is basically a code template or library that houses the blueprint of every aspect of all organisms. It does this by governing the exact structure of the message for the program written with those four bases. That message, stored in the DNA, is copied and transferred to another area of the cell that fabricates the proteins tailor-made for a wide variety of purposes.

The RNA (mRNA) molecule is the messenger, which we previously called Homer. It transfers the message copied from the DNA to the ribosome, where the proteins are manufactured. Both DNA and mRNA carry genetic information in that four-base code. But as we said previously, the proteins carry information in a different language that uses a 20-letter code.

For years, biologists and chemists were stumped trying to find how the gene expression system worked. Some believed that the genes were found in the proteins. James Watson and Francis Crick were convinced it was found in the DNA. Scientists were unable to fathom the connection between proteins and the DNA because there seemed to be no chemical connectedness between one and the other. It was Crick who imagined the idea of a code.

> The breakthrough by Crick and Watson was their discovery of the specific key to life's diversity. It was the extraordinarily complex yet orderly architecture of the DNA molecule. They had discovered that there is in fact a code inscribed in this "coil of life," bringing a major advance in our understanding of life's remarkable structure (Thaxton et al. 1)

This proposal for a code was completely unexpected because it was not dependent on the chemical features of the nucleotides. It was not expected in a randomly generated system. In a flash of brilliance, Crick deduced that there must be some intermediary code that connected the nucleotides in DNA with the proteins.

In other words, this code, an arbitrary intermediate system, is not the product of chemical affinities or necessity. It is not the natural outcome of chemical properties. Instead, it insinuates an arbitrary choice engineered to connect the four-letter language of nucleic acids with the 20-letter language of proteins.

> *Indeed, as Crick imagined this system, nothing about the physical or chemical features of the nucleotides or amino acids directly dictated any particular set of assignments between amino acids and bases in the DNA text. The code could not be deduced from the chemical properties of amino acids and nucleotide bases. It had to be cracked. Just as a specific letter of the English language can be represented by any combination of binary digits, so too could a given amino acid correspond to any combination of nucleotide bases. The assignments are, in both cases, arbitrary....*
>
> *Crick's proposal was striking in its sheer theoretical audacity. Biochemistry had not a shred of direct evidence for the existence of adapter molecules or their corresponding enzymes. Crick simply deduced the need for a code by thinking about what would be needed to make the cell's communication system work. Only a code could facilitate the translation of the information from DNA's four-character base sequences into the twenty-character "language" of proteins. His adapter hypothesis followed logically, and intuitively, from an understanding of the functional requirements of information transfer and the limited informational capacity of the chemical constituents of the relevant molecules themselves (Meyer 118).*

This arbitrary code turns out to be the key to piecing the puzzle together. Stop for a moment and consider the essence of a code. A code is a set of rules for converting information from one useful form into another. For example, if I were to send you this message—ajckdomudnhengslpalkrshextmkhaxedlpezrbaoywdmvui rcnktduossfmuasrmxriwfnaed—what would you think?

Is there any useful information in this set of letters? It is not immediately apparent, but there is, if I were to give you this code: "every third letter, left to right." Without a code, it is gibberish. But if this group of letters were to have a code, then one could decipher the message.

According to the code given, we start from the left and choose every third letter. The first third letter is *c*. The third letter after *c* is *o*. The third after *o* is *d*. The third after *d* is *e*. The third after *e* is *s*. If you continued, you would get this message: codesaretheproductofamind.

Because the reader knows the code of the alphabet of the English language, the first code enables the reader to set the stage for the second code, which stipulates that we only consider every third letter in the sequence (which then subsequently allows us to form words that carry thoughts). Looking at these chosen letters in the code, we can now deduce that it says, "Codes are the product of a mind." But if that code was not specific to every third letter, there would be no useful information carried in that sequence of letters. It is the code that allows us to receive the information.

But if we took this illustration one step further, we see that in the gene expressions system, messages written in "English" found in DNA must be translated to "Spanish" found in proteins. That message must be converted to "los códigos son el producto de una mente." That is, another code must be used to translate from one language to the other.

Perhaps it would be possible to randomly duplicate that sequence of letters, but without the codes necessary to translate it, it is gibberish. How does natural selection engineer a double code? What possible selective pressures could engineer such a marvelous feat? And yet that is precisely what we have between the code of DNA and proteins.

I could have created any number of codes to send the message. There is no law that requires that I should have chosen the code of every third letter. I could have made another choice. It was an arbitrary choice made by the code maker—me. The very nature of the code is that it is an arbitrary system that deciphers what would otherwise be unknowable. But the process of deciphering and knowing it requires a mind to conceive. Dead molecules do not have minds. They cannot create codes, decipher them, or translate them into another code.

Natural processes do not produce codes that pass on information. Only a mind can create a code. In fact, we cannot observe this anywhere in nature outside of living things. How, then, can inanimate matter evolve into living matter without the ability to create a code? Codes are produced only by intelligence, and no empirical evidence exists that can claim otherwise. Dead molecules simply do not magically become alive.

The evolutionary claim that life evolved through simple cumulative chemical processes is based on unfounded and unscientific speculations, which run contrary to all physical processes observed in nature. It is an anachronistic Darwinian idea based on our abject ignorance of the true specified complexity that our modern technology has revealed in the highly complex macromolecules and their ingeniously designed functions.

For example, the idea that the DNA code or the protein code could arise through random chemical recombinations is infinitely less probable than the idea that the Braille method of reading for the blind could have developed by itself or that natural random processes could have produced the Morse code used to communicate through telegraphs.

Information is not created by the medium that transmits it. It is created by the mind that invented the code and the message that is sent. Natural forces do not create complex codes. A code is external and independent of the medium that carries it and cannot be invented outside of intelligence.

The same applies for a program. A program is a planned sequence of steps to accomplish some goal, such as the computer program that I am using to write this book. The idea that information-rich programs could arise through random ordering is nothing more than fanciful speculation and unfounded wishful thinking on the part of evolutionists.

Not only does evolution not account for the hardware, it cannot account for the software code that runs the hardware. The coded information in a specific computer program could not have arisen without the mind of the programmer. What mind existed before life on this planet that could have programmed DNA? It is the irrefutable evidence of intelligent design.

> In the decades since Miller's and Crick's and Watson's reports, however, there have been indications that all is not well in the halls of biology. We have gained a far deeper appreciation of the extremely complex macromolecules such as proteins and nucleic acids. The enlarged understanding of these complexities has precipitated new suggestions that the DNA mechanism may be more complex and the molecular organization more intricate and information-filled than was previously thought.
>
> The impressive complexities of proteins, nucleic acids, and other biological molecules are presently developed in nature only in living things. Unless it is assumed such complexity has always been present in an infinitely old universe, there must have been a time in the past when life appeared de novo out of lifeless, inert matter. How can the mere interaction of simple

> *chemicals in the primordial ocean have produced life*
> *as it is presently understood? That is the question. The*
> *signs do not bode well for the standard answers given*
> *(Thaxton et al. 2).*

The universe is not infinitely old, as previously assumed by evolutionists. It had a beginning. Life, too, had a beginning. Out of lifeless, inert chemicals, the complex codes and chemical structures of living things could not have risen through simple cumulative random reactions. Crick's idea that the DNA information could be passed on by a translator intermediate mechanism that reads the first code and translates it into the second code was, indeed, insightful and revolutionary. But it created an elephant in the room. How could random processes accomplish this complex procedure? What materialistic selective pressure could accomplish this multifaceted, closed-loop system? Ever since, evolutionists have been hard at work to make that great big elephant disappear, to no avail.

The Translation of the Codes

Let us examine in a little more detail how this code that transfers the information in the template from the DNA to the protein works. In this gene expression system, the code in the DNA is converted to an mRNA format (the scribe Homer) so it can be transferred to the ribosome (machine shop) that makes the proteins. The mRNA is a negative copy of the master code within the section of the DNA that it is encoded according to the particular requirement of the kind of protein that is needed in the cell.

It does so by helper proteins that attach to it in order to make sure it begins at the beginning of the appropriate message and not at the middle or the end. The accuracy of the message is critical in creating the right protein. Without this ability for specificity, the cell metabolism would run amuck.

Once the mRNA takes that information to the ribosome, the machine shop goes to work and translates the negative message back into a positive and also translates it from the four-letter code of the DNA to the 20-letter code of the proteins. One by one, the triplets of the mRNA are matched to the tRNAs that carry the corresponding code to a specific amino acid at the opposite end, where they match with the mRNA. These are linked together into a chain, whose order was designated by the initial instructions from the DNA.

We now have a small dipeptide chain of an exactly specified order of amino acids in a particular preordained manner that had been initially commanded by the DNA to give it an exact shape and an exact function for the protein it will produce when completed. The process is repeated over and over again in segments until the protein molecule is complete and the architectural plan brought from the DNA is finished.

Once the assembly is complete, the properly sequenced amino acids are polymerized (linked), and it becomes a single strand—a long chain of amino acids welded together. It is then ejected from the docks to another area of the ribosome where it folds multiple times within seconds in a precise sequence to become the precise shape and character of the protein that the DNA had originally encoded. The ribosome now ejects the folded protein containing the active sites in exactly the right place for the task for which it was designed, and it travels into the cell to go accomplish this specified task.

The thing is that this ribosome does not make just one kind of protein—it makes thousands of different kinds of proteins. It is a marvelous machine shop exhibiting unprecedented organization, preciseness, execution, and delivery systems that boggle the mind.

I highly recommend visiting Stephen Meyer's website at www.signatureinthecell.com. The animation on his site is fantastic and will greatly help you understand this difficult, complex chemical process. I also highly recommend his book *Signature in the Cell* to any who wish to have a more exhaustive understanding of this subject.

He is methodical and sequential in his writing, and his ability to make the complicated understandable is magnificent. I have chosen to extensively quote him because I cannot hope to match his skill or knowledge in this matter.

The thing is that this ribosome (machine shop) is where proteins are made, but the machine shop itself cannot function without many proteins doing specific tasks. In other words, the cell needs many kinds of different proteins in order to make other proteins.

Even in the simplest prokaryote cells, the process of translation utilizes many dozens of separate proteins or protein machines, each one of which is produced during translation. After the messenger RNA reaches the outer cytoplasm, it arrives at the site of a large chemical-processing unit known as a ribosome, the site of protein synthesis. In prokaryotes, the ribosome alone contains fifty separate proteins and three long RNA molecules combined in two distinct but associated subunits.

The process of translation begins as the ribosome subunits dissociate and the messenger RNA (mRNA) binds to the smaller of the two subunits.... Auxiliary proteins known as initiation factors catalyze this disassociation and temporarily stabilize the second subunit in its disassociated state. At the same time, a group of three RNA bases on a transfer RNA (tRNA) molecule binds to the first triplet of RNA bases on the mRNA molecule as it docks in the ribosome. The groups of three bases on mRNA are called codons or triplets. The groups of three bases to which they bind on the tRNA are called anticodons. The sequence AUG constitutes the "initiator codon" at the head of the mRNA transcript.

After the initiator codon (AUG) on the mRNA transcript binds to the anticodon triplet on the corresponding tRNA, then the second and larger subunit of ribosome rejoins the first, forming a large complex of molecules including both ribosomal subunits, the mRNA, and a tRNA molecule carrying its corresponding amino acid. The protein chain can now begin to form. An additional amino acid–tRNA combination (known as an aminoacyl-tRNA molecule) binds to a second and adjacent active site on the ribosome, bringing its amino acid into close proximity to the first. A protein within the ribosome known as peptidyl transferase then catalyzes a polymerization (linking) reaction involving the two (tRNA-borne) amino acids. In the process, the first amino acid, detaches from its tRNA and attaches to the second amino acid, forming a short dipeptide chain. The ribosome then ejects the first and empty tRNA molecule and moves along to "read" the next triplet of bases on the mRNA. Another tRNA–amino acid carrier pairs with the next mRNA codon, bringing a new amino acid into close proximity with the growing chain, and the process repeats itself until the signal for termination is reached on the mRNA. Then a protein termination factor, rather than an aminoacyl tRNA, binds to the second ribosome site and catalyzes hydrolysis (dissolution) of the bond holding the peptide chain to the tRNA at the first ribosome site. The newly assembled protein then detaches (Meyer 127–129).

I think by now the reader can see that from the transcription process where the DNA message is encoded into an mRNA and taken to the ribosome to decode and manufacture any one of thousands of the proteins the body uses, there is a choreographed chemical dance of enormous complexity and elaborate beauty that requires quite specified information in order to produce proteins of specified functions. Each step is interdependent on the other, and no single step could have any useful value or function without the others.

The process is a chain of events that uses the code of DNA and translates it to the code within the proteins through an intermediary—the mRNA and tRNAs. And through the elaborate machinery in the ribosome, this message is miraculously translated into protein language and made into a specific protein molecule. How can random ordering establish such a coordinated system that can produce thousands of different protein molecules, each with a specific blueprint, each with a specified function, all of which are necessary for the structure and metabolism of the living cell?

The complexity and interdependence of these multiple systems are even deeper than Haeckel, Darwin, and Huxley could have ever imagined in their wildest dreams. Both the nucleotides and the proteins are absolutely necessary simultaneously. One cannot exist without the other.

> At each step in the translation process, specialized proteins perform crucial functions. For example, the initial coupling of specific amino acids to their specific tRNA molecules (Crick's adapters) depends upon the catalytic action of twenty specific enzymes, one for each tRNA–amino acid pair. The integrity of the genetic code depends upon the specific properties of these enzymes, known as aminoacyl-tRNA synthetases.
>
> These synthetases are necessary because, as Francis Crick anticipated, there is nothing about the chemical properties of the bases in DNA (or those in mRNA) that favors forming a chemical bond with any specific amino acid over another. In fact the

cloverleaf-shaped tRNA molecule attaches to the mRNA transcript on one end and carries a specific amino acid on the other.... The amino acid and the codon-anticodon pairs are at opposite ends of the tRNA molecule. The distance ensures that neither the codons on mRNA nor the anticodons on tRNA interact chemically with the amino acids. As Crick anticipated, direct chemical interactions between bases (codons) and amino acids do not determine the assignments that constitute the genetic code.

Instead, these associations are mediated indirectly by the enzymatic action of the aminoacyl-tRNA synthetases. The synthetases have several active sites that enable them to: (1) recognize a specific amino acid, (2) recognize a specific corresponding tRNA (with a specific anticodon), (3) react the amino acid with ATP (adenosine triphosphate) to form an AMP (adenosine monophosphate) derivative, and then, finally, (4) link the specific tRNA molecule in question to its corresponding amino acid.... In other words, the synthetases are themselves marvels of specificity (Meyer 129–130).

These tRNA synthetases are ingeniously designed enzymes that are able to grasp just the right amino acid to match with the corresponding tRNA. This ensures that the right message is made without another amino acid falling into the chain and messing up the specificity of the message. It is an intermediary step that connects the right amino acid with the correct tRNA molecule.

But that is not all. To boot, it supplies its own energy to do so (ATP). It's like a battery-powered, wireless drill that provides the energy input necessary to drive forth the chemical linkage. Were it not for this additional intermediary key, the template of the DNA could not be passed on to create a protein.

Here is another example of an irreducibly complex system whose origins could never be adequately explained by a random evolutionary process. What possible selective pressure could engineer such a multifaceted feat that would result in all of these complicated chemical processes appearing in absolute unison when the completion of one without the others is completely useless?

The specific complexity of the (machine shop) ribosome is also something to be admired.

> For their part, ribosomes must also perform many functions. These include: (1) enhancing the accuracy of codon-anticodon pairing between the mRNA transcript and the aminoacyl-tRNAs, (2) polymerizing (via peptidyl transferase) the growing peptide chain, (3) acting as energy transducers converting chemical energy into mechanical energy during translocation of amino acids from tRNA carriers, (4) protecting the growing protein from attack by protease (protein degrading enzymes) possibly by forming a long protective tunnel, and (5) assisting in the hydrolysis (dissolution) of the amino acid–tRNA bond during termination. Further, several separate protein factors and cofactors facilitate various specialized chemical transformations during the three discreet steps of translation: initiation, elongation, and termination (Meyer 130).

By now, I think the reader understands that we are a long way from the simplistic idea held by Darwin, Huxley, and Haeckel that the cell was a simple albuminous gel packet whose origins could be explained through random chemical processes of gradual, small steps from non-living matter. No rational sequence of small steps can randomly reach the level of complexity and interdependent functions that must evolve concurrently in order to be useful at all.

Furthermore, all along this assembly line, the processing of this information requires energy at many discrete steps. This chemical energy is transferred to mechanical energy to accomplish the task of gene expression through the marvel of a specially designed portable battery that can drive forward chemical reactions.

Who Came First, the Chicken or the Egg?

The cell uses a chemical known as adenosine triphosphate (ATP) or a similar one called guanosine triphosphate (GTP) to provide the energy necessary for the many functions of the metabolism in the cell. This is accomplished by using the energy created by breaking off one of the phosphate groups. This release of one or more phosphates can then be used as the power to carry out various tasks. It is the portable battery that pushes forward chemical reactions in the metabolism of the cell.

Normally, inside the living cell, there is an extremely complicated, well-organized chemical powerhouse known as the mitochondria made of specialized proteins. In order for a cell to function, it must be able to create a mechanism for producing usable energy to accomplish the many varied tasks it must perform to stay alive.

But the chemical process involved in the mitochondria is so complex that it is impossible for it to have come first; and yet without it, the cell could not exist. The cell needs energy to create proteins, but it needs proteins to create the mitochondria that create the energy to create proteins. Both are needed simultaneously.

This organic power plant, or powerhouse, allows the cell to do its many metabolic functions. The ingenious way in which the molecules of adenosine triphosphate (ATP) carries energy by giving off one of the phosphates and becoming adenosine diphosphate allows the cell the raw energy to accomplish many of its functions.

ATP is manufactured from glucose through a process known as glycolysis. But this process of glycolysis is accomplished through 10 discrete steps, each catalyzed by a specific protein. And these specific proteins are in turn created from the genetic information of DNA.

Evolution has a few problems here. You cannot have the process of translation and transcription without energy from ATP through glycolysis, but you cannot have glycolysis without DNA. How did DNA develop its complicated double helix structure containing the master genetic code without ATP? Or how did ATP develop through glycolysis without the proteins created by DNA? How did the proteins form without the ribosome with its many specialized proteins necessary to create one protein? Which came first, the chicken or the egg? As we have now observed, there is a variety of places where evolution meets an impossible conundrum. But wait, there is more.

One of the characteristics of life is replication. In single-celled organisms, this is known as mitosis, or the splitting of one cell into two identical ones.

> Besides transcribing and translating, the cell's information-processing system also replicates DNA. This happens whenever cells divide and copy themselves. As with the process of transcription and translation, the process of DNA replication depends on many separate protein catalysts to unwind, stabilize, copy, edit, and rewind the original DNA message. In prokaryote cells, DNA replication involves more than thirty specialized proteins to perform tasks necessary for building and accurately copying the genetic molecule. These specialized proteins include DNA polymerases, primases, helicases, topoisomerases, DNA-binding proteins, DNA ligases, and editing enzymes. DNA needs these proteins to copy the genetic information contained in DNA. But the proteins that copy

the genetic information in DNA are themselves built from that information. This again poses what is, at the very least, a curiosity; the production of proteins requires DNA, but the production of DNA requires proteins (Meyer 131).

It poses more than a curiosity. It means that the DNA language and the double helix metastructure, as well as the protein language and the ribosomal metastructure that manufactures them, and the mitochondria metastructure that produces the fuel must have all evolved simultaneously. There are no small, gradual, and incremental evolutionary steps that can account for the elaborate and multifaceted gene expression system.

This DNA is suspended in a salt solution, the cellular fluid, so it can be accessed in order to replicate itself. Without the ability of DNA to replicate, cells could not divide, and life could not endure beyond the age of a single cell. Life could not replicate without DNA. And DNA also provides the cell with the ability to assemble amino acids into precise types of proteins. Without it, the metabolism of the cell could not exist.

The code (software) and the hardware it uses to function are both highly elaborate and incredibly sophisticated. Through this information-rich code, proteins are fabricated to tailor-made designs that serve an enormous number of specific tasks. But DNA itself needs some of these specific proteins to replicate during mitosis when a cell divides into two. Without these many specified proteins, DNA could not replicate. Which came first? One cannot exist without the other.

The integrated complexity of the cell's information-processing system has prompted some profound reflection. As Lewontin asks, "What makes the proteins that are necessary to make the protein?" As David

Goodsell puts it, this "is one of the unanswered riddles of biochemistry: which came first, proteins or protein synthesis? If proteins are needed to make proteins, how did the whole thing get started?" The end result of protein synthesis is required before it can begin.

The interdependence of proteins and nucleic acids raises many obvious "chicken and egg" dilemmas—dilemmas that origin-of-life theorists before the 1960s neither anticipated nor addressed. The cell needs proteins to process and express the information in DNA in order to build proteins. But the construction of DNA molecules (during the process of DNA replication) also requires proteins. So which came first, the chicken (nucleic acids) or the egg (protein)? If proteins must have arisen first, then how did they do so, since all extant cells construct proteins from the assembly instructions in DNA. How did either arise without the other? (Meyer 134).

It has taken the concerted effort of thousands of brilliant minds continuously working for the span of several decades just to decipher the meaning of the human genetic code. The sheer brainpower and countless hours involved in the Genome Project are quite impressive. It has been stated that its completion is perhaps one of science's most incredible accomplishments in our entire human history.

Cracking the human genetic code is, in fact, one of the most impressive milestones among our scientific accomplishments. Surely, the efforts of the best minds in our generation need to be applauded. But if interpreting the language is that complicated, am I to believe that the creation of this magnificently designed language was merely accidental?

The assertion that this wonderfully complex biological language contained in our DNA, which uses two codes and integrates them in a circular closed-loop system developed by random chemical processes, is nothing more than a statement of blind faith based on no scientific empirical data.

Crick, optimistically entrenched within the naturalistic paradigm and unwilling to concede that there is a previsioned design to this marvelous macromolecule, attempts to superficially piece together a family tree of these macromolecules. But he is obviously frustrated at the incompatibility of the genetic code with a chance and random genesis.

The advancements of our technology have not solved the problem for the evolutionist in applying the idea of natural selection imagined by Darwin as the mechanism for evolution in a naturalistic worldview. On the contrary, the enormous specified complexity found in the molecular level has become even more problematic for the proponents of evolution to explain through random ordering. The more we research the function and complexity of the design of these nucleic acids, we cannot help but be completely amazed at the sheer intricacy of its genius design.

Evolutionists are quick to point out the fact that it is identical in all living things and grasp at this unity to imply that it is evidence of evolution. But the fact that this unity exists without any chemical reason suggests that instead, this "choice" has been made by a single designer. Crick puts on a brave face and, without any empirical evidence to support his thesis, claims it is at least as plausible that the details of the code were decided by purely chemical reasons.

> As we painstakingly collect more and more data from organisms alive today, we can begin to piece together the family trees of certain molecules—transfer RNA molecules, for example—in the hope of being able to deduce the nature of the earliest ancestors of these molecules. Such work is still in progress, but there is one feature, which is so invariant that it

immediately attracts attention. This is the genetic code. With the exception of mitochondria, the code is identical in all living things so far examined, and even for mitochondria the differences are rather small. This would not be surprising if there were an obvious structural reason for the details of the code; if certain amino acids had necessarily to go with certain codons because, for example, their shapes fitted neatly together. Brave attempts have been made to suggest how this could happen, but they all seem unconvincing. It is at least as plausible that the details of the code are mainly accidental. Even if certain early codons were not dictated by chance but had some chemical logic to them, and even if some broad features of the code can be explained in some way, it seems most improbable, at least at the moment, that all the details *of the code were decided by purely chemical reasons (Crick 142-143).*

His optimism is nothing more than bluster. No chemical or structural reasons have been brought forth as evidence to suggest a reason for this particular code, but Crick thinks "it is at least as plausible." Is this not another obvious piece of evidence that points to an arbitrary choice being made by a designer? Yet Crick holds on to the plausible hope that someday, they will find some reason to substantiate his leap of faith.

Again, Crick's use of words in the previous quote belies the underlying reality that he is trying so hard to evade. "It is at least as plausible that the details of the code were decided by purely chemical reasons." He subliminally knows that a decision was made to create the details of this complex code. And this inescapably implies a decider and a reasoner behind the decision. It implies a mind that deliberately chose this ordered and complex language.

Yet his underlying presupposition is that there was no creative mind to engineer this complex metabolic machinery. How can the evolutionary process, a mindless random process, decide anything? How can random ordering decide and create a double code with a translator intermediate?

Is it not true that language is perhaps one of the most sophisticated achievements of the human mind? At least that is what I am led to believe by all the evolutionary books that laud the development of language in humans as one of the crowning pinnacles of evolution. Surely, the intricate aspect of the structure of language requires an enormous brain to develop, decipher, and understand. Then how is it that chemicals, without a brain, developed a language? Content-rich messages are not made outside of a mind. To insist that rational communication can take place outside of a mind is irrational.

Non-specified, low-information systems can be detected arising from natural processes. We can hear the background microwave radiation in our televisions as a hissing sound, but it carries no specified message and little information. That information is meaningless if it is not specific. We can, on the other hand, send a text via microwaves such as those in our cell phones. This gives specific information that can be heard and interpreted by a mind that knows that specific language (code) and can correlate the sounds or the written words in the text with the thoughts they represent.

The insurmountable problem for evolution is how to explain the enormous amount of specified information found within the supposedly simple living cell as originating from random processes. The elephant is still in the room. It is obvious to the objective mind that specific messages are thoughts birthed within an intelligent mind.

The complicated multifaceted overarching system of gene expression is composed of other complicated, multifaceted systems within it that are interdependent of one another to function as a whole. It is a complex system of complex systems within it. They cannot be explained through discreet steps of evolution. The whole is necessary in order for the individual parts to be meaningful or functional. Each part is irreplaceable. Each part is necessary in order for the whole to function. All parts had to be engineered to run together in a single, overarching system. No replacements of the parts can be accomplished by the other components.

Here, naturalists leap across the line of despair to the irrational by simply accepting the complex chemical language as being the result of random ordering, when reason acknowledges the obvious absurdity of this position. It is as if they have donned magical glasses that form an invisibility cloak over the elephant. But the elephant is still there, even if they refuse to see it.

Evolutionists immediately dismiss the possibility of intelligent design and hold tenaciously to the presupposition that everything has evolved by pure random chance chemical processes, no matter how improbable and irrational. This is not true science. It is not the pursuit of truth. It is the subjective pursuit of pseudoscientific rationalizations to legitimize a biased deophobic presupposition.

The Darwinian model is not a scientific hypothesis; it is a metaphysical choice propped by a limited number of discordant scientific facts that fail to account for all the empirical data our modern technology has revealed.

Darwin candidly stated that the evolutionary model can be scientifically tested. The fundamental dogma of his evolutionary theory is that all complex structures or organs are the product of gradual selective steps that move from simple forms to more complicated forms through natural selection. He stated:

> *If it could be demonstrated that any complex organ existed, which could not possibly have been formed by numerous, successive, slight modifications, my theory would absolutely break down (Darwin 189).*

That day has come. But when presented with these undeniable facts, modern Darwinists automatically don their horse-blinds and quickly run to the opposite sidewalk to avoid the plain truth.

In light of these facts, how can a supposedly objective scientist whose job description inherently assumes the objective pursuit of truth maintain personal integrity and still hold on to the idea of the formation of a living cell by pure chance, by random coincidence, by chemical serendipity?

Chemical Serendipity

Even Crick has to swallow hard here. In considering the high improbability of randomness to account for the formation of life due to the sheer complexity found in every level of the structure of the living cell, Crick confessed:

> When we do this we cannot help being struck by the very high degree of organized complexity we find at every level, and especially at the molecular level (Crick 49).

The high degree of complexity is astounding "and especially at the molecular level" where one would expect, in an evolutionary system, that it would be the most simple. The complexity would then build up from the more simple components. But this is absolutely not the case in the real universe.

It is not at all how Darwin, Huxley, and Haeckel envisioned life could evolve from simple to complex. The complex cell has no evolutionary lineage. Oparin's idea of evolving coacervates fails to account in any way for the development of DNA and the ribosome gene-expression system within the cell. Even in his revised version, it cannot account for information-rich systems evolving through natural processes.

Moreover, it can be shown mathematically that the odds for this imagined chemical, abiogenic origin of life are, for all practical purposes, simply and utterly impossible. What would be the mathematical odds that random chemical reactions could produce a gene that would be capable of replicating a single small protein?

We must first consider that at the very minimum, it takes a DNA of 300 "letters" to produce a single small protein of only 100 amino acids.

> *Getting the order of the amino-acids correct in the protein molecule is the job of the gene for that protein. The gene, a length of DNA (deoxyribonucleic acid) which carries the genetic code for a protein, is coded in such a way that three DNA 'letters' are needed for each amino-acid. In other words, it takes a length of DNA 300 letters long to carry the genetic instructions for a protein of a hundred amino-acids.*
>
> *To appreciate the complexity of this fundamental but essential biochemical process, and the possibility of it occurring by chance to give the first primitive protein, we can make use of a well-known illustration. Imagine a tireless monkey trying to type out the 300-letter word of his single 300-letter gene, remembering that there are four different letters. The odds against getting the first letter correct are 4–1. But the odds against getting the first two letters correct are 16–1 (4x4). For the first three letters, the odds are multiplied by 4 again to give 64–1. And so on for the remaining 277 letters of the code for the gene. Since some DNA letters can be replaced by alternatives and still give the correct amino-acid, in the end it turns out that for every attempt to spell out the complete gene-word code, the odds against getting it correct are approximately 1 in 10^{130} (10 followed by 130 zeros).*

The monkey could of course type the correct word-code at the first attempt or the ten thousandth or any time after that, if he goes on for long enough. But what these odds are really illustrating is not to expect it, even if you could have a thousand million monkeys on each square inch of the Earth's surface typing at the rate of a thousand million words per second for a thousand million years. Even with this highly powered monkey set-up, the odds against the correct gene-sequence turning up are still 1 in 10^{80}. This illustration considers just one gene with a mere 300-letter code. But if we try to extend our reasoning to DNA present in a simple virus, which could have a 20,000-letter code, the average simple bacterium with about 4.5 million-letter code and the genetic information of a human being with roughly 5,000 million, the complexity and statistical chances of forming such genes approaches infinity; even mathematicians must consider it unlikely (Brooks 83–84). [Dr. Brooks is a geochemist working in oil exploration for Britoil and was vice-president of the Geological Society.]

The statistical challenges for the probability of chemical abiogenesis are simply insuperable. Very remote is the chance that it is in every respect an unrealistic consideration. In the final analysis, the scientist who leaps across this chasm does so not by reason, but by irrational faith. It is a subjective choice predicated on a metaphysical preference—an antipathy to a God that could hold them morally accountable.

The Miracle of Life from Light

In this analysis of the formation of these organic molecules, we are not even considering the much more complex basic metabolic processes necessary for these organic compounds to form the machinery of the cell. These mechanisms of providing energy for the cells to live, such as the process of directing energy from light in order to sustain the metabolic processes of life, are extremely complicated.

The chemistry of photosynthesis is immensely complex, involving a huge number of interlocked processes. It is a series of interwoven chemical reactions so tedious that I have decided not to include it for fear of boring the non-technical reader (something, I fear, I may have already inadvertently accomplished).

Much is now known regarding the utterly amazing process of photosynthesis. It is a biological means of taking light energy and making life energy, or sugar, and creating free oxygen as a by-product. But much remains to be discovered regarding this cryptic, wonderfully miraculous process. Imagine a mechanism that can take simple water, sunlight, and carbon dioxide and somehow incredibly produce organic molecules of great complexity. The complex nature of the process cannot be reduced to simple fortuitous chemical reactions that piled up on one another until *Voila!* Photosynthesis!

I heard a biologist the other day on the Science channel speaking about the origin of life coming from the prebiotic soup in our supposedly methane-rich atmosphere. He said that all you need is a reducing atmosphere and a prebiotic soup, and with some energy input, like a lightning bolt, you have life. Such speculative statements unproved by any experimental data must not be allowed on a channel calling itself *Science.*

Even more astounding is that evolutionists expect us to believe that the intricate process that uses carbon dioxide and sunlight for fuel and gives off our life-giving oxygen as a by-product somehow evolved into a process that uses oxygen for fuel and gives off carbon dioxide as a by-product. Now that is one hell-of-a U-turn! What selective pressure concocted that miraculous reversal?

All aspects of the chemical pathways in both these processes are complex and sophisticated engineering wonders. Consider the molecule of the protein hemoglobin, which is equally necessary for all animals, including humans. It is the vehicle through which oxygen is transported to the 75 trillion cells of our body.

Generally speaking, covalent bonds are quite strong, and it takes an enormous amount of energy to unlock them. But it just so happens that the bond between the protein hemoglobin and oxygen has been designed (or if you prefer the naturalistic explanation, fortuitously arranged) in such a way that the bond is rather weak. And therefore, the oxygen carried by the hemoglobin is able to be easily released to the oxygen-starved cells of the body. There are more bonafide miracles in the evolutionary yarn than in the entire Bible.

> *Haemoglobin is only able to bind and carry oxygen because of the presence of a non-polypeptide unit, namely a heme group. (The heme gives hemoglobin its distinctive color.) Haemoglobin is made up of amino acids joined together in twisted chains to make its biochemically-unique structure. Each amino-acid is uniquely linked together in a specific sequence of 574 components forming four principle chains, which are interwoven around each other to form the complex 3-D haemoglobin molecule.*
>
> *A healthy human has about 60 million million million ($6x10^{21}$) identical haemoglobin molecules of which 400 million million ($4x10^{14}$) are destroyed every second and replaced by identical molecules synthesized by the body. The human cells do not synthesize such compounds by random chemical processes, but specific enzyme-controlled biochemical reactions.*
>
> *It seems to me that even if there were primeval soups of chemicals on the primitive Earth (or in the oceans), no random/chance abiogenic process operating at the time could possibly have given molecules*

as complex as haemoglobin, nor any other complex protein molecule such as chlorophyll—let alone a living cell (Brooks 86).

After several centuries of concerted scientific work, the magic wand that would make evolution true has not been found, either in a lab or in the field. There is no *Voila!* In fact, there is not enough time or resources in our universe to give chance the opportunity through random processes to make one protein, as we shall now see.

CHAPTER 4

●●●

IS THERE A CHANCE FOR CHANCE?

s far back as 1966, many mathematicians, physicists, and engineers were beginning to express grave doubts about the probability of mutations through chance combinations generating the information necessary to produce new forms of life. The idea that random mutations could change one species into another through accumulated changes is the very heart of the modern neo-Darwinian hypothesis. It was becoming apparent that mutations not only failed to create a different species, but they could not account for the formation of the subcomponents of the gene expression system. We will deal with the process of mutations more thoroughly in the fourth book of this series, *The Descent of Man*, but for now, let's return to the probability challenge.

The probability challenge to the evolutionary hypothesis is not new knowledge. It has been known and discussed for five decades. A conference called Mathematical Challenges to Neo-Darwinism to discuss this probability challenge was hosted by the Wistar Institute in Philadelphia, a prestigious medical research center. It was chaired by Sir Peter Medawar, a Nobel laureate from England. At the conference, they discussed the combinatorial problem that the mutation mechanism faced in creating functional proteins or nucleic acids.

The challenge is that for every combination of amino acids that produces a functional protein, there are much larger numbers of potential combinations that will produce a non-information-carrying polypeptide chain; that is, a non-protein molecule that is unusable to a living cell. In order for the amino acids to form a protein, they must be placed in specified sequences, or they are absolutely useless. In order to show the huge probability problem, Stephen C. Myer, advocate for intelligent design, chose to calculate what the odds would be to create a very small protein molecule of only 150 amino acids. Mind you, most proteins contain thousands of amino acids.

> And as the length of that required protein grows, the number of possible amino-acid sequence combinations of that length grows exponentially, so that the odds of finding a functional sequence—that is, a working protein—diminish precipitously.
>
> To see this, consider the following. Whereas there are four ways to combine the letters A and B to make a two-letter combination (AB, BA, AA, and BB), there are eight ways to make three-letter combinations (AAA, AAB, ABB, ABA, BAA, BBA, BAB, BBB), and sixteen ways to make four-letter combinations, and so on. The number of combinations grows geometrically.... And this growth becomes more pronounced when the set of letters is larger (Meyer 205).

Since proteins are made from only 20 specific amino acids, the probability is overwhelmingly high that other amino acids would foil the attempt to create a protein carrying only the 20 specific amino acids required to make a functional protein. Nevertheless, for the sake of argument, let's pretend that only the 20 specific amino acids are available for this process. But because there are 20 amino acids, the computation would require a much more complicated progression, as Myers explains:

> For protein chains, there are 20^2, or 400, ways to make a two-amino-acid combination, since each position could be any one of 20 different alphabetic characters. Similarly there are 20^3, or 8,000, ways to make a three-amino-acid sequence, and 20^4, or 160,000, ways to make a sequence four amino acids long, and so on. As the number of possible combinations rises, the odds of finding a correct sequence diminishes correspondingly. But most functional proteins are made of hundreds of amino acids. Therefore, even a relatively short protein of, say, 150 amino acids represents one sequence among an astronomically large number of other possible sequence combinations (approximately 10^{195}) (205).

However, there are even further complications to the chance production of a ridiculously small protein of just 150 amino acids:

1. **The first challenge is making a peptide bond.** "First, all amino acids must form a chemical bond known as a peptide bond when joining with other amino acids in the protein chain.... If the amino acids do not link up with one another via a peptide bond, the resulting molecule will not fold into a protein. In nature many other types of chemical bonds are possible between amino acids. In fact, when amino-acid mixtures are allowed to react in a test tube, they form peptide and nonpeptide bonds with roughly equal probability. Thus,

with each amino-acid addition. the probability of it forming a peptide bond is roughly ½. Once four amino acids have become linked, the likelihood that they are joined exclusively by peptide bonds is roughly ½ x ½ x ½ x ½ = 1/16, or $(1/2)^4$. The probability of building a chain of amino acids in which all linkages are peptide linkages is $(1/2)^{149}$, or roughly one chance in 10^{45}" (Meyer 206).

2. **The second challenge is having exclusively left-handed amino acids in the chain.** As we have already discussed, amino acids are found naturally in two versions, one with the active site on the left and as a mirror image, and the other with the active site on the right. However, proteins are made exclusively from left-handed amino acids; hence, the probability computations must include the chances of creating a protein exclusively of only left-handed amino acids. "The probability of attaining, at random, only L-amino acids in a hypothetical peptide chain 150 amino acids long is $(1/2)^{150}$, or again roughly 1 chance in 10^{45}" (Meyer 207).

3. **The third challenge is to have all the amino acids in a functional sequential arrangement.** "Functioning proteins have a third independent requirement, the most important of all; their amino acids, like letters in a meaningful sentence, must link up in functionally specified sequential arrangements. In some cases, changing even one amino acid at a given site results in the loss of protein function. Moreover, because there are 20 biologically occurring amino acids, the probability of getting a specific amino acid at a given site is small—1/20. (Actually the probability is even lower because, in nature, there are also many nonprotein-forming amino acids.) On the assumption that each site in a protein chain requires a particular amino acid, *the probability of attaining a particular protein 150 amino acids long would be $(1/20)^{150}$, or roughly 1 chance in 10^{195}*" (emphasis added) (Meyer 207).

Mind you, this number is unrealistically concluded by excluding the possibility of bonding with the numerous naturally occurring non-protein-forming amino acids, which abound in our world. It is also computing the chance probability of a rather small 150 amino-acid protein, which is the exception to the rule. And yet the odds are 1 in 10^{195}.

That enormous probability of creating a useful protein is a staggering 1 in 1,000,000,000,000,000,000,000,000,000,000,000,00 0,000,000,000,000,000,000,000,000,000,000,000,000,000,0 00,000,000,000,000,000,000,000,000,000,000,000,000,000, 000,000,000,000,000,000,000,000,000,000,000,000,000,000,0 00,000,000,000,000,000.

This number is so large that most of us have great difficulty appreciating its true impact. The number of water molecules in a drop of water is more than 1,000 billion. Let me illustrate the immensity of this probability with an example that may bring some understanding of its ridiculous nature. There are three atoms in a water molecule— two hydrogen atoms and one oxygen atom. These atoms are so small that there are more than 3,000 billion atoms in just one drop of water. Can you imagine how many atoms there would be in an Olympic-sized pool?

Imagine how many drops of water it would take to fill the Great Lakes. I have stood on the shores of Lake Michigan and wondered at its immense size. From the shore, it seems like an ocean. Even from the height of an airplane, I could not see the far shore.

How many drops of water would fill the Atlantic Ocean? Flying from America to Europe at 600 miles per hour, one begins to appreciate the immensity of the Atlantic Ocean, but it is merely an oversized lake compared to the great Pacific Ocean. How many drops of water would fill all the oceans? How many drops of water would fill the volume of the entire Earth from the stratosphere above the North Pole, through the core, and to the stratosphere above the South Pole?

Earth is a rather small rocky planet in our solar system. There are seven other planets and a host of moons, asteroids, and comets that circle our sun. Jupiter is the biggest planet and 1,400 times the volume of Earth. How many drops of water would fill Jupiter? How many would fill all the planets, moons, asteroids, and comets in our solar system? But the sun dwarfs Jupiter; the sun is 1,300,000 times the volume of Earth. How many drops of water would fill the sun and all the components of the entire solar system?

If we were to travel in a spaceship that could cruise at the speed of light—186,360 miles per second—it would take us 120,000 years to fly from one end of our Milky Way galaxy to the other. Astronomers estimate that within this galaxy are 200 billion to 400 billion stars. Can you imagine how many drops of water would fill all the stars, planets, asteroids, and comets in our galaxy? Remember, there are more than 3,000 billion atoms in just one drop of water. Can you imagine how many atoms are in everything that encompasses the Milky Way?

Let's suppose that we bought a ticket in the "Milky Way Lottery," and every atom in our galaxy also bought a ticket. Our chance of winning would be 1 to the number of atoms that exist in our galaxy, which is 10^{65}. In other words, if we had randomly placed one imaginary red tag on one lonely atom somewhere within the entire galaxy, the odds of us being able to pick that one atom would be 1 in 10^{65}.

If we bought a ticket for two galaxies, our chance of finding the one red-tagged atom would decrease to 1 in 10^{130}.

The odds of creating a rather small protein of 150 amino acids through random ordering, even after making unrealistic concessions, are much less than our chances of picking the right red-tagged atom among all the atoms that exist in two galaxies the size of our Milky Way; it is 1 in 10^{195}. In fact, it would not be equal until we widened our search to three galaxies the size of our Milky Way galaxy.

How much money would you bet that you could find that single red-tagged atom among the atoms of three galaxies the size of our

Milky Way? Now that is really a needle in a haystack of astronomical proportions.

James F. Coppedge, the Director of the Center for Probability Research in Biology in Northridge, California, noted an impressive, interesting study on the statistical probability of the formation of the simplest theoretical living cell with only left-handed amino acids by pure random chance. Mind you, this is not an actual living cell but the simplest cell theoretically possible, which they estimate should contain 239 proteins. Again, this is a theoretical cell. No such cell has ever been found.

> *Dr. Harold J. Morowitz of Yale University has done extensive research for the National Aeronautics and Space Agency to discover the theoretical limits for the simplest free-living thing which could duplicate itself, or, technically, the minimal biological entity capable of autonomous self-replication.... From these important studies, the conclusion is that the smallest such theoretical entity would require 239 or more individual protein molecules (Coppedge 71–72).*

Morowitz, taking into account certain metabolic processes and the minimum size necessary for these processes to exist within a cell, has deduced this theoretical model of the smallest possible cell. At the time he did his research, the smallest living cell known in our planet was the Mycoplasma hominis H39, which contains 600 proteins. Today, the simplest extant cell has been found to be the Mycoplasma genitalium. This is a tiny bacterium that lives in the human urinary tract and has 482 proteins to perform its necessary functions. It has 562,000 bases of DNA to assemble the proteins. But the act of creating a functional theoretic protocell includes an enormous amount of integrated components without which that cell could not function.

Based upon minimal-complexity experiments, some scientists speculate (but have not demonstrated) that a simple one-celled organism might have been able to survive with as few as 250–400 genes.

Of course building a functional cell—at least one that in some way resembles the cells we actually observe today—would have required more than just the genetic information that directs protein synthesis. It would also have required, at the very least, a suite of preexisting proteins and RNA molecules— polymerases, transfer RNAs, ribosomal RNAs, synthetases, and ribosomal proteins, for example—to process and express the information stored in DNA. In fact, there are over 100 specific proteins involved in a simple bacterial translation system; roughly 20 more are involved in transcription and over 30 in DNA replication. Indeed, although the information in DNA is necessary for building proteins and necessary for expressing and processing the information in DNA.... Extant cells, therefore, need both types of information rich-molecules—nucleic acids and proteins—functioning together in a tightly integrated way. Therefore, any minimally complex protocell resembling cells we have today would have required not only genetic information, but a sizable preexisting suite of proteins for processing that information.

Building such a cell also would have required other preexisting components. For example, both proteins and DNA are necessary for building and maintaining the energy-production and -processing system of the cell, the ten-enzyme glycolysis pathway that produces high-energy ATP from its low-energy precursor ADP. But information-processing and protein-synthesis—and just about everything else in the cell—depends upon a preexisting supply of ATP or one of the closely relative energy-carrying molecules. Thus, for life to arise in the first place, ATP (or related molecules) must have also been present along with genes and proteins.

Beyond that, the first cell would have required some kind of semipermeable membrane and a cell wall to protect itself and the chemical reactions taking place inside it. In modern bacteria, the protective barrier is constructed by proteins and enzymes that polymerize (link together) the smaller molecules out of which both the phospholipid bilayer and the cell wall are composed. Cells require a variety of these small molecules—phosphates, lipids, sugars, vitamins, metals, ATP—in addition to proteins and nucleic acids. Many of these small molecules are synthesized with the help of proteins in the cell, but proteins also need these molecules in order to accomplish many of their enzymatic functions. Thus, any protocell likely would have required a preexisting supply of these smaller molecules to establish and maintain itself as well.

The integrated complexity of even a "minimally complex cell" has made it difficult to calculate the odds of all the necessary components of such a system arising in close association with one another by chance alone (Meyer 201–203).

Coppedge, using figures furnished by Morowitz, calculates that the average protein in such a theoretical cell would contain around 445 amino acid units of the usual 20 kinds found only in proteins. He computes the odds of such a protein being formed with only left-handed amino acids through random chemical combinations and, unrealistically, also begins from a matrix containing only the 20 amino acids found in protein.

Other naturally occurring non-protein amino acids would be present in a real evolutionary genesis, which would completely interfere with the process. A more realistic computation could be made by working out the chances of only 20 amino acids being chosen out of the entire naturally occurring number. Nevertheless, he unrealistically chooses, for the sake of the argument, to begin with only the exactly exclusive 20 amino acids found in proteins.

> The probability that an average-size protein molecule of the smallest theoretically possible living thing would happen to contain only left-handed amino acids is, therefore, 1 in 10^{123} on the average (Coppedge 74).

It is hard to put into perspective that the statistical chance for just one protein to have been produced by only left-handed amino acids is 1 in 10^{123}. Such large exponential numbers evade our mind's ability to truly grasp their immensity. Let me use another illustration to help us understand the ridiculousness of believing that chance could account for the formation of a protein.

Evolutionists claim that our universe is about 15 billion years old. Even this number is difficult to put into perspective. But follow me in a simple progression to better understand the huge nature of exponential numbers, which is not immediately apparent to the observer who is not familiar with these huge numbers.

There are 60 seconds in one minute, 60 minutes in one hour and 24 hours in one day. Therefore, each day has 60 x 60 x 12 = 86,400 seconds. Since there are roughly 365 days in one year, then there are 86,400 seconds x 365 days in one year = 31,536,000 seconds in one year.

A year is really 365¼ days long. For this reason, we add one day every four years as our leap year. But in order to stay with round numbers, we will use 365 days for this illustration. At the writing this book, I am 60 years old, so on the day of my 60th birthday, I had lived 31,536,000 seconds in one year x 60 years = 1,892,160,000 seconds in 60 years. That is a lot of seconds. I hope I have not wasted too many of them.

Imagine the number of seconds that have elapsed in 100 years or 1,000 years or 1 million years or 1 billion years or in the presupposed 15 billion years of the history of the universe. The number of seconds that have elapsed since the Big Bang is merely 10^{17}. That number includes leap years.

Keep in mind that we did not compute the odds of creating a cell. We only computed the odds that this average-sized protein of the smallest theoretical cell would be composed of only left-handed amino acids. What would be the chances of creating this smallest theoretical cell of only 239 proteins?

For the sake of our discussion, we will assume that we can begin with a matrix containing only left-handed amino acids. The next step, then, would be to calculate the chances of the smallest hypothetical cell to be created by random chance containing only 239 proteins. Remember that no such cell exists. It is simply the smallest theoretical living cell proposed by Morowitz.

Coppedge, at this point, allowed for 14 different concessions to assist chance in this random arrangement process. In other words, Coppedge does not in this computation attempt to refute any of the fundamental assumptions made by evolutionists. A realistic computation would, in fact, consider the odds of the many evolutionary assumptions fundamental to their conclusion. For example, their need for a reducing atmosphere is necessary for the combination of amino acids in the naturalistic hypothesis, but the geologic evidence refutes that our planet ever had a reducing atmosphere for any appreciable length of time. We will look at this further in the section on Chemical Abiogenesis and Organic Compounds.

Coppedge, in his computation, simply takes for granted every fundamental evolutionary assumption they make and even makes it better than reality could provide for them so the possible calculations would have every conceivable advantage imagined by evolutionists and more.

I realize that these concessions are of a technical nature and difficult for the layperson to follow. But I have chosen to include them for the sake of the interested few. I hope you are one of those interested readers.

The 14 Concessions

1. **Assume that the primitive atmosphere was a reducing atmosphere** (hydrogen-rich), as evolutionists claim, although there is much new geologic evidence to the contrary.

2. **Assume that all 20 amino acids were formed naturally and in the right proportions** by the action proposed by evolutionists: ultraviolet rays, lightning, and heat.

3. **Assume that the amino acids were formed in only the left-handed configuration**, even though that is, for all practical purposes, impossible in a random-processed evolution.

4. **In the following calculations, the average protein molecule will be considered to be 400 units in length**, disregarding Morowitz's calculation that it would probably consist of 445 amino acid units.

   He [Morowitz] took into consideration the minimum operating equipment needed and the space it would require Also, attention was given to electrical properties and to the hazards of thermal motion.... Using figures that were furnished by Morowitz, it can be calculated that the average protein molecule in the theoretical minimal living thing would contain around 445 amino acid units of the usual 20 kinds (Coppedge 72).

5. **Assume that every atom in the entire Earth is used in the recombination process.** That is, all the carbon, nitrogen, oxygen, and hydrogen atoms in the air, water, and crust of Earth have been made up into amino acids that could then be combined in this all-out shuffling effort to create proteins from random alignments.

6. **Assume that this entire batch of amino acids has been conveniently grouped in sets, and each set contains one of each kind available at each position of the forming chain.** (This may be pictured in Oparin's suggested coacervate droplets, and hence, this computation is acceding a point, which in reality could not happen.)

7. **Assume that these groupings are supernaturally protected from the destructive forces that they claim created them, such as the lethal ultraviolet light.** Again, such a concession is quite unrealistic since organic compounds exposed to long-wavelength ultraviolet light would be destroyed. "Ultraviolet light would also destroy many organic compounds in the ocean since it would penetrate some tens of meters beneath the ocean surface. Ocean currents periodically would surface even in the deep water, thus exposing its organic content, too, to destructive ultraviolet light" (Thaxton et al. 45). For this reason, all simulation experiments use only short-wave ultraviolet light, an artificial situation that could not have been reproduced in the early Earth.

8. **Concede that the amino acids would automatically unite,** even though this would require going against an energy gradient, and the complex system which unites them in all known living things would be absent.

9. **Concede that in the active site one substitution is allowable in each chain;** that is, it will be considered permissible for any amino acid to substitute for any other at any point.

10. **Assume that the actual rate of chain formation is so rapid that an entire chain requires only one-third of a ten-million-billionth of a second**. This is an astronomically impossible rate, considering that it is 150 thousand trillion times the normal rate in real life.

11. **For each set of amino acids, figure that every usable chain is immediately dismantled and another one is made to maximize the use of the amino acids**. That is, it would be dismantled at the same rate of 30 million billion per second, which amounts to 10^{24} per year in each set of amino acids.

12. **Assume that nothing will interfere so that chance will have an ideal opportunity** and that if a usable sequence is ever obtained, the action will stop so it may be preserved. Such a feat would be miraculous, to say the least.

13. **Assume that if a workable number of proteins (239) in contiguous form is ever obtained, they will be able to merge into one group of proteins ready to work together in a living system**. In other words, by piling up the proteins, it would become alive spontaneously—a ridiculous assumption, to say the least.

14. **Assume that the age of Earth is the 15 billion years that evolutionists propose for the age of the universe**. Evolutionists believe that Earth is no more than 4 billion to 5 billion years old. Hence, in this computation, we are increasing the actual life of Earth over threefold from their accounting. (These concessions were distilled from Coppedge 105–108).

Given all these unrealistic concessions in order to sweeten the pie, here is what Coppedge said about the chance of creating a minimum set of 239 proteins by random ordering:

> *The odds against one minimum set of proteins happening in the entire history of the earth are 10^{119775} to 1 (Coppedge 111).*

That is an absolutely astronomical number. If I could write a thousand zeros every second, there would not be enough time in the supposed 15 billion years of the history of the universe to write down all the zeroes in that number.

Again, compare this number to the number of seconds that have elapsed not in a year, not in a century, not in a millennium, not in a million years, not in a billion years, but for the entire 15 billion years that evolutionists propose our universe has existed: 10^{17}.

Let's take this imaginary scenario one step further to aid evolutionists. Again, conceding all the physical prerequisites evolutionists claim as necessary parameters for the evolution of life to have taken place, let's suppose that we pack every square inch of the entire visible universe with a supposedly simple form of life—bacteria.

Next, we then break down all their chemical bonds and mix all the atoms in order to allow the recombination of these through chance chemical processes in an attempt to create a cell of 600 proteins.

If we were to repeat this process at the amazing rate of a billion times a second and allow the process to go on for 20 billion years, which is 5 billion years more than the age evolutionists give to our universe, and furthermore, if we were to concede the temperature and pressure gradients, which would be favorable to the recombination of these atoms throughout the entire universe, *the odds of a single cell of 600 different proteins to be made would be 1 to an astronomical $10^{99,999,999,873}$*. (Morowitz 2–12, 44–75).

That is a 1 with a staggering 99 billion, 999 million, 999 thousand, 873 zeroes after it. Again, this number is so fantastic that we have difficulty grasping its immensity.

Suppose we took a tape measure and traveled from one end of the universe to the other, and we would document its diameter, not in light years, but in inches. The number would be 10^{28}. To accept random order as the mechanism that created a single cell requires a blind leap of faith, which is absolutely irrational in nature. Such a proposition is not a scientific proposition but rather a speculation grounded on nothing more than a metaphysical choice to believe that there is no Creator and we must have therefore evolved through materialistic random chance, no matter how irrational the leap of faith.

Not Enough Time, Not Enough Matter

What if we were able to calculate the total amount of possible physical transitions that could take place in the most elementary particles throughout the entire history of our universe using all the available matter within it?

> *Due to the properties of gravity, matter, and electro-magnetic radiation, physicists have determined that there is a limit to the number of physical transitions that can occur from one state to another within a given unit of time. According to physicists, a physical transition from one state to another cannot take place faster than light can traverse the smallest physically significant unit of distance (an individual "quantum" of space). That unit of distance is the so-called Planck length of 10^{-33} centimeters. Therefore, the time it takes light to traverse this smallest distance determines the shortest time in which any physical effect can occur. This unit of time is the Planck time of 10^{-43} seconds (Meyer 216).*

If we are to calculate the odds of proteins being formed from amino acids, then we must determine how fast these chemical transitions could take place. Instead of using the real-time duration of such transitions, we will, in order to give chance every chance possible, use instead the smallest theoretically possible time that a transition could take place—the Planck time of 10^{-43} seconds, or one jiffy.

Knowing this, Demski was able to calculate the largest number of opportunities that any material event had to occur in the observable universe since the big bang. Physically speaking, an event occurs when an elementary particle does something or interacts with other elementary particles. But since elementary particles can interact with each other only so many times per second (at most 10^{43} times), since there are a limited number (10^{80}) of elementary particles, and since there has been a limited amount of time since the big bang (10^{16} seconds), there are a limited number of opportunities for any given event to occur in the entire history of the universe.

Demski was able to calculate this number by simply multiplying the three relevant factors together: the number of elementary particles (10^{80}) times the number of seconds since the big bang (10^{16}) times the number of possible interactions per second (10^{43}). His calculations fixed the total number of events that could have taken place in the observable muniverse since the origin of the universe at $10^{139.4}$. *This then provided a measure of the probabilistic resources of the entire observable universe* (emphasis added) (Meyer 216–217).

In other words, the upper limit, the largest possible number of physical reactions that could have taken place in the entire history of our universe using every elementary particle in our universe is $10^{139.4}$. This number documents that the universe does not contain the probabilistic resources necessary to allow chance random ordering to formulate even the most basic building block of life—the protein.

But, the evolutionary hypothesis does not claim that life on Earth evolved using particles from the Andromeda galaxy or from any other part of our universe outside our planet. It can only use those elements found within our much more limited Earth, even if they originated from elsewhere. Life on Earth supposedly "evolved" on our blue planet. So a more realistic calculation would only consider those particles that are limited to the surface of our rocky planet.

Furthermore, proteins are made of amino acids. There are many fewer amino acids in the world than there are elementary particles. Moreover, the components that could have produced proteins are only the amino acids on the surface of the planet, which are considerably fewer in numbers than all the amino acids in the world.

In addition, of all the amino acids in the world, life is only composed of 20 of them. Thus, the total number of amino acids available for such a computation would be considerably less. Then, there is the fact that life only contains left-handed amino acids, so even the 20 amino acids that occur equally in both antipodes must be cut in half. The largest realistic number of potential amino acid reactions limited to the Earth would thus be minute compared to all the atoms in our universe, making the odds that much greater for chance to have selected all these parameters randomly to achieve evolutionists' celebrated *Voila!*

Since the odds of developing one cell of 600 proteins are *1 to an astronomical* $10^{99,999,999,873}$ but the largest number of potential physical interactions since the beginning of time in the entire universe is $10^{139.4}$, it is literally impossible to conceive that chance could have randomly formulated a single cell of just 600 proteins within the time frame of our universe. To assert otherwise cannot be construed as objective scientific reasoning. It is nothing more than simple blind faith.

Given the fact that Murray Eden has proposed that the number of protein molecules that could have ever existed in the presupposed 15 billion years of evolutionary history is 10^{52}, one can readily appreciate the seriousness of this number. Eden is a retired engineering professor at Massachusetts Institute of Technology and was one of the participants at the now famous Wistar Conference in Philadelphia.

The odds that chance could have produced even the simplest living entity are so remote that it should be recognized as realistically impossible by anyone who is considered an objective observer. These are the odds for just one small cell to form. If all of life were to evolve from this single ancestral forefather, the cell would then have to survive the hostile environment envisioned by the reducing atmosphere of the evolutionists.

What are the chances that this cell would survive such a hostile environment as supposedly required in order for these chemical reactions to take place and replicate itself successfully? The ultraviolet light and cosmic rays that would have been literally blasting down on the surface of this primeval Earth with a reducing atmosphere would have damaged any life forms, since in their proposed reducing atmosphere, there would not have been the ionosphere that normally offers protection against cosmic rays.

To date, no theory has been posited to explain how our atmosphere would have acquired so much oxygen from the supposed primordial reducing atmosphere. But evolutionists must propose a reducing atmosphere because the presence of oxygen would have oxidized the amino acids and kept them from becoming proteins, as they suppose.

The fact is that in nature, amino acids do not naturally link up to create more complex protein molecules outside of living organisms that are able to use directed energy through metabolic motors. In fact, in nature, the opposite is the case. Proteins break down into amino acids.

Moreover, the mechanism, or energy sources such as the Earth's heat, lightning, or solar radiation, which, they propose, were the catalyst for creating proteins from amino acids, have been shown to more readily do the exact opposite, even if they existed in a reducing atmosphere.

> *The conclusion from these arguments presents the most serious obstacle, if indeed it is not fatal, to the theory of spontaneous generation. First, thermodynamic calculations predict vanishingly small concentrations of even the simplest organic compounds. Secondly, the reactions that are involved to synthesize such compounds are seen to be much more effective in decomposing them (Hull 694).*

Furthermore, if Earth formed as evolutionists describe, the radioactivity of uranium isotopes from below would have had disruptive or negative effects on any forming life. Yet those are the conditions evolutionists expect us to accept as conducive to biogenesis. How is it, then, that they consider the view that life could not have evolved in such a hostile environment as unscientific?

Even if we were to give them an entire Earth full of only left-handed amino acids, which would have miraculously filled the Earth with viable proteins, what mechanism could cause the development of a cell, which must simultaneously evolve a membrane to contain its form and the processes of replication and metabolism that even the simplest form of life contains simultaneously? The idea that nucleotides could have randomly formed the DNA helix and randomly developed the four-base-genetic language, which, through the intermediate of a mediator molecule (translates DNA language to the protein language) can communicate with the 20-amino-acid protein language, is a hyper leap of faith that cannot be labeled as anything but irrational.

All these processes must have had to evolve simultaneously in order for it to be able to function as a viable single-celled organism in which the genetic material and the protein systems are integrated in a highly complex and irreducible form.

The idea that life could have evolved by random chemical processes devoid of any external guiding force is so remote that even the most ardent evolutionists must admit that it would have been a miracle of the first order. Francis Crick, co-discoverer of the DNA code and a committed atheist, grudgingly admitted this when considering these facts:

> *An honest man, armed with all the knowledge avail-*
> *able to us now, could only state that in some sense,*
> *the origin of life appears at the moment to be almost a*
> *miracle, so many are the conditions which would have*
> *had to have been satisfied to get it going (Crick 88).*

The fact is that no functional duplicative process can be formed without a mechanism to provide directed energy. Without specially directed energy, there can be no format to formulate systems that store specified information. The proposed mechanisms offered by evolutionists to form a living cell, such as the heat or ultraviolet light energy from the sun, could not supply this directed energy, without the mediation of some form of complex metabolic motor. The undirected energy would, in fact, do the opposite of what they propose and keep it from forming into an organism of complexity. The energy must be channeled and harnessed, a feat that is impossible without a complex metabolic motor with which to begin.

It takes more blind faith to believe that life evolved from lifeless chemical processes governed by pure chance than to acknowledge that the design of these complex and interdependent systems and their specified information could not have been formed without a designer, a mastermind that engineered the vast array of intricately balanced metabolic systems in a living cell. Random chance is incapable of producing any credible procedure to organize such interdependent complexity that exhibits such specificity.

Clearly, the idea that the greater the time elapsed, the greater the possibility for an improbable event to occur is inapplicable in this area, for the 15 billion years evolutionary scientists postulate as the age of our universe are not enough for such a miracle to have taken place. Furthermore, the prebiotic soup, even if it existed, would not be enough to make chance viable.

A. I. Oparin's postulate of gradual evolution by a succession of steps that tries to use the concept of long periods of time to make the impossible appear possible is naïve at best considering the true complexity found in the biochemical processes of the simplest cells. The improbability is so astronomical that no matter what ages evolutionists can invent, it is still impossible.

Our universe had a beginning, and the infinite time that evolution so desperately needed when it was first proposed is no longer available. Yet no concession of eons of time in order to allow the impotence of their chance mechanism to don the garb of intellectual and scientific respectability would make a difference. It has failed the litmus test of reality.

In his intuitive book, *Undeniable*, Douglas Axe a distinguished molecular biologist writes:

> *When it comes to understanding from firsthand experience, the difficulty of making atoms come together to form molecular devices, very few people can match Jim Tour. I certainly can't.... [I]t would be interesting to know what Tour thinks about the casual confidence so many scientists seem to have in the ability of unguided natural processes to build complex molecular devices.*
>
> *Thankfully, we don't have to wonder about this. Speaking of the separation of helpful products from unhelpful ones after each step in a complex synthesis procedure (without which the procedure would fail), Tour says:*
>
>> *If one asks the molecularly uninformed how nature devises reactions with such high purity,*

*the answer is often, "Nature selects for that."
But what does that mean to a synthetic chemist?
What does selection mean? To select, it must still
rid itself of all the material that it did not select.
And from where did all the needed starting
material come? And how does it know what to
select when the utility is not assessed until many
steps later? The details are stupefying and the
petty comments demonstrate the sophomoric
understanding of the untrained.*

*In other words, the only thing people demonstrate
when they assume such things can happen by accident
is that they don't know what they are talking about
(Axe 195).*

The scientific reality is that gradualism is dead. Some evolutionists
have grudgingly conceded this fact. Yet they attempt to sidestep the
obvious necessity of intelligent design by positing that the chemical
processes that govern our world today are different than during the
early development of the evolution of life.

*Dr. N. W. Pirie of the Rothamstead Experimental
Station at Harpenden, England, rejects this whole
concept of spontaneous biogenesis simply on the
well-founded fact that complicated molecules such
as proteins do not, in our scientific experience, arise
spontaneously even by stages.... Dr. Pirie rejects
the idea of accounting for life on earth as a result
of occult or supernatural intervention. He points
out, however, that no less a person than Dr. J. B.
S. Haldane was driven to believe that the laws of
chemistry and physics must have been different in
the Precambrian from what they are now, since*

the ordinary laws of chemistry and physics, as we know them today, do not allow complex proteins to arise spontaneously even by stages. Therefore, such is Haldane's logic, since life did in his view arise spontaneously, the laws of chemistry must have been different when it arose! (Wilder-Smith 18)

So much for uniformitarianism! So much for loyalty to experimental data and observations! So much for the scientific process of extrapolating from the present empirical facts! What the evolutionists need now is a magic wand and some fairy dust from Tinkerbell to seal their deal.

Again, secular individuals are forced to take another irrational leap of faith, when the facts just don't quite fit their underlying naturalistic dogma. Louis Pasteur would turn in his grave if he knew that modern "science" has reverted to the medieval concept of spontaneous generation, albeit deceptively masked in ever so slow, gradual steps, through the march of eons of years in time. Alas, a rose by any other name is still a rose!

The Symmetry between the Universe and Life

Life in the most primitive sense that can be observed is, in fact, complex beyond imagination. Our modern technology has proved that there is no such thing as simple life forms. This uniqueness and specified complexity points to intelligent design.

Lawrence J. Henderson, noted professor of biological chemistry at Harvard University at the beginning of the twentieth century, made a considerable impact on the scientific community with his research into the environment and humans. In his books *The Fitness of the Environment* and *The Order of Nature,* he established an impressive array of scientific documentation on the uniqueness of the properties exhibited by our universe, without which life could not have developed or existed.

Henderson was led to reflect on teleology in the biochemical world through his work on the regulation of acidity and alkalinity in living organisms. He noticed that of all known substances, phosphoric acid and carbonic acid (CO_2 dissolved in water) possessed the greatest power of automatic regulation of neutrality. Had these substances not existed, such regulation in living things would be much more difficult. Henderson searched the chemical literature and uncovered a large number of substances whose peculiar properties were essential to life. Water, for example, is absolutely unique in its ability to dissolve other substances, in its anomalous expansion when cooled near the freezing point, in its thermal conductivity among ordinary liquids, in its surface tension, and numerous other properties. Henderson showed that these strange qualities of water made it necessary for any sort of life. Furthermore, the properties of hydrogen, oxygen, and carbon had a number of quirks amongst all the other elements that made these elements and their properties essential for living organisms. These quirks were discussed in detail in his book Fitness of the Environment. *These properties were so outstanding in the role they played in living things that ... we were obliged to regard this collocation of properties as in some intelligible sense a preparation for the process of planetary evolution... Therefore the properties of the elements must for the present be regarded as possessing a teleological character....*

The chance that this unique ensemble of properties should occur by "accident" is almost infinitely small (i.e., less than any probability which can *be practically considered). The chance that each of the unit properties [heat capacity, surface tension, number of possible molecules, etc.] of the ensemble, by itself and in cooperation with the others, should "accidentally" contribute a maximum increment is almost infinitely small. Therefore, there is relevant causal connection between the properties of the elements and the "freedom" of evolution....*

If the properties of the elements were slightly different, if there were no carbon atoms in the world, if for instance living things attempted to substitute silicon instead, then vastly fewer molecules would be possible, and evolution by natural selection on different genotypes would be impossible. Probably no organisms as complex as a single cell would arise, and certainly no creatures as complex as human beings would evolve (Barrow and Tipler 143, 145).

An almost infinite number is quite a large number. An almost infinitely small number is quite a small number approaching zero, or, as Henderson says, "less than any probability which can be practically considered." And yet, against all odds, evolutionists tenaciously hold to this preposterous article of faith in their evolutionary religion.

How could blind chemical chance account for the incredible system found within each cell that keeps the thousands of chemicals, of which some are acidic and others basic, from reacting with one another and causing metabolic mayhem? The intricate system of chemical barriers and buffers are evidence of intelligent design and cannot be adequately explained any other way.

How could these barriers and buffers have evolved simultaneously, at just the right place and time to prevent chemical reactions from being destructive to the living organism? And how could random ordering manage to simultaneously program this into the DNA so it could be passed on to the next generation, since without the gene expression system, any life created would simply die, and the whole chance process would begin at square one?

The thousands of chemical pathways intrinsic to all living organisms usually involve a long series of complex chemical reactions that must be carried out in specific orders for the organism to live, and which cannot be short-circuited without lethal consequences to the organism. The clotting of blood, for example takes some 30 steps, without which we would die. Those unfortunate souls who do not have the capacity to clot (hemophiliacs) live in constant danger of bleeding to death.

On the other hand, blood clots can also be fatal. A blood clot inside the body can cause a lethal myocardial infarction in the heart, or it could cause a cerebrovascular accident (CVA) in the brain. Maintaining the homeostasis in countless such processes could not have been an accident of nature. They are simply too complex, involving many interdependent steps. Omitting one of these many steps, altering the sequence or timing of a given step, or inserting an unwanted step into this complex metabolic reaction could have lethal consequences.

What selective pressure could, through random processes, engineer the ordering of these chemical reactions in the right timing and sequence and provide a system to replicate it through chance chemical combinations?

It is because the very nature of each of the fundamental elements involved in the process of life is so tailor-made for the job that their marvelous design points to a designer. And for this reason, the difficulty in asserting the chance or accidental evolutionary development of life through purely random processes becomes so infinitely improbable that many secular scientists admit it is below the level of practical consideration. Sadly, instead of admitting the obvious, the Darwinist refuses to admit that this is evidence of design and, indirectly, the Master Designer.

And yet, for this reason, the consensus among evolutionists is that the development or evolution of life is so highly improbable that having supposedly evolved once on our planet, the chances of life evolving again is scientifically irrational.

The drive to explore the planets is fueled largely by those who seek to find life there in order to give credibility to the theory of evolution. But if we were to find life on another planet, it would, in fact, prove that an intelligent designer must have created it since the chances of developing life on another planet through accidental chemical reactions would be even greater than the evolution of life on Earth.

CHAPTER 5

●●●

THE EVOLUTIONARY MECHANISMS PROPOSED FOR THE EVOLUTION OF THE LIVING CELL

In this chapter, we will examine the various proposals for the evolution of the indispensable macromolecules of the living cell such as proteins, RNA and DNA molecules necessary for the gene expression system of the cell to function, and the ATP or GMP molecules that fuel all the metabolic needs of a living cell. If evolution fails to find a credible mechanism for the evolution of these principal macromolecules in the cell, then it is clear that the evolution of the living cell cannot be explained through the gradualist natural selection process of the Darwinian model.

I realize that the nontechnical reader may find some of these biology terms daunting. But I will do my best to explain the marvelously complex macromolecules as simply as God gives me grace. This chapter is where the rubber meets the road. It is what makes the evolutionary model naked of its propaganda trappings and destroys the imaginary concept that dead molecules self-organized to become living cells.

Chemical Abiogenesis and Organic Compounds

The theory of chemical evolution proposed by Alexander Oparin to account for the synthesis of organic prebiotic molecules requires that Earth's primordial atmosphere be free of oxygen and have what chemists refer to as a reducing atmosphere containing free hydrogen.

In 1953, American chemist Stanley Miller conducted an experiment in which he attempted to simulate a reducing atmosphere of the type envisioned by Oparin and J. B. S. Haldane in order to synthesize organic compounds. Miller envisioned an atmosphere containing methane (CH_4), ammonia (NH_3), and hydrogen (H_2). Beyond that, he simply assumed that this primordial atmosphere contained virtually no free oxygen.

To duplicate a reducing atmosphere, Miller subjected methane, ammonia, and water to an electrical discharge. Immediately after the charge, he quickly cooled down the by-product to preserve it.

Through this experiment, Miller was able to produce large molecules of organic compounds known as amino acids. Newspaper headlines around the world optimistically and naïvely heralded the achievement as the creation of life in a laboratory. However, this was quite removed from the actual accomplishment. For example, the creation of a few copper wires does not create a computer.

The production of an organic compound is not in any way even remotely comparable to the creation of life. In fact, although the universe is made up mostly of space, it contains, interspersed throughout most of it, many organic compounds obviously produced by non-living, natural, chemical processes.

An organic compound is made of the four elements: carbon, oxygen, nitrogen, and hydrogen. All living things contain organic compounds, but not all organic compounds are contained in living things. There are many organic compounds that are produced by non-living processes. However, there are no proteins produced by non-living processes.

Through the use of radiotelescopes and by comparing the spectra of elements found in outer space, we have been able to determine that the vastness of space is interspersed with matter. The great majority of it is hydrogen and helium, which, under the temperature conditions of interstellar space, cannot form solid bodies and is therefore found in gaseous or plasma form. There is also an enormous amount of water interspersed throughout the universe, most of which is in the form of ice due to the freezing temperatures in outer space.

But in addition to the water and gases, there are also solid grains of matter called interstellar grains. Most of the interstellar grain material found between the stars and galaxies is composed of compounds made by seven elements: oxygen, carbon, nitrogen, magnesium, silicon, iron, and sulfur. Through the use of optical spectroscopy in analyzing hot-emission nebulae, radio astronomers have been able to identify more than 50 molecules.

The precise and unique frequency characteristics of these compounds have revealed to us that compounds such as carbon monoxide (CO), formamide ($HCONH_2$), acetaldehyde (CH_3CHO), ethanol (CH_3CH_2OH), and even formaldehyde (HCHO), a chemical we commonly use to preserve tissue, are found in dense concentrations of these molecular clouds.

In July 2004, a team of astrophysicists reported the presence of two previously undetected aldehyde molecules through the radio emissions from Sagittarius B2, a nebula near the center of our galaxy. All of these are organic compounds made through non-living processes.

We can readily find amino acids created by natural processes. They may even be found in meteorites, but they are certainly not life in any stretch of the imagination. But never in space are these amino acids linked as proteins. We have already seen the improbability of amino acids coming together to formulate a functional protein through natural chance processes. To date, proteins are found only on Earth and created only by living things.

Proponents of intelligent design do not deny that there are mechanisms to produce organic compounds in the universe that do not require living organisms to synthesize. As a matter of fact, the study of meteorites, or carbonaceous chondrites, has revealed that some of them contain organic compounds such as formaldehyde and formamide. There may even be amino acids of the 20 kinds required for protein synthesis in space, but here is a prediction from intelligent design: You will not find proteins unless they are made by living organisms.

Finding an amino acid is a far cry from *creating* a protein. All the concerted effort of evolutionists around the world has yet to find any natural mechanism for the formulation of proteins in a usable manner that would make them functional in the creation of a living cell.

In 1976, Sidney Fox performed some experiments in which he was able to create a protein-like substance that he called a protenoid. And the newspapers again heralded the achievement as the production of life in a laboratory (Wikipedia, s.v. "Sidney W. Fox").

These so-called protenoids are in no way compatible with the types of polymers necessary for life. They are small chain polymers that are not composed with either the shape or the functionality necessary in order for proteins to form the building blocks of a living cell.

Nevertheless, the achievement has been overly celebrated by evolutionists grasping at straws to promote their cherished hope that proteins can be made within a reducing (hydrogen-rich) atmosphere through an abiogenic synthesis.

We have already discussed the empirical fact that the most significant hurdle evolutionists must clear is the development of a chance, undirected process for creating proteins within the 15 billion years since the Big Bang.

Not only did Fox not create proteins, but what he came up with certainly has not been able to create anything that is exclusively composed of left-handed amino acids without the interference of the experimenter removing the right-handed amino acids first. But the problem for evolutionists is complicated even more by the fact that our fossil record actually contradicts their claim of a primordial reducing atmosphere.

The Early Atmosphere Was Not a Reducing Atmosphere

Since the theory of abiogenic synthesis of organic chemicals requires that an atmosphere be free of oxygen, evolutionists have automatically assumed that our primordial atmosphere, for a considerable length of time throughout the early pre-Cambrian period, must have been a reducing atmosphere.

That has been presumed by most and uncritically accepted as fact, not because the empirical data dictate it, but because without a reducing atmosphere for a very long time period, it is inconceivable that chance random processes could develop organic compounds. The presence of oxygen would be disastrous to the chemical process evolutionists have imagined. And the fossil record simply does not show this to be true. The opposite is actually the case. Sedimentary layers of the earth show evidence of oxidation (the opposite of a reducing atmosphere) in the very lowest regions. This is not speculation; it is empirical data.

> *The Chemical Evolution Theory requires that an oxygen-free atmosphere existed for a considerable period of time on the early Earth. Geologic evidence from the early PreCambrian, however, suggests that such primitive and secondary atmospheres did not exist for any appreciable length of time.*
>
> *Supporting evidence for this comes from studies of the ultra-violet photolysis of methane to give*

polymeric materials. These studies suggest that under primitive-Earth conditions the temperature around the Earth might have been so high that methane would have disappeared. It would have been broken down into high-molecular-mass carbon polymer—deposited on the Earth's surface, and hydrogen—escaping instantaneously into space. So an oxygen-free atmosphere on primitive Earth, if it existed, would probably have broken down in too short a time for a living system or chemicals of life to have formed in it. These observations led Shimizu to conclude, in 1976, that the previous optimistic conclusions as to primitive Earth's atmosphere should be cautiously re-evaluated.

And what of the 'primitive-soup' required for Chemical Evolution? If such an environment ever existed on Planet Earth for any appreciable time, it would require relatively large quantities of nitrogen-containing organic compounds (amino-acids, nucleic acid bases and so on). It is likely that such nitrogen rich soups would have given significant quantities of 'nitrogenous cokes', trapped in various PreCambrian sediments. (The formation of such 'cokes' is the normal result obtained by heating organic matter rich in nitrogenous substances.) No such nitrogen-rich materials have yet been found in early PreCambrian rocks on this planet. In fact the opposite seems to be true: the nitrogen content of early PreCambrian organic matter is relatively low (less than 0.15%).

From this we can be reasonably certain that:

- there never was any substantial amount of 'primitive soup' on Earth when ancient PreCambrian sediments were formed;

- *if such a 'soup' ever existed it was only for a brief period of time (Brooks 117–118).*

The numerous ponds of scum, teeming with the "prebiotic soup" we have been nearly forced to believe in throughout the decades of evolutionary propaganda, are absolutely impossible without a reducing atmosphere. But the assumptions made were by necessity and not due to the geologic evidence. As evidence for the geologic condition of primitive Earth is analyzed, it turns out to strongly suggest that neutral gases such as carbon dioxide, nitrogen, and water vapor—not methane, ammonia, and hydrogen—predominated Earth during its history.

> *If there is any merit to the view that methane was an important constituent of the primitive atmosphere, hydrocarbons surely must have formed in the atmosphere under the influence of ultraviolet irradiation and fallen into the ocean. Hydrocarbons would then be brought to rest on the ocean bottom by absorption on sedimenting clays. The earliest Precambrian deposits would be expected to contain unusually large proportions of hydrocarbon material or its carbon remains. They do not, however* (emphasis added) *(Thaxton et al. 57).*

The fundamental component for evolutionists' theory has been shown to be false. The presence of neutral gases means that reaction among the gases in the atmosphere would not allow the formation of biologically significant molecules. Significantly, if even a small amount of oxygen were present, it would quench the production of any biologically significant molecules; it would simply oxidize them.

> *To make matters worse, an accumulating body of geochemical evidence has shown—perhaps, not surprisingly, in light of the previous discussion—that*

there likely never was a prebiotic soup. Two leading geochemists, James Brooks and Gordon Shaw, argued that if an ocean rich in amino and nucleic acids had existed, it would have left large deposits of nitrogen-rich mineral (nitrogenous cokes) in metamorphosed Precambrian sedimentary rocks. No evidence of such deposits exists, however. In the words of Brooks: "The nitrogen content of early Pre-Cambrian organic matter is relatively low (less than .015%). From this we can be reasonably certain that: there never was any substantial amount of "primitive soup" on earth when Pre-Cambrian sediments were formed; if such a soup ever existed it was only for a brief period of time." ...

The chance hypothesis envisioned DNA and proteins arising from random process of chemical "roulette" in a favorable nitrogen-rich prebiotic ocean. If no such environment had ever existed, then whatever specificity the chance hypothesis might have once had was now lost. If there was no "chemical roulette" in which life would emerge as an inevitable if improbable outcome, chance could no longer be considered a substantive hypothesis; it would instead be just a vacuous notion that at best concealed ignorance of the true cause of life's origin....

Simulation experiments of the type performed by Stanley Miller had repeatedly demonstrated this. They have invariably produced nonbiological substances in addition to biological building blocks such as amino acids. Without intelligent intervention, these other substances will react readily with biologically relevant building blocks to form biologically irrelevant compounds—chemically insoluble sludge. To prevent this from happening and to move the simulation of chemical evolution along a biologically promising trajectory, experimenters often remove these chemicals that degrade or transform amino acids into nonbiologically relevant compounds. They also must artificially manipulate the initial conditions in their experiments. For example, rather than using both short- and long-wavelength ultraviolet light, which would have been present in any realistic early atmosphere, they use only short-wavelength UV. Why? The presence of the long-wavelength UV light quickly degrades amino acids (Meyer 225, 226).

Little evidence exists for a reducing atmosphere in early Earth other than the evidence of necessity due to the simulation experiments performed in order to create amino acids through "spark" and "traps" methods as devised by Miller. Since Miller's groundbreaking experiment, many other simulation experiments have been devised, some using UV, others through heat, and yet others by shock waves. It must be noted that a great variety of amino acids have been created using a variety of mixtures of these reducing gases, but the simulation experiments in no way reflect the actual conditions that would have occurred on early Earth, even if there had been a reducing atmosphere, because without their several intentional interventions, the chemical reactions would have resulted in sludge.

Here are a few ways in which evolutionists intervene in order to stack the deck:

1. **Ultra Violet light** – Invariably, experiments using ultraviolet light have chosen the short-wavelength (<2000A) exclusively and have intentionally excluded the long-wavelength (>2000 A) because of its destructive nature. This unnatural separation of the ultraviolet light spectrum does not accord with random ordering as prescribed by the naturalistic

model. Rather, it reflects the exogenous input of intelligence (external intelligent manipulation) into the equation in order to engineer the results toward their favored outcome.

There are no known natural processes that could duplicate this artificial interference manipulated by the experimenters. The suggestion that the ocean could provide such a harbor for these synthesized molecules falls short of the mark. Long-wave ultraviolet light would reach tens of meters below the ocean's surface and destroy the molecular structures quite efficiently. Not even the deep waters of the ocean could protect them very long, for the deep ocean currents eventually bring these waters to the surface periodically.

2. **Spark Discharge (lightning simulators)** – Electrical discharge simulations are designed to represent lightning strikes in these supposed prebiotic soup ponds or in reducing atmospheres. However, the actual lightning leader is much too hot to accomplish what Darwinists propose. The temperature is 20,000 K, which would effectively destroy or incinerate anything it hits. And yet the corona discharges are too low. So experimenters use an energy gradient that is nine times in magnitude what could represent natural processes. The idea that such magnitude represents speeded up evolution is also unrealistic. The long ages and lower temperatures could not have achieved the continuity in the reactive process created in their simulation experiments.

Much milder electrical discharges, the so-called corona discharges from pointed objects, have also been simulated in experiments. The energy density used in these experiments is, however, nine orders of magnitude too great to be called a simulation of natural phenomena. In more imaginable terms the Miller spark experiment adds so much energy that "two days of sparking represent an energy input into the system comparable to some 40 million years on the surface of the primitive Earth." Another geologically implausible feature of electrical discharge experiments is the fact that they are closed systems containing as much as 75% hydrogen. (While they are begun with more plausible hydrogen concentrations, hydrogen is generated in the reaction and not allowed to escape as it would from an open system) (Thaxton et al. 102).

3. **Traps** – Traps are essentially an artificial construct that cannot be generally reproduced in nature. Traps perform several functions that are not representative of a natural environment. First, traps protect the product of the discharge experiment in a reservoir that maintains their chemical integrity by preventing cross-reactions with other chemicals that would have been present in the prebiotic soup. This is an extraneous input of intelligence that is not representative of random processes. Second, traps concentrate the by-products, unnaturally allowing for a greater rate of reactivity. In a prebiotic soup pond, the by-products would be diluted into the mix. Third, traps artificially remove and cool the by-product from the actual energy catalyst that would otherwise cause the disintegration of the molecules produced. All three of these artificial interventional acts are, again, the result of non-natural exogenous inputs of intelligence, which in no way corresponds to random chemical activity. It is not natural selection at work but rather unnatural election by the chemist.

All prebiotic heat, electrical discharge, and ultraviolet light (including photosensitization) experiments use traps. Traps allow for greater yields of product from equilibrium reactions in which dissolution would otherwise far outweigh synthesis.... Traps function by continually removing the small fraction of product formed by the reactions. As products are removed from the zone of their formation, additional reaction is continually required to reestablish equilibrium. In this way, reactions can be productively prolonged until one of the reactants is finally consumed.

This technique functions in accordance with Le Chatelier's Principle, which states that when a stress is applied to a chemical reaction at equilibrium, in this case by the trap, the reaction will shift in the direction that relieves the stress and reestablishes equilibrium. Like the practice of concentrating chemical reactants, this technique is a legitimate means of collapsing time to manageable amounts.

This removal process also shields the products from subsequent destruction by the energy source which produced them. However, Carl Sagan has aptly commented on this shielding effect in the experiments:

"The problem we're discussing is a very general one. We use energy sources to make organic molecules. It is found that the same energy sources can destroy these organic molecules. The organic chemist has an understandable preference for removing the reaction products from the energy source before they are destroyed. But when we talk of the origin of life, I think we should not neglect the fact that degradation occurs as well as synthesis, and that of course of reaction may be different if the products are not preferentially removed. In reconstructing the origin of life, we have to imagine reasonable scenarios which somehow avoid this difficulty." *(Thaxton et al. 102–103).*

Synthesizing Progenitor Aggregates Is Light Years from Synthesizing a Living Cell

The task of synthesizing aggregates that may or may not be possible progenitors of proteins is far removed from the much more intricate task of creating more than 200 proteins that would each have to be synthesized with a unique shape and function in order for a living cell to be produced. But this is quite impossible without the DNA molecule. And the DNA molecule cannot be made without these enzymatic properties in the proteins that polymerase, edit, and help bind the mRNA as well as the tRNA. So which came first, the chicken or the egg?

There are three key features present in all living cells:

1. Each cell is comprised of a membrane barrier called a lipid-protein membrane.
2. Each cell undergoes the process of metabolism.
3. Each cell contains a genetic system. The problem for the evolutionist is that since these lipid-protein membranes are impermeable to ions and polar molecules, then if the membrane developed first, how could the first protocell take in the necessary nutrients for any form of protometabolism to develop within the membrane?

If the lipid-protein membrane developed first in order to create a zone of integrity controlled by the barrier, it would make sense from an evolutionary standpoint. It would provide a region in which the genetic material could be stored and protected. But without the genetic material, what mechanism could have produced these many types of proteins necessary for the membrane to function in the selective way that allows the needed ingredients not to leak out and the needed raw material to enter? If a liposome did form first, all the necessary chemicals would have to have already been present. But how could they have been made?

It may be possible for us to imagine that a protocytosol miraculously developed first before encapsulation by a lipid-protein membrane. But on a practical level, a genetic system is extremely complex, and it is absolutely unfathomable that it could have arisen by chance chemical combinations, as we have already discussed. There is no valid way to evolve in small incremental steps into a cell. All the components are required in unison in order for life to exist, and Darwinists have no system to do so. Natural selection could not function in this capacity until there was a replicating system.

> *The widespread recognition of the severe improbability that self-replicating organisms could have formed from purely random interactions has led to a great deal of speculation—speculation that some organizing principle must have been involved. In the company of many others, Crick has considered that the neo-Darwinian mechanism of natural selection might provide the answer.* An entity capable of self-replication is necessary, however, before natural selection can operate. Only then could changes result via mutations and environmental pressures which might in turn bring about the dominance of entities with the greatest probabilities of survival and reproduction.
>
> *The weakest point in this explanation of life's origin is the great complexity of the initial entity which must form, apparently by random fluctuations, before natural selection can take over. In essence this theory postulates the chance formation of the "metabolic motor," which will subsequently be capable of channeling energy flow through the system* (emphasis added) *(Thaxton et al. 146).*

All they are left with in the Darwinian model is "random fluctuations." But, these random fluctuations are influenced or controlled by the second law of thermodynamics, which predicts the exact opposite. The energy flow of any system in time always moves energy flows toward a uniform distribution (equilibrium) and not toward specified concentrations of energy. Therefore, the probability of specified information arising through natural processes is a physical improbability.

> Clausius, who formulated the second law of thermo-
> dynamics, summarizes the laws of thermodynamics
> in his famous concise statement, "The energy of the
> universe is constant; the entropy of the universe tends
> toward a maximum." The universe moves from its less
> probable current arrangement (low entropy) toward
> its most probable arrangement in which the energy
> of the universe will be more uniformly distributed....
>
> Since the important macromolecules of living
> systems (DNA, protein, etc.) are more energy rich
> than their precursors (amino acids, heterocyclic bases,
> phosphates, and sugars), classical thermodynamics
> would predict that such macromolecules will not
> spontaneously form.
>
> Roger Caillois has recently drawn this conclusion
> in saying, "Clausius and Darwin cannot both be right"
> (Thaxton et al. 116).

The Need for a Metabolic Motor

The use of undirected energy such as heat, UV, or shock waves is incapable of creating higher specifications of energy in a system without a metabolic motor to direct that energy. It is simply too blunt an instrument. It can no more form a DNA molecule than a laser beam from an orbiting satellite can turn a pile of bricks into a house.

The unsolvable riddle for the evolutionists is that a metabolic motor is needed to direct the energy in order to create a metabolic motor. But this metabolic motor is no simple mechanism like a water-driven wheel that runs a mill.

There are many different types of proteins necessary to build the DNA and RNA molecules, which are needed to carry out the process of replication, transcription, and translation. In transcription, the RNA builds these proteins in specific patterns according to the template (architectural plan) of the DNA molecule. The enzyme RNA polymerase attaches to the DNA molecule and opens up a short section of the double helix. Remember, the DNA is in a long double helix structure in which one leg is the antipode of the other. The enzyme RNA polymerase opens the so-called zipper.

As the mRNA moves along one strand of the double helix DNA to which it is attached, it builds an mRNA complementary molecule of the DNA template. The lengthening mRNA strand being created peels off the mother DNA and, once free, creates a new exact replica DNA strand by dehydration synthesis. That is, it attaches the complementary nucleotides, exactly matching the mother DNA helix strand it copied.

But these DNA and mRNA molecules are made from genes. It is the protein enzymes that are used by the genes for their synthesis. The mRNA and tRNA build these complex proteins, but these complex proteins are needed to build an mRNA or tRNA molecule. So we find ourselves back in the riddle of who came first, the chicken or the egg?

What does all this technical stuff mean? It means that without the DNA code, proteins cannot be made, but proteins are essential in the process of transcribing that code and translating it to the protein being made. Were it not for the proteins, the DNA code would be useless. Do away with the DNA, and you cannot produce proteins. Do away with the proteins, and you cannot make DNA or proteins.

In other words, the cycle cannot be broken without destroying the purpose of both DNA and proteins. It is also a fact that proteins cannot be made without proteins.

Beyond that, the DNA code is also necessary to make ATP (the fuel that drives the chemical processes). But without ATP, the DNA cannot be made. Again, the cycle cannot be broken. Both are necessary for the functioning of each. In fact, in order to make ATPs, you need ATPs. The cycles are all interdependent. It is a cycle of multiple intertwining cycles, which are absolutely interdependent on each other, not only to be created but just to function.

In other words, there is no logical sequence in which these features can evolve independently. They must evolve simultaneously and function in synchrony in order for the cell to function at all. Natural selection cannot help until the "selection" can be replicated and passed on to the next generation. Natural selection is a principle of differential reproduction that favors the fittest. Without reproduction, there is no evolution. Theodosius Dobzhansky acknowledges this irrational and perhaps even self-deceptive use of natural selection by Darwinists, describing the evolution of prebiological systems: "I would like to plead with you, simply, please realize you cannot use the words 'natural selection' loosely. Prebiological natural selection is a contradiction of terms."

Dobzhansky is not alone in this criticism. Ludwig von Bertalanffy agrees completely: "Selection, i.e., favored survival of 'better' precursors of life, already presupposes self-maintaining, complex, open systems which may compete; therefore selection cannot account for the origin of such systems" (Bertalanffy 82).

Even if we allowed them to use their holy mantra of "natural selection" prior to the fabrication of the DNA gene expressions system, what selective pressure could have engineered that multifaceted feat? The elephant in the room is now growing in size as we learn more about the complex metabolic motor of the gene-expression system in the cell and all the interdependent metabolic processes that must function together in order for a single cell to live and reproduce.

Affinity and Necessity as the Cause for Self-Organization

Evolutionists have been scratching their heads to come up with an evolutionary process that either begins with DNA or begins with the protein that would eventually evolve into the gene-expression system of the cell. Some have postulated that certain chemical affinities might favor one simple process over another that could, through time, evolve into a more complex system.

Others have looked for some law-like process to provide some external hidden force to organize these molecules. None have been able to succeed. None have been able to explain how the specified complexities of the message in the genes or the proteins have evolved. But before we consider these attempts, let us examine exactly what this *specified complexity* in the gene really means.

One of the earliest science experiments I did as a child intrigued me. I took an empty can and filled it with a saltwater solution. I took a string and tied it to a pencil. I then placed that pencil across the top of the can, dipped the string into the saltwater, and placed my can in the sun. As time passed and the water evaporated from the can, I saw salt crystals forming on the string.

This white lattice structure exhibited a highly repetitive form and was beautiful to observe. Later on, I understood that the energy of the sun and the mutual electrostatic attraction forces among the atoms were able to take that saltwater solution and make a more ordered crystalline structure as the water evaporated.

Many years later, walking along the shore of the Dead Sea in Israel, I saw miles of this phenomenon, some standing in pillars as tall as a person. In fact, I had to wear my flip-flops to walk into the sea because the floor was riddled with these salt crystals. The reason for this crystallization comes from the electrostatic forces between sodium ($Na+$) and chloride ($Cl-$) ions, which cause them to form repeating structures of ordered complexity. If you remember our discussion of information theory, repeating information carries very little information.

But the information in the genes is not in a redundant order like the crystals. It is aperiodic and yet highly sequential. The order must be exact, yet it is not a repetitive order. This is an aperiodic- or asymmetrical-specified complexity and has a great potential for storing information. But the problem is that nothing we have observed in the chemicals found in nature can reproduce this, outside of an already living organism. Only an intelligent engineer can conceivably invent a system that exhibits this aperiodic-specified complexity. Dead molecules simply do not evolve into living organisms.

Evolutionary Biochemical Predestination?

What if there is some chemical affinity that can account for the self-organization of dead molecules? If nature can produce order through this chemical affinity, perhaps the difference in the nature of the reactivity in the units growing various amino acids could explain a defined process for the formation of a growing peptide chain through a naturalistic process. Could a protein perhaps be made through the natural affinities that might choose one chemical link over another? In other words, the natural properties of these amino acids may cause them to be predestined to join in a certain fashion. If this is so, then the specificity of their order could be explained while remaining within the naturalistic framework.

In the early 1960s, Dean Kenyon and Gary Steinman proposed that these differences in affinity imposed constraints on the sequencing process of amino acids being formed into proteins. Their model claimed that proteins came first. Since "chance" undirected abiogenesis (random fluctuations) had taken such a beating from recombinant statistics, they were now in need of some outside force that could possibly engineer the seemingly impossible task of creating a protein from amino acids in a naturalistic universe, a force that could, by necessity, cause what chance could not. That is, they needed a force that could circumvent the second law of thermodynamics in the evolution of prebiological inanimate matter toward life.

> *They wanted to see whether specific amino acid bond more readily with some amino acids than others. Their experimental results suggested that they do. For example, they discovered that glycine forms linkages with alanine twice as frequently as glycine with valine. Moreover, they discovered that these differences in chemical affinity seemed related to differences in chemical structure. Amino acids with longer side chains bond less frequently to a given amino acid than do amino acids with shorter side chains. Kenyon and Steinman summarized their findings in a table showing the various differential bonding affinities they discovered.*

> *In the wake of these findings Kenyon and Steinman proposed that these differences in affinity imposed constraints on the sequencing of amino acids, rendering certain sequences more likely than others. As they put it, "It would appear that the unique nature of each type of amino acid as determined by its side chain could introduce nonrandom constraints into the sequencing process." They further suggested that these differences in affinity might correlate with the specific sequencing motifs typical in functional proteins....*

> *Kenyon and Steinman did not attempt to extend this approach to explain the information in DNA, since they favored a protein-first model. They knew that proteins perform most of the important enzymatic and structural functions in the cell.*

They thought that if functional proteins could arise without the help of nucleic acids, then initially they need not explain the origin of DNA and RNA and the information they contained. Instead, they envisioned proteins arising directly from amino acids in a prebiotic soup. They then envisioned some of these proteins (or "proteinoids") forming membranes surrounding other proteins. Thus, the two were convinced that only later, once primitive metabolic function had arisen, did DNA and RNA need to come on the scene (Meyer 233, 234).

The theory of protein predestination then became instantly popular with naturalists. They believed that the formation of these macromolecules was chemically inevitable. Their self-organization theory sky-rocketed to acceptance almost overnight, but by the 1980s, new empirical findings began to shed doubt on the actual relevance of these "nonrandom constraints into the sequencing process."

Kenyon and Steinman had shown that certain amino acids form bonds more readily with some amino acids than with others, but the new studies showed that these actual affinities did not correlate with the actual sequencing patterns in large classes of known proteins.

Although the differential bonding affinities do exist, they have nothing to do with the actual specific sequencing of the amino acids. The idea that these intrinsic affinities could explain through natural causes the complex structure of the protein came to a sudden death.

Of course, you would not know that outside the framework of the biologists involved in these studies. Many university biology classes still speak as though the affinities can be used to explain the sequences in the proteins. Such is the nature of the beast of the evolutionary paradigm, which grimly hangs on to the propaganda, even after it has been scientifically discredited. Even Kenyon began to doubt his own theory.

Kenyon's doubts first surfaced in discussions with one of his students at San Francisco State University. In the spring of 1975 near the end of a semester-long upper-division course on evolution, a student began to raise questions about the plausibility of chemical evolution. The student—ironically named Solomon Darwin—pressed Kenyon to examine whether his self-organizational model could explain the origin of the information in DNA. Kenyon might have deflected this criticism by asserting that his protein-first model of self-organization had circumvented the need to explain the information in DNA. But by this point he found himself disinclined to make that defense.

For some time Kenyon himself had suspected that DNA needed to play a more central role in his account of the origin of life. He realized that whether functional proteins had arisen before DNA or not, the origin of information-rich DNA molecules still needed explanation, if for no other reason than because information-rich DNA molecules exist in all extant cells. At some point, DNA must have arisen as a carrier of the information for building proteins and then come into association with functional proteins. One way or another, the origin of genetic information still needed to be explained.

Now he faced a dilemma. Having opted for a self-organizational approach, he had only two options for explaining the information in DNA. Either (a) the specific sequences of amino acids in proteins had somehow provided a template for sequencing the bases in newly forming DNA molecules or (b) DNA itself had self-organized in much the same way he and

Steinman supposed proteins had. As he reflected more on Solomon Darwin's challenge, Kenyon realized that neither option was very promising. First, Kenyon knew that to propose that the information in proteins had somehow directed the construction of DNA would be to contradict everything then known about molecular biology. In extant cells, DNA provides the template of information for building proteins and not the reverse. Information flows from DNA to proteins. Moreover there are several good reasons for this asymmetry. Each triplet of DNA bases (and corresponding RNA codons) specifies exactly one amino acid during transcription and translation. Yet most amino acids correspond to more than one nucleotide triplet or RNA codon. This feature of the genetic code ensures that information can flow without "degeneracy," or loss of specificity, in only one direction, from DNA to proteins and not the reverse.

Additionally, Kenyon realized that for structural and chemical reasons, proteins made poor candidates for replicators—molecules that can function as easily copied informational templates. Unlike DNA, proteins do not possess two antiparallel strands of identical information and thus cannot be unwound and copied in the way DNA can. Further, proteins are highly reactive once they are unwound (due to exposed amino and carboxyl groups and exposed side chains). For this reason, most "denatured" (unwound) proteins tend to cross-link and aggregate. Others are quickly destroyed in the cell. Either way, denatured proteins tend to lose their structural stability and function. Moreover, they do not regain their original three-dimensional shape *or activity once they lose it. By contrast, DNA is a stable, chemically inert molecule that easily maintains its chemical structure and composition while other molecules copy its information. For all these reasons, it seemed difficult to envision proteins serving as replicators of their own stored information. Indeed, as Kenyon later told me, "getting the information out of proteins and into DNA" would pose an insuperable conceptual hurdle (Meyer 234–236).*

Kenyon therefore concluded that the information in the DNA did not originate from the proteins. The DNA must have self-organized on its own. Hence, there must be chemical laws or forces of attraction between the constituent monomers that led to their organized state. But this left him in a quandary. Based on his knowledge of DNA structure, he doubted that it could self-organize. Realizing that proteins were not the ideal candidate for the first complex molecule containing specified information, the attempt to find DNA-first evolutionary models began in earnest.

Meyer had met Dean Kenyon in 1985, 16 years after the publication of *Biochemical Predestination,* his seminal work that established the protein-first, self-organizational model as the most popular in evolutionary circles. In a conference held in Dallas, Texas, Kenyon announced that he had come to doubt all current chemical evolutionary theories of the origin of life—including his own. (I must interject here, that it is this kind of objective honesty in science that makes a true scientist.)

Nevertheless, at that point, Meyer did not quite appreciate the reasons for Kenyon's admission. It was not until after arriving at Cambridge that Meyer became aware of Michael Polanyi's work. In 1968, Polanyi published an essay about DNA in the journal *Science,* titled "Life's Irreducible Structure." The year before, Polanyi had published another essay in *Chemical and Engineering News* titled "Life Transcending Physics and Chemistry."

> *Polanyi's answer turned the classical reductionism-vitalism debate on its head. He did this by challenging an assumption held by reductionists and vitalists alike, namely that "so far as life can be represented as a mechanism, it [can be] explained by the laws of inanimate nature." Whereas vitalists had argued against reductionism by contesting that life could be understood mechanistically, Polanyi showed that reductionism fails even if one grants that living organisms depend upon many mechanisms and machines. To show this, Polanyi argued that even if living organisms function like machines, they cannot be fully explained by reference to the laws of physics and chemistry.*
>
> *Consider an illustration. A 1960s vintage computer has many parts, including transistors, resistors, and capacitors. The electricity flowing through these various parts conforms to the laws of electromagnetism, for example, Ohm's law ($E = IR$, or voltage equals current times resistance). Nevertheless, the specific structure of the computer, the configuration of its parts, does not result from Ohm's or any other law. Ohm's law (and, indeed, the laws of physics generally) allows a vast ensemble of possible configurations of the same parts. Given the fundamental physical laws and the same parts, an engineer could build many other machines and structures: different model computers, radios, or quirky pieces of experimental art made from electrical components. The physical and chemical laws that govern the flow of current in electrical machines*

do not determine how the parts of the machine are arranged and assembled. The flow of electricity obeys the laws of physics, but where the electricity flows in any particular machine depends upon the arrangements of its parts—which, in turn, depends on the design of an electrical engineer working according to engineering principles. And these engineering principles, Polanyi insisted, are distinct from the laws of physics and chemistry that they harness.

Polanyi demonstrated that the same thing was true in living things. He did this by showing that communication systems, like machines, defy reduction to physical and chemical law and by showing further that living organisms contain a communication system, namely, the gene-expression system in which DNA stores information for building proteins.

Polanyi argued that, in the case of communication systems, the laws of physics and chemistry do not determine the arrangements of the characters that convey information. The laws of acoustics and the properties of air do not determine which sounds are conveyed by speakers of natural languages. Neither do the chemical properties of ink determine the arrangements of letters on a printed page. Instead, the laws of physics and chemistry allow a vast array of possible sequences of sounds, characters, or symbols in any code or language. Which sequence of characters is used to convey a message is not determined by physical law, but by the choice of the users of the communications system in accord with the principles of engineering.

Thus, Polanyi concluded, communications systems defy reduction to physics and chemistry for much the same reasons that machines do. Then he *took a step that made his work directly relevant to the DNA enigma: he insisted that living things defy reduction to the laws of physics and chemistry because they also contain a system of communications—in particular, the DNA molecule and the whole gene-expression system....*

Polanyi went further, arguing that DNA's capacity to convey information actually requires a freedom from chemical determinism or constraint, in particular, in the arrangement of the nucleotide bases. He argued that if the bonding properties of nucleotides determined their arrangement, the capacity of DNA to convey information would be destroyed. In that case, the bonding properties of each nucleotide would determine each subsequent nucleotide and thus, in turn, the sequence of the molecular chain. Under these conditions, a rigidly ordered pattern would emerge as required by their bonding properties and then repeat endlessly, forming something like a crystal. If DNA manifested such redundancy, it would be impossible for it to store or convey much information. As Polanyi concluded, "Whatever may be the origin of a DNA configuration, it can function as a code only if its order is not due to the forces of potential energy. It must be as physically indeterminate as the sequence of words on a printed page" (Meyer 238–240).

In other words, the laws of physics and chemistry do not build the hardware. They dictate how it functions once it is made, but they do not create the hardware. Neither do these laws create information-rich codes that allow the hardware to function in a specified way. In other words, a message sent on radio waves is not created by any laws or by the components of the radio itself but by the intelligence transmitting it. Hence, laws do not create messages. Laws could not have created the genetic language.

If the bonding affinities of the DNA determined the code, it would not be an aperiodic and asymmetrical code that could carry information in the form that a living cell requires for its complex metabolic system. It would become a repetitive code like that of a crystal that could not carry information-rich codes.

Richard Dawkins arrogantly claimed that the discovery of the DNA dealt the killing blow to the belief that living material is deeply distinct from non-living material. He was dead wrong. The opposite is the case. As we learned more and more about this sophisticated gene expression system, it became clear that the opposite is true. Dawkins failed to realize that it was the language of DNA that dealt the killing blow to reductionism.

If the arrangement of the nucleotide bases in the DNA were determined by affinities or chemical properties, the message would become a rigid, repeating code that could convey little information. It would end up looking much like the crystal of salt I saw on my string— perhaps beautiful, but incapable of information-rich language.

It is the freedom from such constraint that allows the variability of the nucleotides to convey rich information in an aperiodic fashion. It is that freedom from chemical affinities that actually allows for the aperiodic sequencing to carry specified information.

Simply put, the language of DNA defies reduction and implies that intelligence engineered the language through previsioned arbitrary choices that conveyed an enormous amount of specified information.

Consider for example, what would happen if the individual nucleotide bases (A, C, G, T) in the DNA molecule did interact by chemical necessity (along the information-bearing axis of DNA). Suppose that every time adenine (A) occurred in a growing genetic sequence, it attracted cytosine (C) to it, which attracted guanine (G), which attracted thymine (T), which attracted adenine (A), and so on. If this were the case, the longitudinal axis of DNA would be peppered with repetitive sequences ACGT. Rather than being a genetic molecule capable of virtually unlimited novelty and characterized by unpredictable and aperiodic sequences, DNA would contain sequences awash in repetition or redundancy—much like the arrangement of atoms in crystals (Meyer 250).

Meyer recounts the day he had an epiphany while looking at a slide of the double helix DNA. It allowed him to understand why Polanyi was right.

I remember vividly the day the breakthrough came. I was listening to a colleague, a biologist at Whitworth College, teach a college class about the discovery of the double helix when I noticed something about the chemical structure of DNA on the slide that she had projected on the screen. What I noticed wasn't anything I hadn't seen before, but somehow its significance had previously escaped me. It not only confirmed for me Polanyi's conclusion about the information in DNA transcending physics and chemistry, but it also convinced me that self-organizational theories invoking bonding affinities or forces of attraction would never explain the origin of the information that DNA contains....

There in the classroom this elementary fact of DNA chemistry leaped out at me. I realized that explaining DNA's information-rich sequences by appealing to differential bonding affinities meant that there had to be chemical bonds of differing strength between the different bases along the information-bearing axis of the DNA molecule.

Yet, as it turns out, there are no differential bonding affinities there. Indeed, there is not just an absence of differing bonding affinities; there are no bonds at all between the critical information-bearing bases in DNA. In the lecture hall the point suddenly struck me as embarrassingly simple; there are neither bonds nor bonding affinities—differing in strength or otherwise—that can explain the origin of the base sequencing that constitutes information in the DNA molecule. A force has to exist before it can cause something. And the relevant kind of force in this case (differing chemical attractions between nucleotide bases) does not exist within the DNA molecule.... Instead, the same type of chemical bond (an N-glycosidic bond) occurs between the base and the backbone regardless of which base attaches. All four bases are acceptable; none is chemically favored (Meyer 241–243).

The magnificent design of DNA is such that no physical or chemical law can explain its intricate design. Meyer realized that "There are no chemical bonds between the bases along the longitudinal axis in the center of the helix. Yet it is precisely along this axis of the DNA molecule that the genetic information is stored" (Meyer 243). No chemical affinity or external force can account for the origin of this complex and yet utterly efficient way to transfer information through a four-letter language. It is completely arbitrary.

Not only is the language arbitrary but it has 17 dialects. Each of the dialects is arbitrary and points to an intelligent choice rather than an inevitable, predetermined, chemically induced order. In fact, the

17 dialects show the obvious creativity of the designer. The elephant in the room is now bursting out of the windows.

> *Thus, chemical affinities between nucleotide codons and amino acids do not determine the correspondences between codons and amino acids that define the genetic code. From the standpoint of the properties of the constituents that compose the code, the code is physically and chemically arbitrary. All possible codes are equally likely; none is favored chemically.*
>
> *Moreover, the discovery of seventeen variant genetic codes has put to rest any doubt about this. The existence of many separate codes (multiple sets of codon-amino acid assignments) in different microorganisms indicates that the chemical properties of the relevant monomers allow more than a single set of codon-amino acids assignments. The conclusion is straightforward: the chemical properties of amino acids and nucleotides do not determine a single universal genetic code; since there is not just one code, "it" cannot be inevitable (Meyer 248).*

Instead of finding an underlying cause that allowed self-organization, what scientists have found is that a complex intermediary group of some 20 proteins are responsible for joining the correct amino acid to the tRNA molecule. And yet these proteins are themselves created by the template, which they help translate. The process is a completely closed loop without a beginning.

There is no way to evolve a closed loop process in discrete steps since all parts need to be functioning independently from the start.

> *Instead scientists now know the codon–amino acid relationships that define the code are established and mediated by the catalytic action of some twenty*

separate proteins, the so-called aminoacyl-tRNA synthetases (one for each tRNA anticodon and amino-acid pair). Each of these proteins recognizes a specific amino acid and specific tRNA with its corresponding anticodon and helps attach the appropriate amino acid to that tRNA molecule.

Thus, instead of the code reducing to a simple set of chemical affinities between a small number of monomers, biochemists have found a functionally interdependent system of highly specific biopolymers, including mRNA, twenty specific tRNAs, and twenty specific synthetase proteins, each of which is itself constructed via information encoded on the very DNA that it helps to decode.

But such integrated complexity was just what needed explanation in the first place. The attempt to explain one part of the integrated complexity of the gene-expression system, namely, the genetic code, by reference to simple chemical affinities leads not to simple rules of chemical attraction, but instead to an integrated system of large molecular components. One aspect of the DNA enigma leads to another (Meyer 248).

Evolutionists, when faced with the incalculably improbable chances for random ordering to manufacture proteins, imagined that certain chemical laws or affinities among molecules could account for their sequencing miracle. What we have discovered is exactly the opposite. No laws or chemical affinities could be used to correspond to the sequencing order, either in the proteins or the nucleotides in DNA and RNA without destroying its ability to pass on genetic information.

Order Out of Chaos?

Ilya Prigogine's idea that external lawlike forces could bring order out of chaos has attempted to provide another credible means to substantiate the naturalistic formulation of complexity in living things. Noting that an input of energy into a given system sometimes creates a more ordered state, Gregoire Nicolis and Prigogine extrapolated that DNA could have been ordered from chaos through natural processes.

Evidence for this assumption is given by the elaborate convection currents in thermal baths, which seem to spontaneously create a more ordered system from a more chaotic system. While it is true that an input of energy (i.e., high winds) could create the eye of a hurricane, this type of order is no different from that of crystals. It is a repetitive order that cannot provide the aperiodic or asymmetrical matrix indispensible for carrying functional information.

Prigogine failed to make the connection between his examples of order from chaos and the formulation of DNA. It reminds me of Darwin's sleight of hand linking light-sensitive freckles to eyes. They are two separate and disconnected systems. One displays simple repetitive order, and the other displays non-repetitive, aperiodic order that can express complex language.

Without specifically directed energy, complex metabolic motors cannot be formed. Examples such as vortexes and ripples are not directed energy but are, instead, undifferentiated energy. Trust me, pieces of wood flying around the ordered eye of a hurricane do not self-organize into houses in midair. Instead, the opposite takes place. Although the external may take on a given symmetrical shape, the internal is creating more disorder by ripping all things apart and mixing them violently. I have been through the eye of many hurricanes in South Florida, and I can tell you that a hurricane is an engine of disorder and not the opposite.

The astrophysicist Fred Hoyle had a similar way of making the same point. He famously compared the problem of getting life to arise spontaneously from its constituent parts to the problem of getting a 747 airplane to come together from a tornado swirling through a junkyard.

An undifferentiated external force is simply too blunt an instrument to accomplish such a task. Energy might scatter parts around randomly. Energy might sweep parts into an orderly structure such as a vortex or funnel cloud. But energy alone will not assemble a group of parts into a highly differentiated or functionally specified system such [as] an airplane or cell (or in the informational sequence necessary to build one).

Kenyon's self-organizational model had already encountered this problem. He came to realize that, although internal chemical affinities might produce highly repetitive or ordered sequences, they certainly did not produce the information-rich sequences in DNA. Now a similar problem reemerged as scientists considered whether lawlike external forces could have produced the information in DNA. Prigogine's work showed that energy in an open system can create patterns of symmetrical order. But it provided no evidence that energy alone can encode functionally specified information-rich sequences—whether biochemical or otherwise....

In Prigogine's convection baths, an energy source established a pattern of motion throughout the system that affected all the molecules in a similar way, rather than arranging them individually and specifically to accomplish a function or convey a message.

Yet character-by-character variability and specific-ity of arrangement are hallmarks of functional in-formation-rich sequences. Thus, as Yockey notes:

"Attempts to relate the idea of order ... with biological organization or specificity must be regarded as a play on words that cannot stand careful scrutiny. Informational macromolecules can code genetic messages and therefore can car-ry information because the sequences of bases or residues is affected very little, if at all, by [self-organizing] physicochemical factors."

(Meyer 257)

I find it curious and ironic that those who champion relativism are turning to lawlike forces as determinants when they realize the failure of randomness to explain reality. And yet the irony is even deeper, for what is a law? A law is not a cause. A law does not affect an outcome; it only describes the determined outcome. A law is simply a human convention that describes an absolute physical phenomenon. The phenomenon is not the law. It is simply a description of a characteristic of the physical universe.

If there were no minds, the characteristic would still be there, but the law is a pattern recognized in the mind of the observer. Now if we observe that that characteristic is universal, is it reasonable to conclude that chaos and randomness could create a universal and specified characteristic? And if that characteristic existed before the human mind, then is it not reasonable to conclude that a higher mind that preexisted the characteristic engineered it?

In fact, it is irrational to believe that randomness could have produced any absolute laws. Only a transcendent mind could design and engineer a universe that contains universal laws, those universal physical characteristics we recognize as absolute laws of science.

But more to the point, laws, by their very nature, are rigidly deterministic; that is, they reduce or explain a system with precise and deterministic parameters. If the origin of the codes were due to either chemical affinities in the molecules or lawlike physical forces, it would create molecules that are deterministic and repetitive with little ability to carry any useful information. In fact, it is precisely the indeterminacy of the code that allows it to carry information.

> In the case that a lawlike physical or chemical process determines that one kind of event will necessarily and predictably follow another, then no uncertainty will be reduced by the occurrence of such high-probability event. Thus, no information will be conveyed....
>
> Polanyi appreciated this point but also its converse. He knew that it was precisely because the sequences of bases in DNA were not biochemically determined (or predestined) that the molecule could store and transmit information. Because any nucleotide can follow any other, a vast array of sequences is possible, which allows DNA to encode a vast number of protein functions. As he explains, "It is the physical indeterminacy of the of the sequence that produces the improbability of occurrence of any particular sequence and thereby enables it to have meaning—a meaning that has a mathematically determinate information content equal to the numerical improbability of the arrangement" (Meyer 251).

Because the nucleotides (anticodons) at the bottom of the tRNA that bond with the message brought from the DNA in the mRNA (Homer) are positioned at the opposite end of the tRNA molecule from the amino acids they carry at the top (the sombrero), they do not interact chemically in any direct way. While it is true that the amino acids do react with the specific nucleotides at the head of the tRNA (where the sombrero attaches), these nucleotides remain the same triplet for all 20 amino acids (ACC).

In other words, there is no direct chemical affinity between the amino acids (sombreros) and the anticodons at the bottom of the tRNA. That means the properties of the nucleotides in the tRNA do not directly determine chemically which amino acid should bond. All 20 amino acids are equally preferred. The code was an absolutely arbitrary choice that cannot be attributed to anything other than a choice by a mind.

> *Thus, chemical affinities between nucleotide codons and amino acids do not determine the correspondences between codons and amino acids that define the genetic code. From the standpoint of the properties of the constituents that comprise the code, the code is physically and chemically arbitrary. All possible codes are equally likely; none is favored chemically (Meyer 248).*

The genetic code is therefore necessarily characterized by an unpredictable aperiodic sequencing potential that alone is capable of novelty in the choices of the sequences, which can subsequently be rich in the capacity to carry information. If, instead, some lawlike force or some chemical affinity potential drove the nucleotide codes, it would create a molecule that is not aperiodic but instead filled with rigid, repetitive redundancy without the capacity to carry any useful information.

That purely arbitrary choice, once again, necessarily points to a master chooser—that is, an intelligent designer, and it disqualifies some randomly generated accident of nature that through purely materialistic mechanisms could self-organize through subtle chemical or physical reasons. Having failed to show any viable chemical pathway of self-organization with protein-first and DNA-first attempts, some postulated that perhaps the RNA was the first to evolve.

The RNA World

Scientists proposed next that the earliest stages of biochemical evolution evolved in RNA-rich environments. Carl Woese, a microbiologist at the University of Illinois, first championed this idea. Later on, Walter Gilbert, a Harvard biophysicist, coined the term "RNA world." The RNA world model has become arguably the most popular origin-of-life theory in evolutionary circles today. Its popularity comes from the claim that RNA sequences can serve either as catalysts (like proteins) or as information carriers like DNA with the ability to self-replicate.

Since the RNA-first model claims that it could perform the catalytic functions of proteins and the information-storage function of DNA, proponents thus circumvented the need for either DNA or proteins to begin the process. They envisioned that chance associations with nucleotides, sugars, and phosphates in a prebiotic soup allowed the first RNA to replicate itself. Eventually, the RNA enzymes were replaced by the more efficient proteins, or so their story goes.

> For that to occur, the RNA-replicating system first had to begin producing a set of RNA enzymes that could synthesize proteins. As Gilbert has explained, in this step RNA molecules began "to synthesize proteins, first by developing RNA adapter molecules that can bind activated amino acids and then by arranging them according to an RNA template using other RNA molecules such as the RNA core of the ribosome." Finally, DNA emerged for the first time by a process called reverse transcription. In

this process, DNA received the information stored in the original RNA molecules, and eventually these more stable DNA molecules took over the information-storage role that RNA had performed in the RNA world. At that point, RNA was, as Gilbert put it, "relegated to the intermediate role it has today—no longer the center of the stage, displaced by DNA and the more effective protein enzymes" (Meyer 300).

The first assumption in this theory is that the primitive earth needed to have a prebiotic soup containing three basic ingredients:

1. the four nucleotide bases: adenine, cytosine, guanine, and uracil
2. ribose (sugar)
3. phosphate molecules, the main components of RNA

The second assumption is that these components could, by chance, synthesize (come together) to form an RNA molecule in early Earth, with high-temperature conditions claimed by evolutionary models.

However, the problem for RNA world advocates is that the first two components of RNA arise through two chemically incompatible pathways. They could not have evolved side-by-side.

1. **The four nucleotide bases**

It turns out, however, that both synthesizing and maintaining these essential RNA building blocks, particularly ribose (the sugar incorporated into nucleotides) and the nucleotide bases, has proven either extremely difficult or impossible to do under realistic prebiotic conditions.

Consider first the problems with synthesizing the nucleotide bases. In the years since RNA world was proposed, chemist Robert Shapiro has made a careful study of the chemical properties of the four nucleotide bases to assess whether they could have arisen on the early Earth under realistic conditions. He notes first that "no nucleotides of any kind have been reported as products of spark-discharge experiments or in studies of meteorites."

Stanley Miller, who performed the original prebiotic simulation experiment, published a similar study in 1998. Moreover, even if they did somehow form on the early Earth, nucleotide bases are too chemically fragile to have allowed life enough time to evolve in the manner Gilbert and other RNA-first theorists envision.

Shapiro and Miller have noted that the bases of RNA are unstable at temperatures required by currently popular high-temperature origin-of-life scenarios. The bases are chemically subject to a chemical process known as "deamination," in which they lose their essential amine groups (NH_2). At 100 degrees C, adenine and guanine have chemical half-lives of only about one year; uracil has a half-life of 12 years; and cytosine a half-life of just 19 days.

Because these half-lives are so short and because the evolutionary process envisioned by Gilbert would take so long—especially for natural selection to find functional ribozymes (RNA molecules with catalytic activity) by trial and error—Stanley Miller concluded in 1998 that "a high temperature origin of life involving these compounds [the RNA bases] therefore is unlikely."

Miller further noted that of the four required bases, cytosine has a short half-life even at low temperatures thus raising the possibility that "the GC pair" (and thus RNA) "may not have been in the first genetic material."

Shapiro concurred. He showed that it would have been especially difficult to synthesize adenine and cytosine at high temperatures and cytosine even at low temperatures. Thus he concluded that the presumption that "the bases, adenine, cytosine, guanine and uracil were readily available on the early Earth [is] not supported by existing knowledge of the basic chemistry of these substances" (Meyer 302).

2. **Ribose (sugar)**

Producing ribose under realistic conditions has proven even more problematic. Prebiotic chemists have proposed that ribose could have arisen on the early Earth as the by-product of a chemical reaction called the formose reaction.

The formose reaction is a multistep chemical reaction that begins as molecules of formaldehyde in water react with one another. Along the way, the formose reaction produces a host of different sugars, including ribose, as intermediate by-products in the sequence of reactions.

But, as Shapiro has pointed out, the formose reaction will not produce sugars in the presence of nitrogenous substances. These include peptides, amino acids, and amines, a category of molecules that includes the nucleotide bases (Meyer 302–303).

In other words, if the prebiotic soup contained nucleotides or amino acids (nitrogenous substances), then ribose could not have been formed through the formose reaction. But without sugar, there would be no RNA or DNA. If the prebiotic soup was capable of creating ribose, then there could be no amino acids or nucleotides present.

Without amino acids, there would be no proteins, and there would be no protocellular membranes to enclose the RNA into the cell as proposed by RNA world advocates. Without nucleotides, there would be no RNA or DNA. The processes that derive the two chemical substances (sugars and nitrogenous substances) are incompatible in the same prebiotic soup.

In addition, the formose reaction that produces sugars also creates many undesirable by-products that must be actively removed by chemists in order to keep them from reacting with one another in ways that would inhibit the chemical pathways that would be compatible with their desired objectives. In a natural environment, no such manipulation could be mimicked by random natural forces.

> As Dean Kenyon explains, "The chemical conditions proposed for the prebiotic synthesis of purines and pyrimidines [the bases] are sharply incompatible with those proposed for the synthesis of ribose." Or as Shapiro concludes, "The evidence that is currently available does not support the availability of ribose on the prebiotic earth, except perhaps for brief periods of time, in low concentration as part of a complex mixture, and under conditions unsuitable for nucleoside synthesis."
>
> Beyond that, both the constituent building blocks of RNA and whole RNA molecules would have reacted readily with the other chemicals present in the prebiotic ocean environment. These "interfering cross-reactions" would have inhibited the assembly of RNA from its constituent monomers and inhibited any movement from RNA molecules toward more complex biochemistry, since the products of these reactions typically produce biologically inert (or irrelevant) substances (Meyer 303).

Sifting these RNA molecules in order to protect and preserve them from cross-reactions is not a process of random ordering. It is a process that inputs specified knowledge. Since molecular engineers know the end product they desire, they choose to select those that lead to that path. That is not natural selection but rather unnatural, willful election by a mind.

Yet their intercession in these simulations is necessary to avoid interfering cross-reactions. For this reason, Kenyon is quite critical of the laboratory simulations that do not in any way realistically parallel the conditions of the early Earth as envisioned by evolutionists.

> *In most cases the experimental conditions in such studies have been so artificially simplified as to have virtually no bearing on any actual processes that might have taken place on the primitive earth. For example, if one wishes to find a possible prebiotic mechanism of condensation of free amino acids to polypeptides, it is not likely that sugars or aldehydes would be added to the reaction mixture.*
>
> *And yet, how likely is it that amino acids (or any other presumed precursor substance) occurred any-where on the primitive earth free from contamination substances, either in solution or the solid state? The difficulty is that if sugars or aldehydes were also present polypeptides would not form. Instead an interfering cross-reaction would occur between amino acids and sugars to give complex, insoluble polymeric material of very dubious relevance to chemical evolution. This problem of potentially in-terfering cross-reactions has been largely neglected in much of the published work on the chemical origins of life (Thaxton et al. vi).*

In a nutshell, the conditions required for a prebiotic soup would not favor the creation of proteins, RNA, or DNA. Any intermediate forms could not last for any appreciable amount of time before being destroyed by interfering cross-reactions. The prebiotic soup model is incapable of chemically cooking the right recipe in a natural environment. Only through discrete steps of artificial interference, engineered by an intellect, can the intermediate forms be protected and cajoled to accomplish the desired and purposeful goals of the chemist. That is hardly the stuff of dysteleology.

> *In a similar fashion, growing polypeptides would be terminated by reactions with amines, aldehydes, ketones, reducing sugars or carboxylic acids. If by some remote chance a true protein did develop in the ocean, its viability would be predictably of short duration. For example, formaldehyde would readily react with free amino groups to form methylene cross-linkages with proteins. This would tie up certain reactive sites, and retard the reaction of protein with other chemical agents.... This tying up process is the principle of the well-known tanning reaction, and is used similarly to retard cadaver decay....*
>
> *If we assume some small amount of nucleic acids formed in the primitive ocean, they too would be vulnerable to immediate attack by formaldehyde, particularly at the free amino groups of adenine, guanine, and cytosine. Some of the bonds formed with nucleic acids would be so stable that hydrolysis to liberate free formaldehyde would take place only by boiling with concentrated sulfuric acid. As with proteins, it is difficult to conceive of a viable nucleic acid existing in the primordial soup for more than very brief period of time (Thaxton et al. 55–56).*

For these reasons, Thaxton concludes:

> *It seems probable that in an oceanic chemical soup the synthesis of RNA and other essential biomolecules would have been short-circuited at nearly every turn by many cross-reactions (Thaxton et al. 57).*

The Impotence of RNA

Besides the impossibility of arriving at the basic components of RNA in a single prebiotic arena, RNA has been shown to perform only a handful of the thousands of catalytic functions that modern proteins perform.

> *Beyond that, RNA can perform only a few minor functional roles and then usually as the result of scientists intentionally "engineering" or "directing" the RNA catalyst (or ribozymes) in question.*
>
> *For this reason, claiming that catalytic RNA could replace proteins in the earliest stages of chemical evolution is extremely problematic. To say otherwise would be like asserting that a carpenter wouldn't need any tools besides a hammer to build a house, because the hammer performed two or three carpentry functions (Meyer 304).*

There is an impassable abyss between the relatively few functions that RNA can perform and the complex machinery of the gene-expression system in the cell, which the RNA world model does not explain. To pass through that abyss, the RNA world model would need to explain how RNA could develop a coding and translation system based entirely on RNAs, which would at the same time generate the specified information required to build many specific proteins that would supposedly later replace it. That includes the complicated machinery of the ribosome (the machine shop that builds proteins).

The machinery of the ribosome and the many other protein functions, which are determined by their specific and sequential order of amino acids, are many and varied with great complexity. The idea that trial and error could accomplish this feat is absurd from a statistical viewpoint.

> To evolve beyond the RNA world, an RNA-based replication system eventually would have to begin to produce proteins, and not just any proteins, but proteins capable of template-directed protein manufacture. But for that to occur, the RNA replicator first would need to produce machinery for building proteins.
>
> In modern cells it takes many proteins to build proteins. So, as a first step toward building proteins, the primitive replicator would need to produce RNA molecules capable of performing the functions of the modern proteins involved in translation....
>
> Presumably, these RNA molecules would need to perform the functions of the twenty specific tRNA synthetases and the fifty ribosomal proteins, among the many others involved in translation. At the same time, the RNA replicator would need to produce tRNAs and the many mRNAs carrying the information for building the first proteins.
>
> These mRNAs would need to be able to direct protein synthesis using, at first, the transitional ribozymes-based protein-synthesis machinery and then, later, the permanent and predominantly protein-based protein-synthesis machinery.... This is a tall order. The cell builds proteins from the information

stored on the mRNA transcript (i.e., the copy) of the original DNA molecule.

To do this, a bacterial cell depends upon a translation and coding system consisting of 106 distinct but functionally integrated proteins as well [as] several distinct types of RNA molecules (tRNAs, mRNAs, and rRNAs) (Meyer 305).

Again, the chasm that needs to be crossed is that the function of these numerous proteins of the gene-expression machinery of the cell is integrated into one closed loop system. The evolution of such a system could not happen in discrete steps because the function of the whole is interdependent on the function of all the independent proteins.

Showing that one component, the hammer, can drive a few nails and pull out some others does not provide the mechanism to pour a slab, lay out the plumbing, and wire the house with electricity. In other words, the single hammer (RNA) is not sufficient to build a house (cell).

RNA has not been shown to accomplish all these important and vital steps necessary for replication in a cell. Although ribozymes have been shown under laboratory conditions to have the capacity to catalyze representative examples of the three main types of chemical reactions involved in translation, the gap between the total number necessary for the reactions within these general classifications is much greater.

For example, RNA has not been demonstrated to catalyze aminoacyl bonds with the other 18 protein-forming amino acids. Proteins are not made by only two types of amino acids, but rather 20. Establishing a genetic code requires molecules that can form aminoacyl bonds for each of the 20 amino acids that are required in order to build proteins with the specificity necessary to both transcribe and translate.

The catalytic functions required of the gene-expression system cannot be met with ribozymes, which can perform only one subfunction of the several integrated functions that protein enzymes serve.

> *Thus, synthetases help form molecular complexes with a specificity of fit and with specific binding sites that enable translation to occur in the context of a whole system of associated molecules.*
>
> *The RNA catalyst proposed as a precursor to the synthetase cannot do this. It does not couple ATP to amino acids as a precursor to catalyzing aminoacylation. Instead, the ribozyme engineer provides "preadenylated" amino acids (amino acids already linked to AMP molecules).*
>
> *Nor does the RNA catalyst couple an amino acid to a specific tRNA with a specific anticodon. The more limited specificity it achieves only ensures that the RNA catalyst will bind a particular amino acid to itself, a molecule that does not possess the specific cloverleaf shape or structure of a tRNA.*
>
> *Moreover, this RNA does not carry an anticodon binding site corresponding to a specific codon on a separate mRNA transcript.* Thus, it has no functional significance within a system of molecules performing translation (emphasis added). *(Meyer 308–309).*

Without the interference of the ribozyme engineers (lab scientists), the ATP energy necessary to catalyze would not even be available to allow the RNA to catalyze. The protein catalysts (enzymes) are able to drive forward reactions that are not chemically favored by storing the necessary energy (ATP, AMP). This allows them the ability to coordinate both energetically favorable and energetically unfavorable reactions. Ribozymes cannot do so.

The ribozymes will simply not produce a molecule with the functional specificity necessary to perform the coordinated reactions necessary for the translation of the genetic code. Last, but not least, freestanding RNA cannot force amino acids to link into a single linear strand, which is an indispensible need in creating proteins.

The fact is that the RNA world model was not proposed as a way to explain the enigma of the DNA code but as an explanation of the evolution of the interdependent systems in gene-expression, which, as previously noted, has failed to adequately do so.

Most remarkable is the fact that RNA already possesses sequence-specific order, which is the necessary component for gene-expression. The RNA world model has not answered the fundamental enigma of the origin of the code. It begins with the code in place in the RNA.

Some advocates have attempted lately to provide an evolutionary scenario for RNA. We should note that in order for natural selection to take place, replication is required. There can be no selective progression without replication to pass on the genetic traits. Bane attempts to show a progression due to natural selection from short chains (oligomers) arising by chance and eventually acquiring the ability to self-replicate ignore this fundamental reality.

What increments in complexity acquired by natural selective pressures can be passed on without replication? There are no forward steps in small increments possible without replication to preserve them. How could the accidental choice be remembered? The progression from simplicity to complexity would have to be connected into a single bond within the lifespan of that molecular structure.

Moreover, even the fully formed RNA has not been shown to be a fully replicating system.

> Indeed, experimental studies indicate that RNA molecules with the capacity to replicate themselves, if they exist at all, are extremely rare among possible RNA base sequences. Although no one has yet

produced a fully self-replicating RNA molecule, some researches have engineered a molecule that can copy a part of itself—though only about 10 percent of itself and then only if a complementary primer strand is provided to the ribozyme by the investigator. Significantly, the scientists selected this partial self-replicator out of an engineered pool of 1,000 trillion (10^{15}) other RNA molecules, almost all of which lack even a limited capacity for self-replication. This suggests that sequences with this capacity are extremely rare and would be especially so within a random (nonengineered) sample (Meyer 313–314).

Attempts to explain how RNA evolved into an information-rich molecule has proved to be no different than for DNA. But that is understandable when one considers that the nucleotides in RNA are no different than DNA in that neither manifests any bonding affinities that could cause them to self-organize.

To date, no one has attempted to build RNA from the basic components in a prebiotic context. As a matter of fact, even if it did magically come together, it could not readily replicate. RNA is a single-stranded molecule that would have to fortuitously find another magically produced RNA that would luckily be near enough to it to interact and would also fortuitously contain a highly specific sequence of nucleotides that match the original miracle RNA. When one considers the cross-reactions that would take place in a realistic prebiotic soup, the chances of RNA replicating are infinitesimally small. The elephant is bursting out of the room, and the house is falling apart.

RNA Mutants

Much has been learned about the RNA molecule. Adherents to the RNA world model have designed new RNA molecules that possess functional capacities not observed in the natural world. They hope to provide evidence for RNA to be capable of accomplishing the tall order granted to it by the RNA world model.

Chemists artificially attempt to improve the efficiency of the ribozymes or create brand new ones with different capabilities. They randomly mutate some part of the sequence of the RNA and assess and select the most functional models. This process is repeated over and over again, hoping to find an increase in the desired function. Each time a batch is screened by engineers, a quantum of intelligence is input into the product. The natural world has no such selective process until replication has been achieved.

Each time scientists cause a mutation and separate the ones that are more functional, they are adding another quantum of intelligence to a process that is supposed to be randomly executed. Each time they remove the less functional, they are again generating intelligent information into their by-product, which nature cannot do. There are no natural processes that can parallel their intrusions into the chemical properties naturally appearing in these ribozymes. If they manage to artificially design an RNA molecule that can perform all the basic processes necessary of a gene expression system, all they will prove is that intelligent design is a valid proposal for the creation of life, because without the intelligent engineering of scientists, it could not have been created.

No credible bridge across that impassable abyss has been offered by the RNA world model in natural conditions. Moreover, the chance development of the complicated code for RNA and for DNA is, as previously noted, a statistical improbability. But to imagine that the complex interface with the 20 amino acid–protein code, which is indispensible in building proteins, could develop through trial and error from RNA is even less realistic.

The laboratory has failed miserably to support the Darwinian abiogenesis model for the origin of life.

CHAPTER 6

●●●

EVOLUTION "PROVED" BY COMPUTERS?

After years of failing to find evidence for self-organization in labs, some scientists turned to computers as a way to "prove" that order could come from disorder. Richard Dawkins (perhaps one of the most stridently vocal attackers of intelligent design) and Bernd-Olaf Küppers developed computer simulations that attempted to demonstrate how information could rise from a disordered state.

It is not surprising that Dawkins believes his computer program proves that evolution is a fact. In his book *The Greatest Show on Earth*, he goes to great lengths to insist that the theory of evolution is not a hypothesis but a fact. He wrote, "This is a book about the positive evidence that evolution is a fact" (6). He added, "Nowadays it is no longer possible to dispute the fact of evolution itself – it has graduated to become a theorem or obviously supported fact" (17).

He fails to understand that his worldview is an overarching construct that interprets the facts and not the facts themselves. My response to Dawkins is this: Your book is about the positive evidence that evolution has failed to explain the facts. It has not explained the origin of life, the origin of the universe, and the symmetry it contains universally. It fails to explain the intrinsic nature of humans. It fails to explain how such information-rich molecules as DNA, RNA, and proteins evolved and formulated a closed loop system, without which life could not exist. It fails to acknowledge the elephant in the room. It simply fails, and your computer program is no different.

Dawkins arrogantly calls all who accept the intelligent design model "history deniers." In elitist overtones, he characterizes Jews and Christians who believe in intelligent design with derogatory terms and whines at the vast number of ignorant people in our nation.

> *I shall be using the name "history-deniers" for those people who deny evolution.... To repeat, they constitute more than 40 percent of the American population. The equivalent figure is higher in some countries, lower in others, but 40 percent is a good average and I shall from time to time refer to the history-deniers as the "40-percenters."...*
>
> *If the history-deniers who doubt the fact of evolution are ignorant of biology, those who think the world began less than ten thousand years ago are worse than ignorant, they are deluded to the point of perversity (Dawkins 7, 85).*

Dawkins's portrayal of scientists that happen to differ with his worldview as ignorant and perversely deluded hardly constitutes a scientific critique. What is even more astounding to me is the audacity he flaunts in turning the truth around by making the proponents of intelligent design the persecutors of truth in our age. Using Holocaust-deniers as examples of the type of people that promote intelligent design, he builds a picture of them as ignorant bullies who threaten the noble defenders of evolution with being fired from their jobs as teachers.

The exact opposite is the real situation in our nation. Any who doubt my words should watch the documentary *Expelled: No Intelligence Allowed* starring Ben Stein. Instead of empty, hot rhetoric, the film documents many scientists who have been expelled for coming to the scientific conclusion that this universe bears intelligent design.

In the film, tenured professors have been fired from universities, and scientists of impeccable reputation have been drummed out of government agencies. It is the evolutionary paradigm that has feverishly harassed, curtailed, and impeded the free expression of the human mind through tyrannical censorship in the public institutions of learning. To insinuate otherwise is simply a bold-faced lie. Such is the convoluted mind of Dawkins when he compares us to Holocaust-deniers:

> *Imagine that, as a teacher of European history, you are continually faced with belligerent demands to 'teach the controversy' and to give 'equal time' to the 'alternative theory' that the Holocaust never happened but was invented by a bunch of Zionist fabricators. Fashionably relativist intellectuals chime in to insist that there is no absolute truth: whether the Holocaust happened is a matter of personal belief; all points of view are equally valid and should be equally 'respected.'*
>
> *The plight of many science teachers today is no less dire. When they attempt to expound the central and guiding principle of biology; when they honestly*

place the living world in its historical context – which means evolution; when they explore and explain the very nature of life itself, they are harried and stymied, hassled and bullied, even threatened with loss of their jobs (Dawkins 4).

It is unconscionable that Dawkins would have the gall to compare Jews and Christians to the Nazi and Islamic elements that have promoted the hatred of Jews and Christians. We are the ones who are being burned in their ovens because they have taken to heart the theory of evolution and put it into political practice. We are the ones who suffer under the iron fist of tyranny because the only matrix to reality to which they give credence is the survival of the fittest. It is our genes they tried to expunge from the genetic pool of humanity to bring forth their master race spawned in the mind of those who believe in the mantra of survival of the fittest.

We are the ones whose heads are being chopped off by Muslims. We are the ones persecuted in Islamic countries. And exactly when have the deniers of absolute truth ever come to support the proponents of absolute truth? Quite the opposite is the absolute truth. It is the "fashionably relativistic intellectuals" who have "harried and stymied, hassled and bullied, even threatened with loss of their jobs" any who stray from the evolutionary paradigm of our age. What planet is Dawkins living on? In this blue planet, reality is 180 degrees from Dawkins's convoluted words.

In addition, what institution of higher learning does not teach the main elements of Nazism and communism and every other kind of "ism"? Teaching the elements of opposing views is not wrong. It is what separates education from indoctrination. Censorship belongs to book-burners like Hitler, not in our American public schools. Why does Dawkins fear the expression of our worldview so it can be censored from the public square? Could it be that Dawkins fears that the truth always rises to the top?

It is an unfortunate fact that the public education system in the United States and most of the Western world unilaterally teaches only one perspective of the argument for our genesis. The scientific evidence for intelligent design is simply banned or censored from the schools of higher learning. This is not true science.

There is a not-so-silent, very real, and palpable bias against any scientist who dares to question the status quo. Receiving grants and moving up the ladder in the scientific disciplines is almost impossible if one does not tow the party line. Scientists who have dared to question the paradigm of evolution and offer scientific evidence for intelligent design have met with rash and unjust expulsion from the scientific community. As I have already noted, this monolithic and unconscionable censure of well-established, well-recognized scientists within their professions has been exposed and documented in *Expelled* released in the spring of 2008.

In a very real sense, what we have in our school systems is not education, but rather unabashed, plain, and unadulterated indoctrination. An education presupposes the teaching of all possible viewpoints. Contrary to the scientific process, indoctrination subverts the scientific process by stacking the deck and teaching only one viewpoint.

The scientific model proposed by scientists who opt for intelligent design is the only model that truly accounts for the empirical facts observed in our universe. Yet teachers are prohibited from teaching the bare scientific elements, even without espousing any creed. This censorship is not only immoral and biased, but it is also in direct contradiction to the scientific process.

The scientific process, by definition, explores all possible alternatives. Anything less is nothing more than censorship and the root of evil that has attempted to bind the minds of free thinkers throughout human history.

Let us now look at Dawkins's "facts" about evolution. In an attempt to "prove" that evolution is a fact, Dawkins and his colleague Küppers came up with separate computer algorithms to illustrate the process of evolving order from chaos. Their goal was to provide proof that the code within DNA could have evolved by random chance.

Each provided their computer programs with a target sequence that is a short code. By using the code of the English language, they illustrated how the code in DNA could have developed by random ordering. Küppers chose the English phrase *natural selection.* Dawkins chose the English phrase *methinks it is like a weasel.* The phrase was borrowed from Shakespeare's play *Hamlet.* Of course, the sequence length chosen by both men were infinitesimally short compared to the sequence found in DNA.

Küppers's sequence had 16 characters. Dawkins's sequence had 23 characters. Inside the human DNA, there are more than 6 billion nucleotides. Nevertheless, I can see that their point was to show that a small increment can happen by chance. What were the results?

After 35 generations Küppers's computer program produced the intended phrase *natural selection.* After 43 generations, Dawkins's computer program produced the intended phrase *methinks it is like a weasel.* Evolutionists everywhere heralded their computer programs as evidence for random ordering in natural selection.

But was it evidence? They actually proved the opposite. The following is a step-by-step account of this process after careful inspection:

1. They programmed their software with target phrases.
2. They programmed their software to generate alphabetical sequences of the same length as their target phrase.
3. The program then randomly generated a crop of variant phrases.
4. The software programs then selected from those variant phrases the ones that best matched their target phrases.
5. The software programs then preserved those phrases.
6. The software programs then amplified the production of those selected phrases.

7. The software program then eliminated the undesirable variants.

8. The process was then repeated until the target was acquired.

What Dawkins and Küppers failed to realize (or perhaps consciously evaded) is that with each of these steps, except step 3, they inputted specific information into their software programs. Seven of the eight steps added external information into the system. It is that specific information that allowed their software programs to achieve the target sequences. There was no randomness to that sequential approach.

Even their basic assumption is irreconcilable with the supposed random natural selection process. Their very first step is an incredibly audacious deception. Natural selection cannot see a target sequence in the future. It cannot fathom an ordered state that would be advantageous. It is a simple random process that has no goal and no purpose. It is blind both to purpose and design according to the theory of evolution. Dawkins ought to know that creating a teleological process to prove evolution is an oxymoron.

For example, we can illustrate that with a thief who tries to rob a safe. Let us suppose that it takes 16 characters (like Küppers's target sequence) to open the safe. If the thief blindly attempts to find the combination by random ordering without any external information, what are the chances of the thief coming up with the code? The code could be anywhere from 1 to an infinite number of characters long.

However, if you provide the thief with the first step, the knowledge that it is exactly 16 letters long, you have significantly narrowed the number of possibilities. The robber's chances have now improved significantly. In addition, if at every choice you provide the thief with random variations that are closest to the actual combination, you are again adding more information that the thief has no ability to gather internally. Furthermore, if at every choice you throw out all the bad guesses, you are again adding more external information to the process. Each addition of external information cumulatively impacts the equation.

So from the onset and quite the opposite of their propagandistic intention, their example actually evidences that an external intelligence must exist to create a target. Without "knowing" that exact sequence target, none of the eight steps they designed their software to perform could have been performed.

Moreover, without the specified information written into the software program to elect one variant over another, their programs could not have produced the target sequences. This selective programming is without any scientific justification in a natural environment because there is no functional advantage to an incomplete code. Hence, random ordering could not have selected any subcomponents of the whole in this progressively advantageous manner. Their computer experiment fits better in Las Vegas than in the halls of science.

Ironically, Dawkins inadvertently provided evidence for intelligent design rather than natural selection.

Küppers should have chosen as his target phrase *unnatural election*—unnatural because material nature cannot foresee future advantages and election because there were conscious choices elected by the minds of the programmers, not random patterns that haphazardly ruled their algorithm. Unnatural election more aptly represents what their programs actually accomplished.

In a natural environment, there are no such selective steps that correlate to their software program. This deceptive technique is called *displacement*. Since information is necessary to create information, they simply disguise the initial information and thus displace it from sight.

Such displacement problems plague all attempts to show self-organization through random processes. These programmers are essentially preselecting the result when they input their intellectual foreknowledge of the end result to curb the intermediate results. Dawkins is using teleology and not dysteleology to purposefully generate the previsioned, designed, and desired results.

> *Clearly it is impossible to distinguish sequences based on considerations of comparative functional advantage when the sequences in question have no function whatsoever. Such determinations can be made only if considerations of proximity to possible future functions are allowed, but that requires foresight, the very thing natural selection lacks (Meyer 282).*

Methinks Dawkins is a fact-denier. Perhaps the evolutionary history Dawkins imagines is simply a hologram projected by a subliminal subjective desire to deny the existence of a higher authority. Perhaps he is projecting a deep antagonism to a moral authority above him, which could be diagnosed as latent deocide. Perhaps we would be wise to consider that arrogance is ignorance, a lesson I have been learning the hard way all my life.

Ev is not Eve

Following Dawkins's and Küppers's algorithms, Thomas Schneider, a research biologist at the National Institutes of Health, proposed another software program he called *Ev*. Ev also supplies a target sequence, a particular sequence of nucleotide bases that function as a binding site. Following are the steps in that program:

1. A target sequence is chosen by the programmer.
2. The Ev algorithm is then programmed to favor sequences that resemble the general profile of a bonding site. In other words, the program applies a filter that chooses or elects those sequences that best match their target.

3. It then applies a fitness function to the remaining sequences.
4. This fitness function then analyzes and measures the degree of divergence between the mutated sequences and the target sequence assumed at the beginning.
5. It now gives an error value to each of the mutated sequences.
6. The program then preserves those sequences with less error and allows them to replicate and mutate.
7. The process is then repeated until the desired outcome is achieved.

Again, each of these steps is adding external information into the system. The second step, which filters the sequences, is dependent on Schneider's knowledge of the functional requirements of bonding sites. Nature has no such foreknowledge in a truly random evolutionary process. The displacement factor here is once again exemplified as information is added surreptitiously. It is another disguised teleological experiment that in no way resembles the supposed dysteleological process of random evolution.

Avida's Vida Comes from the Intelligence of the Programmers

Perhaps the most popular evolutionary algorithm to date is *Avida* (A – artificial; vida – life). It was proposed by three computer scientists: Christopher Adami and C. Titus Brown of Caltech and Charles Ofria of Michigan State University. In 2003, Adami and Ofria, in cooperation with biologist Richard Lenski and philosopher Robert Pennock, both from Michigan State, published an article in *Nature*.

Their conclusions were that digital organisms such as those produced by the *Avida* program can explain how random mutations and natural selection could produce complex features and functions from a simpler form. The more acceptable feature of the *Avida* program was that it does not provide the system with a target sequence and thus claims to avoid the sticky teleological factor for evolutionists, or so they claim.

Although on the surface it seems the scientists evaded the teleological problem of the previous evolutionary algorithms, as we shall see later, they did not. *Avida* is still plagued with the same displacement problem.

> *Avida consists of two main parts, the Avida world and the Avida organisms that populate this world. Avida organisms have two basic parts: software and hardware. Each Avida organism has a small software program consisting of a loop of instructions composed from a set of twenty-six predefined commands. Additionally, each digital organism also consists of virtual hardware that can execute each of the twenty-six command among the set of possibilities.*
>
> *These commands direct Avida organisms to perform various operations on two fixed input strings of binary digits, thus producing various output strings. The loop of instructions contains a program that has been written to replicate the loop (initially this is all the instructions in the loop do). Upon replication, the loop of instructions is mutated as the Avida world makes random changes to the loop by inserting, deleting, or switching commands, thus making it possible for the Avida organisms to generate new output strings from the two fixed input strings.*
>
> *These Avida organisms exist within a larger Avida "world." The Avidaworld represents the rules by which the digital organisms operate and compete with each other for survival. The Avidaworld contains an evaluation algorithm—what a colleague of mine calls the "sniffer"—that determines whether one of nine logical relationships exists between the input*

strings given to each digital organism and the output strings they produce.

Another way to think of this is that the sniffer is evaluating whether a "logic function" has been performed on the input strings to produce the output strings... If all the binary digits in an output string are consistent with any of the nine logic functions having been applied to each pair of binary digits along the two input strings, then the sniffer will recognize that a logic function has been performed.

In that case, the Avida organism that performed the logic function is rewarded with resources that improve its ability to replicate itself. Replication is imperfect, meaning that the "offspring" of an Avida organism may carry random changes to the instructions in their program loops. These changes involve replacing a command with another (from the set of twenty-six), inserting a command (making the loop longer), or deleting a command (making the loop shorter)....

Their simulations showed that after many generations Avida produced digital organisms capable of performing both simple and compound logic functions (Meyer 287–288).

The glaring problem is that *Avida* still displaces information. It begins with a digital organism that already has the capacity to replicate, when this is the very essence of the problem that confronts the evolutionary hypothesis. How can random processes engineer the code in DNA, RNA, and proteins that are responsible for the gene-expression system? The elephant is dancing in the room, and no one sees it.

The engineers of the *Avida* program obviously understand that without replication, there can be no natural selection. Hence, they begin with replication already established.

The elephant in the room is that the volume of specified information necessary for replication to be performed is enormous. The authors simply insert replication at the beginning, assuming it in order to provide natural selection an opportunity to work. Not only does it already contain the software to replicate, but it also contains a highly specific hardware that allows it to replicate. This hardware also represents a significant amount of specified information to engineer—the second deception in this program.

In other words, the *Avida* organism is, in fact, from the onset imbued with the properties of life and cannot be used as evidence of how life began. To be fair to its inventors, they did not intend it to be an explanation of how life evolved but of how a disordered state can become more complex through random processes. However, it has been widely and repeatedly used to justify the evolutionists' notion that life could have developed in such a fashion. Given that the computer program was rigged to accomplish its goal, it can hardly be considered anything but the result of the human intelligence that programmed the computer.

Furthermore, it actually fails to do what the authors intended. There is no progression from a disordered state to a more complex state through random processes. The *Avida* program adds an enormous amount of information in the 26 discrete instructions that command the organism. These instructions, that input of specified information, did not arise through random ordering. They came from the minds of the programmers.

Moreover, the changes allowed by the program kept the commands intact. They may have switched one for another, subtracted one or added another to make the sequence shorter or longer, but the discrete commands did not mutate. Each command represents a quantifiable amount of specified information, which, in a random world, would have degraded. The program does not represent random ordering but rather the preservation of specified complexity, which requires further specified complexity.

The *Avida* software may not provide a target sequence, but it provides target functions—the nine logic functions that, once again, integrate an enormous amount of information and at the same time establish a standard that blind evolutionary randomness cannot "know." Again, a teleological model is disguised to supposedly prove dysteleology.

In addition, the *Avida* software provides a sniffer that evaluates the results of the digital organisms against these nine functions and elects which organisms are to be rewarded. There are four information-rich steps in this action: recognition, analysis, comparison, and reward.

Somehow I am not able to understand how these four functions of the sniffer are purposeless. No such counterpart exists in inanimate nature. No such progression can be arrived through random ordering. In other words, the programmers did not completely avoid the teleological problem. They just hid it better, but the elephant is still in the room.

If anything, these computer simulations have shown that intelligence is absolutely necessary to obtain a net gain of information in any system. Each program began with or added along the way an enormous amount of external information without which the results would not have been as the programmers designed them. Without this infusion of information, all these programs would have totally failed.

Each piece of information reduces the information requirements of the search in order to diminish it to levels that are manageable. If these reducing agents were not there, the statistical improbabilities would be insuperable by any software program. That, Mr. Dawkins, is a fact that no one can deny.

CHAPTER 7

●●●

THE EVOLUTION OF IRREDUCIBLE AND COMPLEX ORGANS: DARWIN'S BLACK BOX

The lack of understanding of the immense intricacy and vast complexity of these organs at the time Darwin proposed his theory allowed evolutionists to oversimplify the process of the evolution of these organs in order to make evolution seem plausible. In their naïveté, they glossed over inconsistencies. In their haste to prop up the naturalistic theory of evolution, they leaped blindly over impossible chasms. No better example of this ignorance and naïve misconception can be found than their proposed mechanism for the evolution of the eye.

The fossil record shows that complex biological structures (organs) such as feathers and eyes are found fully formed. After all, what possible selective advantage could a half-feather or half-evolved eye possess?

The eye to the evolutionist in Darwin's time was like a simple black box into whose metabolic intricacies we could not peer. A "black box" is an unexplainable mystery that functions outside our understanding, which we tend to simplify out of ignorance. It seemed simple on the surface, but as technology advanced our understanding of the process of vision, we discovered how complex and multifaceted the biochemical processes is. It is so incredibly sophisticated that the Darwinian assumption has been shown to be absolutely naïve.

There is, I think, a mystical quality to eyes. Some say they are a window to the soul. I know when I look into the eyes of my wife, my soul is stirred. There seems to be something mystical to the process of vision. It is a biochemical miracle of immense complexity.

The ability to sense an object through light bouncing off of it and entering into our eyes is an incredible engineering feat. We see this same engineering concept, albeit in a different medium, in bats through the use of bouncing sound waves. Their ability to fly swiftly and catch their prey in complete darkness is a marvelous engineering design. It is mirrored by radar systems that use bouncing radio signals to "see" objects.

Is it scientifically credible, then, to postulate a theory that proposes that random ordering created the sophisticated electromechanical components of radar tracking systems? If that seems preposterous to your logical mind, then how can an even more complex system such as vision be entertained as such?

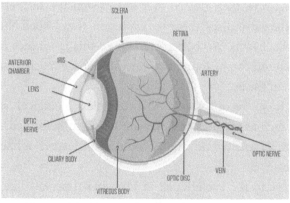

A diagram of the human eye

As we will see, the irreducible system of the biochemical process known as vision is undeniable evidence of the failure of the evolutionary process to explain the development of the eye through accidental steps guided only through selective pressures. The staggering number of steps that would have had to evolve simultaneously, without any known selective pressure to do so, makes the biochemical process of vision impossible to emerge in gradual steps, as proposed by the theory of evolution. It is more logical to assume that such complexity and structured biochemical pathways, each with no special advantage until the whole is completed, had to be intelligently designed.

The Evolutionary Riddle of the Eye

For the eye to function adequately, a minimum of eight steps would have to evolve simultaneously in order to create just the structural components of the eye. The lens, which focuses light on the retina, and the muscles that control it would have to evolve in synchrony. What good is a lens if it cannot focus according to the distance of the object being observed? The tear glands that clean and keep the eye moist, together with the eyelids to protect and moisten the eye, would also have to evolve simultaneously.

The cornea, a transparent protective outer covering, and the iris, the self-adjusting aperture that controls the amount of light that comes into the eye, would also have to evolve at the same time that all these other structures were being developed. Without these features, light could not be properly focused on the retina to reproduce the image of the object being observed.

But this is not yet vision. It is only the engineering wonder that allows the eye to focus light and adapt to changing conditions, like no camera could ever mimic. But we are still not talking about vision. We are only referring to the superstructure of the eye and the capturing of light.

The retina would also have to evolve with its 130 million light-sensitive rods and cones that interpret light through chemical reactions into electrical impulses. At the same time, the optic nerve, which carries that impulse to the brain, must have been coincidentally evolving. The capturing and sensing of light would be utterly useless if there were no mechanism to connect it to the brain, which would interpret these impulses.

What is being described here in a few simple paragraphs is no simple biochemical task, as we shall see. Can we seriously consider that all these conditions evolved simultaneously, in parallel, without a conductor to orchestrate the process for the purpose of converging in the end, and only in the end, to produce the ability of the eye to see? And are we supposed to accept that all of these multifaceted functions came together merely by chance? What possible selective pressure could have engineered such a feat?

Each part of the eye's structure is completely useless as an individual part until the entire process is completed. Can rational, objective people propose that all of these processes were developed simultaneously, in parallel, without any selective advantage in each process until the final outcome was complete?

Is it really credible to assume that all of this was fortuitously accomplished through random chemical processes of chance recombinations? The naïveté of this assumption is made even more glaring the more we understand the true nature of the chemical process that gives us the miracle of sight. Beyond the magnificent structural components of the eye, the biochemical process of detecting an image is staggering in sophistication.

Evolutionary biologists routinely gloss over this problem by suggesting that the eye evolved from a light-sensitive spot. But the empirical truth is that no intermediates can be truly presented that can document the evolution of the eye, as we shall see. There is a tremendous difference between the structure of a light-sensitive spot and the eye.

Michael Behe, associate professor in biochemistry at Lehigh University, in his enlightening book *Darwin's Black Box* addressed

Darwin's response to this specific question about the complexity of all the interrelated parts of the eye. I have chosen to quote him entirely in deference to his ability to say the difficult simply. The following quote is of a technical nature but essential in understanding the incredible fallacy of Darwin's simplistic evolutionary argument.

> *Charles Darwin knew about the eye, too. In The Origin of Species Darwin dealt with many objections to his theory of evolution by natural selection. He discussed the problem of the eye in a section of the book appropriately entitled "Organs of Extreme Perfection and Complication." In Darwin's thinking, evolution could not build a complex organ in one step or a few steps; radical innovations such as the eye would require generations of organisms to slowly accumulate beneficial changes in a gradual process. He realized that if in one generation an organ as complex as the eye suddenly appeared, it would be tantamount to a miracle. Unfortunately, gradual development of the human eye appeared to be impossible, since its many sophisticated features seemed to be interdependent. Somehow, for evolution to be believable, Darwin had to convince the public that complex organs could be formed in a step-by-step process.*
>
> *He succeeded brilliantly. Cleverly, Darwin didn't try to discover a real pathway that evolution might have used to make the eye. Rather, he pointed to modern animals with different kinds of eyes (ranging from the simple to the complex) and suggested that evolution of the human eye might have involved similar organs as intermediates....*
>
> *Here is a paraphrase of Darwin's argument: Although humans have complex camera-type eyes,*

many animals get by with less. Some tiny creatures have just a simple group of pigmented cells—not much more than a light-sensitive spot. That simple arrangement can hardly be said to confer vision, but it can sense light and dark, and so it meets the creature's needs....

Darwin convinced many of his readers that an evolutionary pathway leads from the simplest light-sensitive spot to the sophisticated camera-eye of man. But the question of how vision began remained unanswered. Darwin persuaded much of the world that a modern eye evolved gradually from a simpler structure, but he did not even try to explain where his starting point—the relatively simple light-sensitive spot—came from. On the contrary, Darwin dismissed the question of the eye's ultimate origin: "How a nerve comes to be sensitive to light hardly concerns us more than how life itself originated."

He had an excellent reason for declining the question: it was completely beyond nineteenth-century science. How the eye works—that is, what happens when a photon of light first hits the retina—simply could not be answered at that time. As a matter of fact no question about the underlying mechanisms of life could be answered. How did animal muscle cause movement? How did photosynthesis work? How was energy extracted from food? How did the body fight infection? No one knew.

To Darwin, vision was a black box, [a black box is an unexplainable mystery that functions outside of our understanding which we tend to simplify out of ignorance], but after the cumulative hard work of many biochemists, we are now approaching answers to the question of sight. The following five paragraphs give a biochemical sketch of the eyes [sic] operation....

When light first strikes the retina a photon interacts with a molecule called 11-cis-retinal, which rearranges within picoseconds to trans-retinal. (A picosecond is about the time it takes light to travel the breadth of a single human hair.) The change in the shape of the retinal molecule forces a change in the shape of the protein, rhodopsin, to which the retinal is tightly bound. The protein's metamorphosis alters its behavior. Now called metarhodopsin II, the protein sticks to another protein, called transducin. Before bumping into metarhodopsin II, transducin had tightly bound a small molecule called GDP. But when transducin interacts with metarhodopsin II, the GDP falls off, and a molecule called GTP binds to transducin. (GTP is closely related to, but critically different, from GDP.)

GTP-transducin-metarhodopsin II now binds to a protein called phosphodiesterase, located in the inner membrane of the cell. When attached to metarhodopsin II and its entourage, the phosphodiesterase acquires the chemical ability to "cut" a molecule called cGMP (a chemical relative of both GDP and GTP). Initially there are a lot of cGMP molecules in the cell, but the phosphodiesterase lowers its concentration, just as a pulled plug lowers the water level in a bathtub.

Another membrane protein that binds cGMP is called an ion channel. It acts as a gateway that regulates the number of sodium ions in the cell. Normally the ion channel allows sodium ions to flow into the cell, while a separate protein actively pumps them out again. The dual action of the ion channel and pump keeps the level of sodium ions in the cell within a narrow range. When the amount of cGMP is reduced because of cleavage by the phosphodiesterase, the ion channel closes, causing the cellular concentration of positively charged sodium ions to be reduced. This causes an imbalance of charge across the cell membrane that, finally, causes a current to be transmitted down the optic nerve to the brain. The result, when interpreted by the brain, [another black box] is vision.

If the reactions mentioned above were the only ones that operated in the cell, the supply of 11-**cis**-retinal, cGMP, and sodium ions would quickly be depleted. Something has to turn off the proteins that were turned on and restore the cell to its original state. Several mechanisms do this. First, in the dark the ion channel (in addition to sodium ions) also lets calcium ions into the cell. The calcium is pumped back out by a different protein so that a constant calcium concentration is maintained. When cGMP levels fall, shutting down the ion channel, calcium ion concentration decreases, too. The phosphodiesterase enzyme, which destroys cGMP, slows down at lower calcium concentration. Second, a protein called guanlate cyclase begins to resynthesize cGMP when calcium levels start to fall. Third, while all of this is going on, metarhodopsin II is chemically modified by an enzyme called rhodopsin kinase. The modified rhodopsin then binds to a protein known as arrestin, which prevents the rhodopsin from activating more transducin. So *the cell contains mechanisms to limit the amplified signal started by a single photon.*

Trans-retinal eventually falls off of rhodopsin and must be reconverted to 11-cis-retinal and again bound by rhodopsin to get back to the starting point for another visual cycle. To accomplish this, trans-retinal is first chemically modified by an enzyme to trans-retinol—a form containing two more hydrogen atoms. A second enzyme then converts the molecule to 11-cis-retinol. Finally, a third enzyme removes the previously added hydrogen atoms to form 11-cis-retinal, a cycle is complete (Behe 16–21).

The staggering complexity required to sense one single photon is a chain reaction of mutually occurring, interdependent chemical processes that, figuratively speaking, require nothing less than a musical conductor to maintain the harmony and a genius composer to design it.

Moreover, once the process is complete, it resets itself for the next encounter with a photon. Without the second phase that returns the chemical balance to the original format, the eye could not see more than one photon. The supply of the chemicals necessary for the process would be depleted.

All these steps would have to evolve by chance simultaneously, while yet mutually independent of one another, in order for this singular photon to be sensed in the eye and transmitted to the neuron for our brain (another black box) to interpret it as vision.

What possible selective advantages could these interdependent processes have during the enormous periods of time necessary for such complex steps to arise from minute changes? How could one of these biochemical processes by itself create a selective advantage for the organism?

Here, again, as in the evolutionary punctuated equilibrium theory that fails to provide any tangible mechanism to evolve from one species into another, the evolutionist simply accepts by faith that it just happened. Since the fossil record shows all species fully formed and no real intermediates, they wave a magic wand and claim that it did so through an unknown mechanism, which was too brief in time to be recorded in the fossil record—Voila!

There are no credible selective pressures or evolutionary mechanisms that would orchestrate the many functions that are obviously a teleological process designed to achieve vision as the final product. Anything short of a real magic wand is intellectually absurd.

It is important to understand that this biochemical symphony set off by a single photon occurs ultimately at the molecular level. We have only begun to understand this. Therefore, a satisfactory explanation of the origin of such biological phenomena as sight, digestion, and immunity can no longer be made by appealing to similarities in superficial anatomical structures, as early Darwinists were prone to do.

Evolutionary explanations must include the molecular level, where the real work is being done. External similarities of anatomical structures simply have no bearing on whether or not evolution could take place at the molecular level where the real action is. If it fails at this level, then it fails altogether.

Yet evolutionists are still using Darwin's antiquated nineteenth-century argument because they lack any other alternative. There are no molecular pathways that evolutionists can point to that document the evolution of sight. Each of these anatomical steps that Darwin thought was so simple to traverse has been shown at the molecular level to be staggeringly complex beyond our wildest imaginations.

The evolution of the eye can no longer be explained away with empty rhetorical language and simplistic analogies with light-sensitive spots. Hard empirical data are the only acceptable explanation that can be called science.

The empirical reality is that modern biochemists have discovered that these supposedly simple anatomical steps that Darwin theorized could gradually develop are surprisingly complex and multifaceted at the molecular level. They could not have evolved in simple steps of progression as Darwin posed because there is no evolutionary advantage to the system until it is totally complete.

In fact, if Darwin were alive today, armed with our present knowledge of the staggering complexity of these multi-staged biochemical processes, I seriously doubt that he would have proposed his theory of gradual evolution. At the very least, he certainly would not have dismissed the eye so cavalierly.

There is no simple way to describe this nine-stage, very intricate biochemical dance that allows a single photon to register in the brain. The chemical chain of events that must happen in order for a single photon to be sensed and a message transferred to the brain is difficult to grasp when described in words. But I have found that illustrations sometimes serve to visualize the process and help create a clearer picture of the otherwise laborious process.

This, of course, must take into account that the transmission of this message must also be carried through an optical nerve that transmits this chemically or neurally split image to the brain. It must then be further integrated in the occipital cortex of the human brain, and somehow, these chemical signals must be interpreted by someone behind the brain. In other words, this chemical signal must be reintegrated into an image and interpreted at the occipital cortex level by a person.

There are some unfortunate individuals who have had a stroke in this area of the cortex, and although their eyes and optical nerves are functioning perfectly, they are unable to interpret what they see and are consequently cortically blind. The occipital cortex's ability to interpret this signal, not as a two-dimensional image in a television screen but as a three-dimensional image, is another black box.

The Irreducible Eye

Drawing courtesy of Dr. Paul Rodriguez

There is no doubt that this interpretation of the signals sent by the optic nerve requires an immense complexity in the biochemical process, about which we as yet have no inkling. The truly objective thinker must accede that we have only begun to scratch the scratch on the surface of a scratch.

In the face of empirical evidence discovered by modern science, the gradualist evolutionary process from simple forms to more complex forms is completely deficient as an explanation of the genesis of life and the development of complicated organs that allow life to exist.

We should keep in mind that in Darwin's time, technology had at its disposal only a simple light microscope to study the microscopic world. Darwin's power of observation was greatly limited compared to the arsenal of tools we have at our disposal today.

A microscope cannot resolve two points that are closer together than half the wavelength of light. The wavelength of light happens to be approximately 1/10 the diameter of a typical bacteria. So to Darwin, the cell seemed like a simple organism composed of some nebulous gelatinous material. It was not until very late in the nineteenth century that J. J. Thompson discovered the electron, and it was not until the early part of the twentieth century that the electron microscope was invented.

By illuminating objects with electrons, which have a considerably smaller wavelength than light, a whole world of submicroscopic entities appeared. It was this breakthrough in technology that opened the door for the study of the components of the cell. For the first time, subcellular structures such as the mitochondria appeared.

The mitochondrion is a complex structure that, as previously described, is the power plant of the cell, responsible for the process of creating usable energy in a cell in order to fuel the production of molecules for a variety of needs. It is the powerhouse of the cell that provides the energy necessary for metabolism.

And then holes were seen in the nucleus. The cell was observed to have a double membrane that is selectively permeable, allowing certain molecules to enter and keeping others out. As we have already mentioned, that is an indispensable requirement for the cell so that within its walls, the chemical processes necessary for life can function.

What seemed to Darwin as a simple gelatinous structure turned out to be an amazingly complex, tiny galaxy of unprecedented molecular activity. We have barely scratched the surface in understanding this biological wonder that we have ignorantly called a "simple cell."

A rather new technique called X-ray crystallography is currently being used to study the cell at a molecular level. It allows us to peer at even smaller increments since the wavelength of X-rays is so infinitesimally small. The shapes of molecules are now becoming visible.

All these sub-cellular structures that, for the early evolutionists, seemed simple in shape and function, are now observed to have intricate shapes and utterly complex functions. Even the so-called "simple organisms" are replete with infinitely more complex biochemical processes than what we could have imagined in Darwin's time.

As we are able to peer deeper into this black box we call the living cell, the wondrous complexity of even the smallest organelle is becoming ever so startling. Moreover, the origin of the cell from an evolutionist's standpoint has become convincingly improbable to the critical, objective observer.

The Irreducible Immune System

Now, let's consider the infinitely more elaborate engineering marvel of the entire human body and the enormous degree of improbability that random processes resulted in such extraordinarily specific complexity. For example, the biochemical process of the immune system by which our body resists foreign invaders such as bacteria and viruses is a lengthy, complex biochemical story that would surely bore the nonscientific reader. It is another highly intricate biochemical dance.

The body's magnificent immune system presents another riddle for the evolutionist. Again, the entire process is useless from a selective advantage standpoint if it does not reach completion. It is, as Behe so eloquently claimed, irreducible to small gradual changes that can accumulate through random chance into a complete system.

Like most biochemical processes that occur in our bodies, there are no selective pressures that could account for only partially fulfilling the many steps of this complex, biochemical response. The contention that all these processes developed slowly over time, with simple steps that finally arrived at a complex step by the sequential grouping of the simple steps, is simply impossible.

Moreover, the speculation offered by the punctuated equilibrium theory that some unknown selective pressure caused them to simultaneously evolve instantly is at best absurd in light of our present knowledge. Those who hold tenaciously to this contention are, sadly, guilty of self-delusion of the highest order. I am a skeptic at heart and refuse to take a blind leap of faith into the unknown. I simply do not have enough faith to be an evolutionist.

If neither gradualism nor the supposed instantaneous magical process of punctuated equilibrium can explain the genesis of such irreducibly complex organs, then it must logically follow that these intricately designed systems were, in fact, designed. Ah! But this is the sticky point. Naturalism automatically precludes the idea of a designer by its insistence on the paradigm of a universe functioning as a closed system. But science should be the pursuit of truth, wherever it may lead us. It should be the concerted effort of scientists to pursue truth in observance of true reality. Reason should trump our predispositions.

As a result of our advances in biochemistry, many such organs have been documented that could not possibly have evolved through Darwin's idea of gradualism. These organs of irreducible complexity, as Michael Behe refers to them, are systems composed of several interacting, interdependent, individual components or functions in which the removal of any one of those parts renders the whole system completely ineffective or inoperable.

Examples of such irreducible systems are numerous and can be found in any college textbook on biochemistry (protein transport, cilia, blood clotting, closed circular DNA, electron transport, telomeres, photosynthesis, transcription regulation, etc.) For example, there is a process in the immune system that scientists call *affinity maturation*. This process plays an important role in the immune system by continuously improving its ability to rid our bodies of foreign pathogens. The ingenious method to do this is mind-boggling. Amino acids with appendages that have sticky ends are able to bind with bacteria and viruses that invade our bodies.

> *Once again these are amino-acid appendages. Like all proteins, the entire antibody is bristling with these appendages....*
>
> *You and I owe much to these sticky ends because they have saved our lives, literally, many times. Every time we get an infection, from the common cold to a festering scrape, our bodies go into high gear to fight off microscopic invaders, and antibodies are a key part of winning these fights. Like laser beams guiding missiles to their targets, antibodies tag the invaders for destruction, and the high specificity of their sticky ends is what enables them to do this tagging so effectively. To achieve this specificity, our bodies use an extremely elegant version of selective optimization, where billions of variations on the best sticky ends found so far are reproduced repeatedly, with better sticky ends replacing the previous ones until no further improvement can be made. Adding to the elegance, our bodies retain the best versions of these sticky ends from each of these battles so they can be deployed very quickly the next time the same invader is encountered (Axe 208).*

The incredible specificity of this ingenious system of defense is impossible to reconcile with a randomly generated evolutionary system. Were Darwin alive today, taking him at his word from the statement he made in his book, we would expect him to abandon the concept of gradualism as incompatible with the reality observed in irreducible structures. Perhaps modern evolutionists should take his advice.

But unfortunately, I doubt if the empirical facts would convince anyone of anything they do not want to see. One must first be willing to see.

These are the empirical facts:

1. All parts of these irreducible systems must work in unison to create the function of the whole. And each component part has absolutely no adaptive value by itself, whether in complete or incomplete form.
2. These systems cannot be produced gradually by a slight modification of each part. All parts must be fully functioning and complete in order for the system to operate.
3. There is no observable natural selective pressure that can account for simultaneous numerous gradations from a simple form to a more complex form of these individual parts, when the only working form of this system is operable at the stage when each part is complete. That is, each part of the whole must be complete and intact in order for the system to operate at all as a whole.

Hence, Darwin's idea of gradualism is based on ignorance of the interlocking complexity of these irreducible systems on the biochemical level. Moreover, the punctuated equilibrium idea in these cases becomes even more absurd to contemplate. To accelerate the timetable would not in any way change the miraculous nature of such an event.

Therefore, if there is no possible way for natural selection to account for simultaneous evolution of these parts in order to end up in convergence with the resulting system fully functional, then it stands to reason that the only other alternative explanation to this phenomenon is that a master designer designed it so. Such specific complexity is not found in any natural processes we can observe today.

The scientific process should be the quest for truth, regardless of where it takes us. If the factual physical evidence observed is such that no other explanation for the origin of these marvelously designed systems is possible or logical, then can we consider it reasonable for honest people to exclude the Designer as a possible explanation?

> *Imagine a room in which a body lies crushed, flat as a pancake. A dozen detectives crawl around, examining the floor with magnifying glasses for any clue to the identity of the perpetrator. In the middle of the room, next to the body, stands a large, gray elephant. The detectives carefully avoid bumping into the pachyderm's legs as they crawl, and never even glance at it. Over time the detectives get frustrated with their lack of progress but resolutely press on, looking even more closely at the floor....*
>
> *There is an elephant in the roomful of scientists who are trying to explain the development of life. The elephant is labeled "intelligent design." To a person who does not feel obliged to restrict his search to unintelligent causes, the straightforward conclusion is that many biochemical systems were designed. They were designed not by the laws of nature, not by chance and necessity; rather, they were planned (Behe 192–193).*

It is important here to make a clear distinction; we are concluding that these irreducibly complex systems are designed, *not because of what we do not know, but because of what we do know.*

It is not ignorance that leads us to posit the necessity of a designer, but rather knowledge. It is, in fact, the "ultimate ignorance" to evade the plain facts and opt to accept an answer that is not consistent with our physical reality. It is like attempting to shut out the sun with our thumb.

You may be surprised at how many are holding their thumb up against the sun. In 1999, Kenneth R. Miller wrote *Finding Darwin's God*, in which he attempts to discredit Michael Behe's lucid argument of irreducibly complex systems by simply quoting Darwin's initial presupposition, as if Darwin's words somehow carry some magical quality that makes the absurd become respectably logical.

> *Since the eye could not work properly without all of its parts in place, including the lens, retina, iris, optic nerve, and many others, it is a classical example of an irreducibly complex organ. So, presumably it presents a terrible problem for evolution. But, Darwin already had the answer:*
>
>> *Yet reason tells me, that if numerous gradations from a perfect and complete eye to one very imperfect and simple, each grade being useful to it possessor, can be shown to exist; if further, the eye does vary ever so slightly, and the variations be inherited, which is certainly the case; and if any variation or modification in the organ be ever useful to an animal under changing conditions of life, then the difficulty of believing that a perfect and complex eye could be formed by natural selection, though insuperable by our imagination, can hardly be considered real.*
>
> *Darwin's reasoning cuts right to the heart of the argument from design. It boldly claims that the interlocking complexity of a multipart organ like the eye could indeed be produced by natural selection. How? As Darwin noted, all that we really need to show*

is existence of "numerous gradations" from the simple
to the complex. Then all natural selection has to do
is to favor each step in the pathway from simple to
complex, and we have solved the problem (Miller 135).

Somehow, Behe's clear and substantiated presentation of irreducible systems escapes Miller. He simply ignores the biochemical pathway that is so long and complicated at the molecular level and returns to the nineteenth century simplistic arguments over anatomical similarities.

Miller simply ignores the fact that there are no known evolutionary gradations in the individual parts of these irreducible complex organs that can be shown to be a benefit to the animal until it is completely formed in its present complex state. There is, therefore, no selective pressure that can be brought upon it to develop in this magical fashion, at least outside of evolutionary imagination.

In other words, there is no functional improvement to the animal as a whole by any of the individual and discrete biochemical steps that could allow selection to favor it, since only functional advantages could be selected in a competing environment as envisioned by evolution until all the steps are completed and it is functioning as a whole system. Nevertheless, such fallacious reasoning seems to suffice those who refuse reason in favor of rationalization.

The examples of these supposedly "numerous gradations" are not gradations at all in the evolution of the eye. They are completely separate and independent systems designed to function at that level for the specific need of that particular creature. There is no interconnection between the different designs. That is, to say the least, a deceitful argument.

Miller's allegation that the "eyespots" of bacteria and algae are an adaptive selective pressure that proves gradation toward a fully functional eye is at best ridiculous and at worst deliberately deceptive. He completely avoids answering Behe's argument and says nothing about the intermediate gradations that would have to evolve within the complex biochemical sequential steps that are going on simultaneously in each part of the biochemical processes that make the eye functional.

There is no gradation here. There is a hyper leap of light years, from one simpler system to a completely different system, shored up only by the unverifiable imagination of those whose evolutionary horse blinders keep them from facing the obvious.

Miller has not added anything new to the argument. He has not even given us a plausible selective pressure that could govern the development of intermediate chemical processes of these complex parts simultaneously in gradations. He has completely sidestepped the subject of molecular evolution because there is no evolutionary explanation that can be verifiable.

He has literally just dusted off the old generalized argument of gradation and pawned it off as the magical answer. Using his logic, we could deduce that the sun evolved from a light bulb, which evolved from a candle. Again, the evolutionist must resort to the magic wand and fairy dust.

Miller then proceeds to attack Philip Johnson with the same caustic vehemence. And since he cannot logically and scientifically refute his claim that the only real evolution that takes place is microevolution (evolution within a species, which we will cover in Book 4, *The Descent of Man*), he then resorts to the age-old, underhanded tactic of personal attack by attacking Johnson's credibility and claiming that he is not a "serious scientist." I submit to you that Einstein was a patent clerk in Switzerland and not considered a serious scientist by any of his peers when he blew them all away with the general theory of relativity and changed physics forever.

The Tyranny of Paradigms

As I understand it, a serious scientist is one who, when faced with verifiable observable facts that contradict his or her hypothesis, changes the hypothesis to fit the facts. This is what Copernicus and Kepler and Newton and Einstein did, and it is my prayer that one day Miller will remove his evolutionary paradigm-colored spectacles and become a serious scientist.

The true credential of a serious scientist is not measured by how many degrees he or she has or by what positions he or she holds, but by how honestly that scientist follows the scientific process and conforms to the real physical findings in pursuit of scientific truth. Aristotle did not have a doctoral degree from an accredited university. And neither did Lucretius. Hardly would any evolutionist dare insinuate that either of them was not a serious scientists in every sense of the term.

Our modern culture has unwittingly been programmed to think that if an individual does not have a degree from a secular educational institution, he or she is self-taught and academically inferior. The concept of being self-taught is an improper, deceiving term. No one is truly self-taught. We learn from the accumulated learning of those who have gone before us, through books, conversations, and lectures. Then, we analyze the material we have been exposed to and derive personal conclusions as a product of our experience and inductive and deductive capabilities. That is what Benjamin Franklin did. That is what William Smith did, who, apart from Lyell, was the most influential person in the evolutionary theory regarding geological strata.

It is irrelevant whether the material is learned in a structured environment or in an informal setting. We can say that our learning is self-directed, or other-directed. But no one is truly self-taught. Neither is a structured academic center the end of an education. What we read or learn through experimentation or observation after our formal education is truly the flesh that goes on the skeleton that an academic institution has provided us.

The truth is that structured environments tend to make us have tunnel vision. Other-directed learning has a tendency to become indoctrination rather than education. For this reason, people like Einstein who were independent thinkers did not fare well in other-directed institutions. And for that reason, one of the most intelligent and brilliant physicists in human history could only get a job in a Swiss patent office.

He rejected the status quo that was indoctrinating students in academic institutions and chose to think outside the box. As a consequence, he was able to stand against the tide of his colleagues, who monolithically floated with the prevailing wind of the paradigm of their age.

The paradigms of any era are difficult to overturn. When, for one reason or another, a large group of our society accepts a norm, it is quite difficult to go against the grain and incur the wrath of the powers that be. Human nature being what it is, we seek for the most part to fit in and belong. We are, after all, social creatures.

It is no secret that our postmodern culture has accepted materialism as the fundamental worldview. This is especially so in our academic institutions. Any serious scientist who dares upset the apple cart with an alternative worldview faces a daunting barrage of criticism and is immediately ostracized by the "enlightened" from the scientific community. It seems that true tolerance is not an enlightened position held by the modern priests of scientism. They have turned the tables of science from free thinkers to an elitist cabal steeped in authoritarian dogma and censorship. Many brilliant scientists have paid a dear price for daring to question the scientific dogma of our modern paradigm. Douglas Axe, a brilliant molecular biologist, has felt that personal sting for daring to courageously swim against the current.

Once an embellished view of science becomes established, active suppression of dissent becomes inevitable, with predictable consequences. Everything that opposes the institutionalized agenda is labeled

*'anti-science' by those working to protect the agenda,
and the fear of that label quickly enforces compliance
among the timid (Axe 54).*

But here and there, we find people in history who were willing to think past the paradigm of their age and take a stand against the entrenched dogmas of their culture. They are the illustrious ones of true science who thought outside the box and dared to differ from the status quo.

These people—Copernicus, Kepler, Galileo, Newton—have endured the ridicule of the narrow-minded and truncated thinkers who form the vast majority of every age. And as a result of their courage, truth prevailed, and paradigms were toppled. These are the people who advance our understanding of reality in quantum leaps.

The theory of evolution is the paradigm of our era. It is based on an anachronistic and erroneous notion that complex organs can evolve in simple steps. The very foundation of this theory was predicated on scientists' technical inability to know the true biochemical complexity of even a single cell. Hence, their false assumption that simple progressive steps could theoretically create a more complex entity was adopted as a plausible evolutionary mechanism. Moreover, their second essential false premise of an eternal universe, which would allow the necessary time for these imperceptible changes to accomplish the seemingly impossible, has also been scientifically disproved.

In addition, certain dogmatic aspects of their uniformitarian hypothesis have equally been dismantled through empirical evidence. Catastrophes do happen from time to time, and our geologic processes are not always gradual. Therefore, evolutionists' major dispute with biblical catastrophism, which they ridiculed as mythological, has been scientifically substantiated by the discovery of global catastrophes such as the meteor that made the dinosaurs extinct.

Thus, for those of us who are willing to accept the true empirical data, we are forced to conclude that evolutionists' concept of gradualism has now been shown deficient in three ways:

1. The universe is finite in space-time. Hence, evolution has neither infinite resources nor an infinite amount of time to accumulate these imperceptible, gradual changes.
2. The fossil record shows no gradual change from one species to another. All species appear complete and abrupt. No intermediate forms have been found anywhere in our ecosystem.
3. In light of modern technical advancements in science, the biochemical processes of such irreducibly complex organs as the eye could not have evolved in gradual steps.

Today, we are beginning to understand the marvelous complexity of the "simple cell" and the magnificently engineered organs formed by them in the body, and it is nothing less than mind-boggling. The sheer complexity of every single cell in the body—60 trillion of them—is many times more complex than a modern computer.

The brain is so complex that we are still only scratching the surface of this multifaceted wonder. It is, indeed, another magnificently mysterious black box. An organ that simply looks like three pounds of grey matter has proved to be nothing less than a sophisticated organic computer of amazing capabilities. The unimaginable biochemical complexity of the brain is only now being appreciated through the advancements of our technology.

The human brain contains 10^{14} electrical connections; that is, one hundred thousand billion electrical connections. No humanly contrived motherboard can come close to it. That is more than all the electrical connections in all the electrical appliances that exist in the entire world, all in a single brain that fits inside one skull.

We have mapped certain regions of the brain that correspond to certain functions of the body, but we have absolutely no idea how the brain reasons. We have unlocked the mechanisms of nerve synapses, but we have no idea how a thought is produced or how memory is stored.

> *The amount of information that can be stored in a human brain is estimated to be between 10^{10} and 10^{15} bits, with the lower number assuming there is one bit stored on the average for each of the brain's 10^{10} cells. Now about 1% to 10 % of the brain's cells are firing at any one time, at a rate of about 100 hertz. This gives a computation rate of 10 to 1000 gigaflops (a gigaflop is 10^9 floating point computations per second). The lower bound of 10 gigaflops is about the rate at which the eye processes information before it is sent to the brain. For comparison, the fastest computer in existence today, the Cray-2, has a speed of 1 gigaflop and storage capacity for 2×10^{10} bits (in 64 bit words) (Barrow and Tipler 136).*

Again, compare this number to the number of seconds that have elapsed, not in a year, not in a century, not in a millennium, not in a million years, not in a billion years, but for the entire 15 billion years that they propose our universe has existed, or 10 to the 16th power.

Since Barrow and Tipler wrote their book in 1996, computers have advanced, and it is estimated that in 2020, we may be able to reach the level of the brain through artificial intelligence (AI). The concerted effort of thousands of people spending countless hours in the research and development of computers contributed to this cumulative effort.

Can we be so bold-faced to accept the paradigm of our era that assumes this staggering complexity in design and yet believe that the design of organs, which are far more intricate and advanced than computers, could have evolved by blind random processes void of any purpose and any teleological underlying cause? What possible explanation can humans produce for this phenomenon?

Ironically, any human explanation requires the brain to process an enormous amount of information in a very short period, reemphasizing the absurdity of assuming that such staggering complexity could arise through blind, random chemical processes.

> But only the information which a human being can process consciously, or hold in the forefront of the mind, can be used in forming a humanly acceptable explanation. We don't know exactly how much this would be, but it is comparable in order of magnitude to the information coded in a single book, which is typically 1 to 10 million bits. No explanation humans have ever dealt with has been as complex as this. The content of most science books has been concerned with justifying the explanation rather than explaining it (Barrow and Tipler 135–137).

I mention this marvelous organ we call the brain not to belittle the great strides of science thus far and not to predict that we might never crack that code. On the contrary, humans will one day accomplish this, sooner rather than later, I hope. But my point is that such overwhelmingly specified complexity could not have ever resulted from mere random ordering in a dysteleological fashion. Such outlandish speculation is sheer scientific nonsense. It ranks right up there with Santa Claus and the tooth fairy.

We are just beginning to understand the extremely intricate, complex fashion in which our brain works. In an article published in *Frontiers in Computational Neuroscience* on June 12, 2017, researchers wrote that by using an advanced algebraic system, they discovered that the brain operates in up to 11 different dimensions, creating electrical geometric structures containing cavities within them that appear momentarily and then disappear. The research, called the Blue Brain Project, used supercomputer simulations to study the reactions among various regions of the brain (Reimann et al.).

Using algebraic topology (a system used to describe networks with constantly changing structures and the spaces inside them), they were amazed to discover that the neurons made electrical structures by making specified cliques with other neurons that created precise geometric structures. The more neurons involved in that clique, the higher the dimension created containing cavities within them. Once the brain has finished processing that information, the structure vanishes. Ran Levi, one of the researchers, said, "The appearance of high-dimensional cavities when the brain is processing information means that the neurons in the network react to stimuli in an extremely organized manner" (Osborne). Levi went on to explain, "It is as if the brain reacts to a stimulus by building then razing a tower of multidimensional blocks, starting with rods (1D), then planks (2D), then cubes (3D), and then more complex geometries with 4D, 5D, etc." (Osborne).

Most of us who are used to only seeing three dimensions in our visible reality have great difficulty appreciating the intricacy of structures in higher dimensions. Henry Markam, director of the Blue Brain Project, said, "We found a world that we had never imagined. There are tens of millions of these objects even in a small speck of the brain, up through seven dimensions. In some networks, we even found structures with up to eleven dimensions" (Osborne).

It seems that the brain circuit always responds to brain stimuli by constructing a series of geometrical electrical structures, beginning with low dimensions and then adding progressively higher dimensions until the brain processes the information. Then the structures collapse and become ready for the next stimulus.

I found this research extremely interesting. The brain appears to work in a completely organized manner, which could hardly be considered the product of random ordering. I have a hunch that the Blue Brain Project research team has discovered a monumental truth about how our brain works, because it matches the symmetry of our spatial reality. The mathematics of the M-theory (string theory) tells us that our physical universe is composed of seven invisible spatial dimensions and three visible spatial dimensions that equal 10 spatial dimensions. In addition, all of them are intertwined in the time dimension, making a total of 11 dimensions to our physical reality.

My experience is that God always uses symmetry in His creation to point out to the searching mind that this universe was previsioned and intelligently designed and not just random evolutionary happenstance. It does not surprise me that our brain, which gives us the ability to understand our physical reality, usually works in seven dimensions and, when necessary, also resorts to 11 dimensions. The idea that random ordering could create an organ like our brain that processes stimuli in structures that form 11 dimensional geometric patterns instantaneously and then collapses the structure to make itself ready for the next stimulus is a stretch of blind faith that, in my mind, is logically irrational.

Certainly, modern science has accomplished some astounding achievements. I remember being glued to my television in 1969, when I was a junior at Miami Senior High School when the first man stepped onto the moon. I will never forget that crackling voice of astronaut Neil Armstrong: "That's one small step for man, one giant leap for mankind."

I turned to one of my younger brothers and said something like this: "You have just witnessed a historical milestone in human history. You have heard a man talking to you from another heavenly body beyond our earth." I pointed to the TV and continued, "That is a real human. That is the real moon. And he is speaking as we hear him from the very moon above us."

I can still remember that moment as if it happened this morning. I was lifting weights, part of my regular workout routine back then, when I heard the moon landing and stopped to listen to Neil Armstrong's voice and peer intently at the television. Even now, I get goose bumps thinking about it. What an incredible achievement of the human mind! I still have the *Miami Herald* newspaper for that day that headlined the marvelous accomplishment. I hope I live to see the day a human walks on Mars.

No other animal has that kind of mind. No other animal can reason with the potential to unlock the mysteries of God's creation. We alone of all creatures have been endowed with the grace to do that. Such an engineering miracle could not have been possible without the combined efforts of the brilliant minds of the many scientists involved in that grand venture.

Can we rationally presume that the *Apollo 11* spacecraft could have evolved to contain the specific information necessary to take those astronauts to the moon and back through random, undirected chemical transpositions? Then how can we believe that the much more complex brain that designed that lunar vehicle could have evolved randomly??

Trash the Space Trash Theory

Our modern technological advancements have given us an unexpected and marvelous insight into the deepest recesses of space. The macroworld has unfolded before our eyes in an astonishing fashion that could not have been imagined by humans a few hundred years ago. Copernicus, Kepler, Galileo, and Newton would have been awestruck and thrilled to the core.

It is an understatement to say that the spectacular images of the vast cosmos provided by the Hubble Space Telescope are breathtaking and magnificently beautiful. Where once we thought only stars existed, we now know that these tiny dots of light are, in fact, whole galaxies of differing sizes and shapes.

The grand scale of the magnificently structured universe is almost too vast for our minds to truly comprehend. The massive variety of strange and wonderful things discovered in deep space— quasars, supernovas, black holes—boggle the mind. Such is the majesty of God's creation, the variety and splendor that ought to humble us.

Our advancements in technology have also allowed us to peer more deeply into the molecular structures of the microworld, revealing the immense complexities of the components of the living cell. How that undeniable complexity could develop without a genius designer to invent it first and a genius biochemical engineer to formulate it is difficult to fathom.

Somehow, postmodernists have developed a dichotomy in their reasoning powers that allows them to claim that undirected blind chance chemical processes became the instruments of the evolution of life when considering the origins of the living cell, which is many times more complex than the rocket and lunar vehicle that took the astronauts to the moon and back.

The complexity found at this elemental level is such that even die-hard evolutionists such as Nobel Prize winning geneticist Francis Crick cannot accept that the living cell was a product of chance evolution here on Earth. He believes that, especially given the lack of time necessary for such complex designs to formulate through gradualism and the lack of evidence of the prebiotic organelles that are completely absent within the fossil record.

They insist that there must be some simple organelle, a sort of "proto-cell" from which unicellular cells evolved. But since no such thing exists here on Earth, some, like Crick, in an attempt to bridge this gap, are resorting to a space trash theory called *directed panspermia*. In essence, they are claiming that progenitors of the cell evolved elsewhere and were artificially transplanted to this planet.

Since they cannot substantiate the evolutionary development of the cell from the evidence on Earth, it is conveniently asserted that it developed extraterrestrially. Yes, real scientists, not crackpots, are now claiming that our biology evolved from the trash left behind by some space traveler long ago or perhaps arrived as hitchhikers in some comet or asteroid.

Others have suggested that perhaps a meteorite that was contaminated from another exploding world seeded our planet. But there is good reason to look elsewhere, because the evidence they are looking for just does not exist on this planet.

What the biochemical evidence shows is a wonderfully ordered and complex world that could never have evolved by random, blind, chance chemical processes. This lack of intermediate evidence, which should have been amply represented in the fossil record and the genetic information if, in fact, evolution was the gradual and almost imperceptible change depicted as the means to change from one species into another, is absent even at the unicellular level.

In fact, what we are discovering due to advancements in gene sequencing from the Human Genome Project is that the genetic evidence indicates otherwise. Even within the single-celled bacteria, the uniqueness of each species that evolutionists would regard as evolutionarily connected are found to have a much greater number of unique genes then they had imagined.

One of the great surprises to come from genome sequencing projects is how many unique genes, and therefore proteins, are present in each form of life, including forms that to us look only subtly different. For example, a group of German scientists recently examined the genome sequences from sixteen cyanobacterial strains in an effort to discern all the distinct kinds of genes these strains carry. Since they're all cyanobacteria, you might think they would carry the same set of genes, with perhaps an extra gene here or a missing gene there. The scientists found that they do share a common set of 660 genes, meaning not that these genes are identical from one strain to the next but rather that they are similar enough that we can be quite certain they encode proteins that fold to the same overall structure and perform the same biological function. Much more surprising, though, was their finding that nearly 14,000 genes are unique to individual strains! At an average of 869 unique genes per strain, this makes these bacterial strains more genetically different than alike, despite their overall external similarities.

The proportion of species-specific genes varies from one species to the next, but their existence in large number seems to be a property of all life, not just cyanobacteria. To quote the abstract of a recent technical paper, "Comparative genome analyses indicate that every taxonomic group so far studied contains 10–20% of genes that lack recognizable homologs in other species." In other words, every species has many genes that seem, at first glance, to be one-offs—unlike any gene found anywhere else.

> *The painstaking work of finding the structures of the proteins these genes encode is showing that about two-thirds turn out to resemble previously known proteins, with the remaining third being genuinely new (Axe 182–183).*

It has become more than apparent that each individual species contains such a large percentage of unique genes (more than what they have in common) that the evolutionist has great difficulty explaining this phenomenon. In contrast, that is what we would expect if an intelligent designer who wished to create unique species in fact created life.

The genetic evidence has simply not corroborated the supposedly seamless continuity between one species and another imagined by evolutionists. Efforts to create a common genetic lineage have proved fruitless. But I am not saying anything new here. This fact has been dutifully observed by many evolutionists, including Crick, and consequently used as evidence for his theory of directed panspermia.

Incidentally, he proposes that we should respond in kind gratitude to our space ancestors and send out rockets filled with blue-green algae to inseminate the universe. After all, that is the logical consequence of the space trash theory. If life on Earth came from outer space, then why not return the good deed and disperse the seeds of life throughout the universe?

Crick understands the unbelievable statistical hurdles necessary to believe in the evolution of life on earth by chance. And since no prebiotic evidence has been found to support his naturalistic presupposition, he is forced to postulate that life on Earth was sent here from another planet.

> *An honest man, armed with all the knowledge available to us now, could only state that in some*

sense, the origin of life appears at the moment to be almost a miracle, so many are the conditions which would have had to have been satisfied to get it going (Crick 88).

In explaining the lack of prebiotic evidence, Crick wrote:

Perhaps a better approach might be to ask what special features we might hope to see in the fossil record if Directed Panspermia had indeed occurred. The main difference would be that microorganisms should appear here suddenly, without any evidence for prebiotic systems or very primitive organisms. We might also expect that not one but several types of microorganisms would appear which, although distantly related, would be rather distinct. In particular, it might be difficult to trace intermediate ancestral forms, since these would only have existed on the sender planet, not on Earth. Of these distinct forms we should not be surprised to find one which resembled the blue-green algae, since this has independently been suggested as a good candidate for an effective primitive organism.

Now, it is perhaps remarkable that these are all features of the early fossil record or of the early evolutionary trees deduced from the study of present-day molecules. The earlier fossils, so far, do indeed resemble the blue-green algae. They date to a relatively early time in the life of the earth, so early that one is surprised to find them fully formed at that stage. Attempts to trace back molecular family trees seem, at the present time, to lead back to several distinct families which appear rather distant from each other (Crick 144–145).

What is truly remarkable is the fact that there is not one single species or organism that evolutionists can point to as the first living thing. Crick candidly points out that using their evolutionary presupposition regarding simplicity as a sign of antiquity in the development of the organism, there are several distinct families of organisms, which, from an evolutionary standpoint, are in fact irreconcilable as having come from a common source.

That leaves Crick with only one option: These organisms must have been deposited here simultaneously and fully formed at the time. The problem is twofold. First, these organisms are so complex that there is little chance of such complexity developing by random chance. Second, the organisms at that level are so numerous and impossible to interconnect from an evolutionary standpoint due to their diversity that it is baffling to evolutionists. These organisms could not have come from a single ancestor. If they had, there would be greater similarities among them. That would mean they would have to concede to not one beginning but many beginnings developing at the same time. If the odds were so immense against the formation of one, what would be the odds against the formation of many life forms at once?

Crick is well aware of this difficulty and thus admits that the development of life is "almost a miracle." He uses the term, "almost a miracle" because miracles don't happen in an atheistic evolutionary framework. Well, he is getting there.

Crick also took a blind leap of faith and escaped reason when he came up with his controversial directed panspermia hypothesis in order to explain why life appears suddenly and so complex, even in the supposed relatively simple unicellular level. The difficulty in assuming that by random selection these incredibly complex biological cells were formed invariably points to a designer. Since Crick cannot bring himself to admit the presence of this designer, he must reach beyond reason to try to force his presupposition into the facts, a task that is inconsistent with the scientific process.

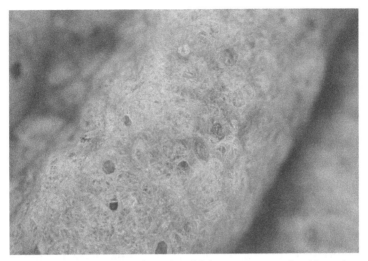

The simple blue-green algae that Crick proposes we should send
into space in his directed panspermia theory

Needless to say, the theory of directed panspermia does nothing
to answer the question of origin other than move the enigma back
one more step. It is, however, a convenient step for evolutionists,
for it is not possible to scientifically observe the evolution of life on
another planet.

Give me a break! Is this supposedly a scientific explanation for
the origin of life having developed on other planets any more testable,
credible, or scientific than intelligent design? By the way, who created
the aliens? Here is another example of presuppositional bias intended
to categorically ignore the obvious? This is another prime example
of displacement rationalization. Certainly, no rational thinker could
consider this assumption as anything less than speculative wish
projection of the highest magnitude.

Junk DNA and Vestigial Organs

On the Science channel, in a program hosted by Morgan Freeman
called "Through the Wormhole," a prominent cosmology theore-
tician said that aliens may have planted within us a code such as

the code we sent to deep space on the gold disks in the *Voyager 1* spacecraft.

This code, he said, could be imbedded in the junk DNA within our cells, waiting for our evolutionary process to reach a point where intelligence will be able to detect it. The assumption is that the DNA that is too difficult to form through random processes must have been given to our world by aliens. Well, he is close. It was, indeed, placed there in order for us to understand the omnipotence and omniscience of our Creator, the only being not bound to our planet or even our universe.

Evolutionists now claim that intelligent design is not a scientific hypothesis because it cannot make predictions. Here are two predictions: (1) There is no such thing as junk DNA; and (2) There is no such thing as vestigial organs. God does not produce junk DNA. God does not design vestigial organs without any purpose or function. Nothing that God does is without significance.

This truth does not negate the fact that some DNA may have been corrupted by mutations. That is evidence of the fall in the garden and the second law of thermodynamics. But the prediction of the evolutionary hypothesis that stipulates that many useless chromosomes in our DNA will be found is false. This does not point to accidental processes but to our ignorance of their true purpose.

If evolutionists could prove that there is such a thing as junk DNA, then they would prove that it has no intelligent design. If they can prove that there is such a thing as a truly vestigial organ without any function, then they could prove that it has no intelligent design. But these evolutionary claims are, in fact, based on ignorance.

Many of these genes erroneously labeled as junk DNA have been found to perform vital functions, including the regulation and expression of the information for building proteins. These non-protein coding regions of the genome function are much the same as a software program that regulates how other information in the system is processed.

As William Dembski explained and predicted in 1988: "On an evolutionary view we expect a lot of useless DNA. If, on the other hand, organisms are designed, we expect DNA, as much as possible, to exhibit function." The discovery in recent years that non-protein-coding DNA performs a diversity of important biological functions has confirmed this prediction. It also decisively refutes prominent critics of intelligent design—including Shermer, Miller, and Kitcher—who have continued to argue (each as recently as 2008) that the genome is composed of mostly useless DNA.

Contrary to their claims, recent scientific discoveries have shown that non-protein-coding regions of the genome direct the production of the RNA molecules that regulate the use of the protein-coding regions of DNA. Cell and genome biologists have also discovered that these supposedly "useless" non-protein-coding regions of the genome: (1) regulate DNA replication, (2) regulate transcription, (3) mark sites for programmed rearrangements of genetic material, (4) influence the proper folding and maintenance of chromosomes, (5) control the interactions of chromosomes with the nuclear membrane (and matrix), (6) control RNA processing, editing, and splicing, (7) modulate translation, (8) regulate embryological development, (9) repair DNA, and (10) aid in immunodefense or fighting disease among other functions. In some cases, "junk" DNA has even been found to code functional genes. Overall, the non-protein-coding regions of the genome function much like an operating system in a computer that can direct multiple operations

> *simultaneously. Indeed, far from being "junk," as materialistic theories of evolution assumed, the non-protein-coding DNA directs the use of other information in the genome, just as an operating system directs the use of the information contained in various application programs stored in a computer (Meyer 407).*

Ken Miller claimed in *Finding Darwin's God* that the genome contains regions evolutionists assume are "gene deserts," which have been proved to be more like regions of "oasis" that are indispensible for life. They regulate multiple biological programs necessary in order for life to exist. The same can be said for these supposedly vestigial organs; as we learn more about the biochemical molecular level of biological processes, we are finding that vestigial organs do have vital functions.

Brilliant people who begin with false assumptions can only arrive at falsehoods.

> *Brilliant and erudite reasoning may produce abhorrent conclusions if they proceed from a faulty starting point. A scientist who refuses to acknowledge facts that he knows are true can hardly be expected to arrive at sound conclusions. Any reasoning process that begins with a denial of the known and proceeds on the basis of prejudice can hardly produce light, no matter how lucid and cogent the argument may proceed after the initial error is made (Sproul 65).*

The renowned Dean Kenyon, professor of biology at San Francisco State University, candidly admits as much in the foreword to Charles Thaxton's landmark book *The Mystery of Life's Origin* that shook the halls of biology to the very core. The book is the product of the combined minds of three men of impeccable reputations in their three respective fields. Charles Thaxton is a chemist, Walter Bradley is a material scientist, and Roger Olsen is a geochemist. Kenyon wrote:

> If the author's criticisms are valid, one might ask, why have they not been recognized or stressed by workers in the field? I suspect that part of the answer is that many scientists would hesitate to accept the authors' conclusion that it is fundamentally implausible that unassisted matter and energy organized themselves into living systems. Perhaps these scientists fear that acceptance of this conclusion would open the door to the possibility (or the necessity) of a supernatural origin of life. Faced with the prospect many investigators would prefer to continue in their search for a naturalistic explanation of the origin of life *along the lines marked out over the last few decades, in spite of the many serious difficulties of which we are now aware.* Perhaps the fallacy of scientism is more widespread than we like to think.
>
> *One's presuppositions about the origin of life, and especially the assumption that this problem will ultimately yield to a persistent application of current methodology, can certainly influence which lines of evidence and argument one chooses to stress, and which are played down or avoided altogether* (emphasis added) *(Thaxton et al. viii).*

Kenyon hits on a very basic truth: If we begin our scientific investigation already convinced of the end results, not much objective science can take place during any experimental investigation. The metaphysical worldview of scientism has *a priori* excluded the possibility of intelligence being a factor in discovering the origin of the mystery of life. That is not true science.

Darwinism is not a scientific theory; it is a metaphysical theory using science as a means to promote its atheistic underlying worldview.

CHAPTER 8

●●●

A DESIGNER MUST EXIST

The monolithic control of public education in our Western culture by the Darwinist paradigm is absolute. Practically all the approved philosophy textbooks treat the intelligent design argument as an anachronistic debate that has been settled by the writings of David Hume since the 1700s.

> Hume refuted the classical design argument in biology by showing that it depends on a flawed analogy between living forms and human artifacts. In his Dialogues Concerning Natural Religion, Hume admits that artifacts derive from intelligent artificers and that biological organisms have certain similarities to complex human artifacts. Eyes and pocket watches both depend on the functional integration of many precisely configured parts. Nevertheless, he argues, biological organisms also differ from human artifacts—they reproduce themselves, for example—and

*the advocates of the design argument fail to take these
dissimilarities into account.* Since uniform experience teaches that organisms always come from other
organisms, Hume argues that analogical arguments
really ought to suggest that organisms ultimately
come from an infinite regress of earlier organisms
or from some eternally existent primeval organism
(perhaps a giant spider or vegetable) not a transcendent mind (emphasis added) *(Meyer 383–384).*

At the time Hume wrote his rebuttal to the classical design
argument, naturalists believed in the steady state theory, which
stipulated that our universe was infinite in space-time. The idea of
an infinite regression of living things was presumed to be possible.
Hume was wrong. Einstein taught us that the universe is not infinite
in either time or space. It had a beginning a finite time ago. Life,
therefore, could not have reproduced from infinity within a closed
universe as he erroneously assumed. Hence, the reproductive
property of life cannot exempt it from a beginning. His argument
is now defunct. At some point after the creation of our universe, life
began, and the geologic record tells us that it was sudden and global.
It's called the Cambrian explosion.

Is it rational to believe that an eternally existent organism of a
lower level life form (such as a spider or tomato) gave forth life and
then died and disappeared, leaving no trace? If it died, it was not
eternally existent. If it was eternally existent, as he so dogmatically
declared, then we would have access to it today. Hume was not
reasoning; he was rationalizing in order to promote his naturalistic
presupposition. That is not called science. It is called propaganda.

The empirical reality is that at some point, the universe was
created. Before that point, nothing existed—not time, not matter or
energy, not even spatial dimensions. At that point, the universe was
without life and then life appeared suddenly and abundantly. If we

are to accept Hume's reasoning that uniform experience shows that life comes only from other life, then the only option left is not his eternally existent primeval organism. That life-giving being must stand outside of our finite cage we call the universe, because nothing in our material universe could have lived through the Big Bang. Our universe began as a hot ball of plasma. That eternally living being that Hume theorized about could only be God, who is not bound to the confines of our universe.

Hume was correct that life only comes from life in our observable reality. Dead molecules do not magically self-organize into a living organism. And since our universe had a beginning, something had to exist before our universe that caused it to begin. If there was truly nothing before the Big Bang, there could be nothing now. Is it not more rational to deduce that it was an eternal living organism that was of higher intelligence than the massively complex nature of the universe it created?

The intellectual absurdities of Hume's anachronistic arguments for a materialistic genesis for life are made evident by our modern scientific knowledge of both the macroworld and the nanoworld. The macroworld is finite and filled with symmetry and universal laws of physics, which directly imply it was not the product of random transpositions but of willful design. The nanoworld is also filled with symmetry and run by universal laws such as the law of conservation. We have seen in the previous chapters that living things in our world are replete with numerous codes that govern their metabolism.

Both symmetry and codes are proof of an intelligent, previsioned, willful design and not a dysteleological or randomly ordered reality. A primeval organism that is not infinite in nature, as Hume suggested and even insisted, does not exist—or more accurately, it cannot exist because our universe is finite. And yet college philosophy textbooks continue to herald Hume's critique as the nail in the coffin of the design argument.

It utterly amazes me that the obvious inference to intelligent design displayed by all living organisms is nonchalantly categorically ignored by evolutionary scientists. In our everyday lives, we are habitually confronted with situations that we automatically understand are due to intelligent design. We could not function in life if our brains could not infer the obvious in daily situations.

In a New York subway, there was once graffiti painted on the wall that said, "Frodo lives." Thousands of New Yorkers filed by those words and read them every day on the way to and from work or school. Some may not have known that Frodo is a character in J.R. R. Tolkien's novel, *Lord of the Rings*. But every person who read that 10-letter message knew, without a shadow of a doubt, that the message was the product of intelligent action.

Not one sane person believed that a paintbrush accidentally fell into a bucket of paint and, through random ordering, fell against the wall and wrote "Frodo lives." Why? Our human experience has taught us that such information-rich code could not arise accidentally. It is not the product of random processes. It is the product of an intelligent mind that wanted to convey a message.

When my children were younger, we visited Stone Mountain in Georgia and ran up the gradual inclined slope all the way to the top. I held the hand of my little David (the youngest at the time), who made it all the way to the top. Stone Mountain is a solid piece of granite that rises into the air just east of Atlanta. Along the way to the top, we saw boulders of many shapes worn down by wind, rain, and time. My four boys had great fun climbing and jumping off the multi-shaped boulders. But from the restaurant at the top, we could see the other side of the mountain, which was a steep, almost perfectly perpendicular cliff.

On the surface of that cliff were the shapes of three men riding on horseback. They took up about three acres on the side of the mountain. The figure on the left was Jefferson Davis, president of the Confederate States of America during the Civil War. In the middle was

Confederate General Robert E. Lee, and behind him was Confederate General Thomas J. "Stonewall" Jackson. Lee's horse was so large that you could fit two school buses end to end on its hindquarter. At the lodge, I saw a photograph of a table on Lee's shoulder at which 12 men were dining (by the way, I am a staunch enemy of any kind of slavery, so do not in any way misread my illustration).

Perhaps millions of people have seen this immense carving over the years. I guarantee you that not one person has left Stone Mountain believing that natural forces through random processes carved those figures.

Why? Can natural forces like wind and rain carve rocks? Of course they can. The many boulders my children and I jumped off during our hike to the top were all carved by natural forces. So why would we not think that the carvings of these three men and their horses were also created by natural forces? Because we recognized immediately that there was specified complexity in those carvings.

We recognized their faces from historical data. From our own memory banks, we recognized that it was horses they were sitting on. That coded information was immediately recognized in our brains, and we automatically inferred intelligent causes for the phenomenon.

We immediately understood that no amount of time could change the outcome of natural forces to create such specified information. Natural forces can create repetitive functions that carry little information. They are mere complexity, not specified complexity. We can see this in the patterns of the rocks in the Grand Canyon. Sometimes the wind carves spectacularly beautiful and odd-shaped rocks, but they do not possess the highly specified information found in the Stone Mountain carvings that carry a coded message.

Sometimes my kids and I would sprawl out on the grass and study the curious shapes of clouds that, in our imagination, resembled the general forms of animals. But the association between the shapes of those clouds was mainly due to imagination and not specific information. In the case of the carvings on Stone Mountain, we can see specifically designed features that allow us to differentiate one face from another. That is specified information and is attributable only to an intelligent cause.

We can also attribute simple complexity to chance. For example, if I toss a silver dollar into the air 20 times, chances are it will land roughly half the time on each side. My chances are one in two every time I toss it. If, however, it lands on the same side all 20 times it could still be chance, although much less probable. At that point, you would be looking at me askance, wondering what trick I'm using. As I increase the number of times I toss the coin, I decrease the chances of it landing on the same side all the time.

If I were to toss a coin a thousand times and each time it landed on the same side, you would immediately know that the coin was weighted. A rational mind would immediately suspect that the coin had been infused with some specified information designed by intelligence from the onset. The point here is that even a single procedure, if it must be sequenced in a specified order, becomes specified complexity, and chance is no longer a plausible mechanism as that sequence becomes large.

> If an object or event is both complex and specified, then we should attribute it to intelligent design. By contrast, Dembski notes that we typically attribute to chance low- or intermediate-probability events that do not exhibit discernible patterns. We typically attribute to necessity highly probable events that recur repeatedly in a regular lawlike way (Meyer 354).

If we go beyond that and deal with more than one procedure, which is sequenced and at the same time interrelated in a closed loop system, the complexity would be dramatically much greater. That is what I call integrated complexity.

What is integrated specified complexity? Let me give you an example of an integrated complex system. Suppose I set up a mechanical lever that, after being cocked from a distance of three feet, could throw a coin to land on a second lever, each time landing heads up. And suppose that upon landing on that second lever, it released a marble down a slide into a spinning, drum-shaped container. The marble is perfectly round and the density is perfectly homogenous. The topless, drum-shaped container is bound by a perfectly smooth, round wall that contains seven holes of the exact same size, equally dispersed and numbered accordingly.

Now suppose I pull the trigger on the first lever, releasing the coin. But it not only has to land on the same side face up, it also has to land on the second lever in order to trigger the marble, which in turn must land in the spinning drum-shaped container and then precisely every time fall into hole number 7. Once the marble lands in hole number 7, the weight of the marble triggers an electric current that releases the next coin in the first lever and starts the process all over again.

Each step requires a great deal of specified information to engineer it and cause it to function perfectly every time. But each step is interdependent on the previous step. Without all the steps functioning precisely as designed through the specified information the engineer had to calculate, the process would not come to fruition. If all but the last step worked, then it would not be a closed loop system. All processes must work as specified in order for the closed loop system to continue the process.

That would be an example of integrated specified complexity, which is much higher in specified information. What are the chances that the coin would be tossed in the air 20 times, land on the lever, and send the marble into hole number 7 as the drum is spinning— each and every time?

If you could quantify the force on that coin, determine the arc necessary for it to land on the lever, create a mechanical arm that could consistently produce that exact force, and time the rate of the spin so you could time the throw at the exact moment the marble would hit the spinning round canister in order for it to enter exactly and only into the seventh hole, then it could be done.

But the enormous amount of specified information necessary that must be calculated in order for this to happen exactly the same way 20 times in a row is enormous. Only through intelligence could it be done. It cannot be accomplished by random chance. This is *integrated specified complexity*, which requires even more specified information than just specified complexity because of the interrelatedness of the several systems within it. And this is exactly what we find in the simplest living cell.

Integrated specified complex systems are super rich in specified information. Random processes cannot create them. They are indicative of intelligent design. There are no known natural causes that can create this super rich amount of specified information. No rational human being would expect such an elaborate system to be formed by accidental means.

In other words, beyond specified complexity is *integrated specified complexity*, which compounds the complexity exponentially because it entails multiple systems of specified information that form a closed loop system in which all the functions are necessary in order for the entire system to function. It therefore must be recognized as undeniable proof of intelligent design. And in fact, we habitually do so every time we are confronted with such systems without any hesitation during our normal everyday experiences. It is logical.

A living cell is a marvel of multiple systems of integrated specified complexity. I am speaking of the many biochemical processes such as the closed loop systems of gene expression and the production of ATP for energy, and so on. Even its individual structural components such as ribosomes and the double helix DNA are complexly specified and integrated systems within the overall integrated gene expression system.

The enormous specificity of the cell and its integrated specified components cannot be blindly resigned to the happenstance of random ordering. The exact sequences of the elements create amino acids. The amino acids must all be left-handed. These left-handed amino acids must each be composed in correctly specified sequences in order to make a specific protein. And this protein must be folded in a specific sequence in order for its shape and active site to be located at the proper place so it will be the right kind of protein, unique from the variety of thousands of proteins that perform all the specific functions within a living cell.

This specified information is carried in the genetic code within the DNA, which is composed of a double helix structure carrying this coded message of specified information that must be transcribed, then translated, and then applied in the synthesis of these exactly ordered proteins by the ribosomal machinery, which is itself made of proteins and uses a variety of specialized proteins in the manufacturing process. The functioning of the whole is interdependent on the sequencing of each of the integrated components.

Although we may find these components independently, there can be no life without the ability to cohesively function interdependently. It is that integration of all the interrelated complex systems that compounds the amount of specified information necessary and roundly disqualifies random ordering as a possibility in its origins.

Here is another example of an integrated system in which several systems of specified complexity are interrelated, such as in a single cell.

Imagine the largest bank vault in the universe.

System 1: It is only one story tall, but it has a door that is 35,700 yards long made of solid steel.

System 2: On the large solid steel door, there are 238 large panels, each 150 yards long.

System 3: Inside these 238 large panels, there are 150 smaller panels, each one yard long from side to side, that fill each large panel.

System 4: Inside each of the 150 smaller panels, there is a variety of spinning tumblers with the letters C, O, N, and H. One set of letters in each tumbler is colored red, and the other set is colored green. By spinning that tumbler, we can land on either the red letters or the green letters.

In order to open the door, each of those spinning tumblers has to have exactly the right combination (System 4) so each of the smaller panels (System 3) can move one tumbler. Each small panel must move its tumbler until that first large panel (System 2) moves its bigger tumbler. This same procedure has to happen for all the 238 large panels (System 2). That is, all of them have to go through the opening of the smaller panels, choosing exactly the right color and letter in order to eventually move each of their bigger tumblers. Then—and only then—will the door (System 1) open.

Let's imagine that inside the vault is a long piece of paper with the exact combination. It would be nice if we had access to that combination in order to open the door, but we must first open the door before we can see the combination. Let's call the combination the software of the program.

System 1 represents the cell. These 238 large panels (System 2) represent the 238 proteins of the smallest theoretical cell. The 150 smaller panels (System 3) represent the number of amino acids in a small protein. The spinning tumblers (System 4) with the letters C, O, N, and H represent the elements carbon, oxygen, nitrogen, and hydrogen, which, in specified sequences, make up the exact amino acid.

Some numbers are in red. They are the ones that produce a right-handed amino acid, which are unusable for life. Although the elements are not actually right-handed or left-handed (that applies only to the amino acid molecule), the illustration represents the chances of these elements coming together in such a configuration. In other words, the combination in the System 4 tumblers must not only always land on green but also land in the right sequence of the elements in order to build that specific amino acid that builds a protein that is exclusively made of left-handed amino acids.

The knob is like a roulette wheel. You can only spin it once and let it arbitrarily land on whatever letter it falls. You cannot consciously choose the number you prefer, or it would not be random ordering. To choose would be intelligent design.

Imagine the odds of going through each panel, tumbler by tumbler and spinning each knob, panel by panel throughout the entire 35,700 yards of that huge vault door. Each spin must land on exactly the right number and right color time after time until all panels have been completed. Then and only then will the vault door open.

Can you honestly say that in this complex integrated system chance could result in the exact combination to open that huge door? More importantly, if you examined the integrated structure of the door and its functionality, would you conclude that random processes could create such integrated, specified complexity in the hardware of the vault?

Since we immediately recognize that the door has a purpose, we assume teleological origins. If life and organs in living things are purposeful, and we can hardly describe an organ otherwise, then how did purposeless random ordering create purpose? Reason shouts to us that a designer must exist.

What these computer algorithms used by evolutionists to prove evolution do is magically reach into the vault ahead of time and get the combination written on the piece of paper. They know before they begin what combination they must end up with. They then input the specified information into the program and select the appropriate sequences that would eventually lead to the proper combination. That is not random ordering and natural selection!

In other words, they devise software to come up with a pre-known precise combination—their target sequence. But this cannot then be ascribed to chance. Intelligence must input the exact combination *a priori* to the equation. I apologize beforehand for being so blunt, but in my mind, that can only be construed as nothing more than cheating and deceptive evolutionary propaganda.

Biomimetics and the Argument from Ignorance

The design of the living cell cannot be accounted for through random ordering. It is the evidence of a master biological engineer. Today, the science of biomimetics, which recognizes the superior design of living organisms and seeks to mimic their engineering in order to produce more efficient designs, is big business.

For example, the invention of Velcro by Swiss engineer George de Mestral was inspired by burrs that stuck to his pants after taking a hike with his dog in 1941. Viewing the spur through his microscope, he was amazed at the tiny hooks at the end of each one that allowed it to stick to surfaces with loops.

Let's look at other examples. The magnificent aerodynamic design of the boxfish inspired Mercedes Benz to design a bionic concept car whose aerodynamic properties boost its gas mileage to 70 miles per gallon. And the amazing design of the whale flipper inspired biomechanist Frank Fish to design a wind turbine blade that enhances its power at slower than conventional wind speeds. And the list goes on ad infinitum.

From an engineering standpoint, the fabulously complex biological systems often baffle people's attempt to reproduce or even understand their ingenious composition. In order for the abalone shell to be so hard, for example, 15 different proteins perform a carefully choreographed dance that several teams of our most intelligent, well-educated scientists had not comprehended as of 2008.

The amazing strength of the spider's silk lies not only in the precise concoction of the proteins of which it is composed but also in the intricate mysteries of its delicate spinnerets. These little creatures have 600 spinning nozzles that weave seven different kinds of silk into incredibly resilient configurations whose tensile strength is unmatched by anything made by humans.

The gecko's uncanny ability to walk on ceilings (without magnetic shoes) is another engineering miracle. Geckos possess billions of tiny nanohairs that grow on slightly larger hairs, which in turn grow on toe ridges, which in turn are part of bigger toe pads, and so on up to the scale of a centimeter. This ingenious, seven-part hierarchy is so intricate that currently we cannot hope to reproduce it. And yet the DNA of the lowly gecko effortlessly reproduces all of this with the precision that a state-of-the-art factory cannot match.

Human beings, with the most advanced brains in the world, still cannot compete with the sophistication of the designs found in nature. If our intelligence is inferior in engineering skill and the creative versatility of the design in such magnificently efficient and elaborate creations, how can we rationally ascribe it to random ordering?

That rational human beings could possibly believe that random and undirected chemical processes have, by chance, fortuitously developed these engineering marvels is amazing to me. It is the very essence of a fanciful fairy tale, complete with magic wands and fairy dust.

The amazing design of living things is so incredible that humans with all their supposedly superior intellect have been forced to admit that they are engineering masterpieces. Even with the use of electron-and-atomic-force microscopes, microtomography, and modern high-speed computers, we are only beginning to peer into nature's magnificently engineered microscale and nanoscale. The evolutionary mechanism of chance is simply not adequate to explain this highly symmetrical and elegant phenomenon. It cannot be denied that an intelligence of unfathomable magnitude designed our genetic code and the marvelous engineering of all living organisms.

When faced with this clear exposition regarding the absence of natural sources for specified complexity, Darwinists religiously turn to their favorite evasion tactic—the argument from ignorance. Claiming that our arguments of intelligent design are based solely on our present absence of any natural or material cause for specified information, they immediately suggest that our arguments are thus based on ignorance. They cleverly insinuate that our foundation for believing in intelligent design is the absence of knowledge.

The opposite is the case. We are not ignorant of how information arises. It is our knowledge of the absence of natural processes to create such structured specified complexity that leads us to propose that intelligence is the most rational alternative as a primal cause. To deny this is to deny what we do know empirically about specified complexity in our real space-time universe. To believe against all known physical data that natural processes can produce specified complexity is to ignore reality. That is ignorance, literally. It is the evolutionist that argues from ignorance.

Based on our accumulated knowledge of established cause-and-effect relationships regarding specified complexity, we can say with certainty that there are no known natural causes that can create specified, information-rich complexity. The cause-and-effect relationship has been thoroughly tested and vetted without being successfully countered even one time. Thus, the argument is not based on lack of knowledge but on the accumulated knowledge of tested experiments.

This argument from ignorance is nothing more than clever semantics. For instance, someone may propose that humans, without any mechanical aid, can jump off a skyscraper and fly like a bird, defying gravity. I could then counter with this: After many trials and tests, there have been no instances in history where a human, relying completely on natural forces, could flap his or her hands and fly.

My opponent would then say this: That is an argument from ignorance. Just because you have no knowledge that humans can fly does not mean they cannot fly. My answer would be this: Show me. I'll bring the ladder. It is the same answer I give to Darwinists: Show me how natural forces can produce specified, information-rich complexity. Show me one single evolutionary mechanism that can be documented to change one species into another.

It is the knowledge garnered from repeated attempts to fly without mechanical aids that has brought me to the rational conclusion that humans cannot fly unassisted by mechanical devices. It is knowledge, not ignorance, that leads us to reason that intelligent design must have created the genetic code.

Using the uniformitarian concept properly, without its superfluous evolutionary-inspired anti-catastrophe component, we can say that repeated and prolonged observations of cause and effect have consistently and without exception shown that no natural causes can produce this information-rich specified complexity.

At the same time, we have also observed and tested that intelligence can cause this information-rich, specified system of complexity. Hence, we can deduce rationally that the present is the key to the past and that intelligence must have been the cause in the past. Intelligence offers a superior explanatory power as a proposed cause and is therefore the more rational choice. That is not ignorance; it is reason based on positive knowledge.

The truth is that naturalists, evolutionists, and Darwinists really know that subconsciously. That is why the gold disk in *Voyager 1* sent our cosmic message in a bottle in codes. They know that if any aliens come upon such specified complexity, they will rationally assume that an intelligence with higher consciousness was the cause of those codes. But because naturalists refuse to give up their moral autonomy, they cannot accept the idea that intelligence brought forth our universe.

Their clever semantic deception by their argument from ignorance is nothing more than a rationalization to fortify their presuppositional bias against the notion of a creator. That, too, is ignorance. Theirs is an argument from ignorance.

Another common argument made by Darwinists is that the proponents of intelligent design are contradicting the scientific process by stipulating that natural causes could never bring forth specified complexity rich in information. Their argument is that good scientists should never say never or they will run the risk of being disproved with later discoveries.

The statement that a good scientist should never say never stipulates that the first *never* is a valid statement. If it is valid in one case, it can be valid in another. And in fact, we can observe this in science.

For instance, I can say that 2+2 can never equal anything other than 4. That is a rational and scientifically verifiable truth. I can say that according to Einstein's equations, matter within our visible spatial dimensions can never travel faster than the speed of light. That is absolutely mathematically accurate and true. I can say that human beings, without the protection of pressurized mechanical assistance to artificially maintain their normal biohabitat such as space suits or space capsules, could never survive the deep space environment. So it is not true that science can never say never.

Nevertheless, what we are stating is not that natural, material causes can never create specified complexity. What we are saying is that thus far, it has never been shown as a model that actually works. Therefore, the more rational proposition is what stands the test of reality, or what has been shown to work.

To believe otherwise is to make a leap of faith unsubstantiated by science. Such a leap of faith, unsupported by empirical data, can only be viewed as unscientific to the core. It is the Darwinist speculation that stipulates that such specified complexity came from random, unscientific ordering because it has no empirical data to support it.

Richard Dawkins in his book *The God Delusion* argues that the intelligent design hypothesis fails to explain anything since it evokes an infinite regress of causes, each necessary to explain the other. In other words, if the specified complexity of life requires an intelligence to design it, then we must ask who designed the designer?

Dawkins fails to understand that the point of the intelligent design argument is not to prove the existence of God but to prove that life could not have arisen from random ordering. Only an intelligent designer could rationally have produced such specified complexity. That is why intelligent design should not be banned from the public school system. It does not invoke God as the primal cause. It simply reflects the scientific evidence that necessitates intelligence as the cause for life.

Dawkins automatically and unwarrantedly assumes that this higher intelligence must also be finite and therefore in need of another designer. But that is nothing more than ignorance.

Since science has shown us conclusively that at a certain point space-time and matter had a beginning, then the primal cause must stand outside of space-time and matter. The primal cause must therefore be infinite if it is not trapped inside of space-time. All other finite causes are therefore irrational. That logical conclusion comes not from lack of knowledge or ignorance but from positive knowledge of empirical reality. The other choice left for Dawkins is that nothing instantly created everything. How is that in any way a rational scientific statement?

He fails to consider that reason leads us to the possibility and the only logical conclusion that this higher intelligence that designed the universe and life must be an eternal being that needed no other designer. But the specific knowledge of all the attributes and who that being is cannot be answered by the intelligent design argument. Only if that eternal being communicated with humans could we know the specifics of who that being is.

The general revelation gathered from the observation of our universe can lead us to understand that this infinite higher intelligence cannot be the god of pantheism because it had to exist prior to the universe. The god of the pantheist is trapped within our finite universe. It can tell us that it is not the god of the deists because of the active role this higher intelligence had to play in the ongoing process of creation.

The evidence of this ongoing activity is the isotropic and homogeneous nature of our universe. Had randomness been the guiding factor in our universe after the Big Bang, it would have created a universe with a lumpy texture that would have led to the overwhelming formation of black holes rather than galaxies. The selection of the fine-tuned parameters that rule our physical universe in such a way that it could be inhabited by life cannot be rationally attributed to random chance. This topic is discussed in greater detail in my second book *Supersymmetry or Chaos* and in *The Ancient Wisdom—The New Age, Occultism, and Pantheism.*

Nevertheless, this general revelation cannot give us the particulars of the character of this higher intelligence. For this, only propositional revelation can bring us to the particulars. Unless this infinite primal cause chose to reveal itself through propositional revelation, humankind could not through reason come to understand the particulars of this higher intelligence's character. That topic will be covered in *The Coming Prince of Peace.*

Nevertheless, Dawkin's argument in no way negates the validity of the intelligent design argument. It does not do away with the statistical improbability of randomness creating such specified complexity as the gene expression system. It does not negate the need for a primal cause that stands outside of space-time and matter. It is not necessary to give a complete explanation of the nature and origin of this higher intelligence or primal cause to prove that it is a legitimate cause. Columbus did not have to have a map of the Americas complete with rivers, mountains, and accurate coastlines to prove that the Earth was not flat.

Einstein did not have to provide the evidence from quantum mechanics to prove that Newtonian physics was flawed. He did not have to provide the specifics of the Big Bang to show that the universe had a beginning. That specific knowledge came later as the mathematics of his brilliant equation was extrapolated to its logical conclusions.

Reason tells us that a designer must exist. Now, even some evolutionists are admitting the obvious while still trying to remain steadfast in their evolutionary presupposition. Since the probability that our universe could have developed through mere chance's chemical processes is so remote that the naturalist must come up with a primal cause that, while being the catalyst of this creation, would still remain within their cherished materialistic paradigm (within a closed system). This in a nutshell is the anthropic cosmological principle.

> A designer must exist. Yet, for whatever reasons, a few astrophysicists suggest that perhaps the designer is not God. But, if the designer is not God, who is? The alternative, some suggest, is man himself.
>
> The evidence proffered for man as the creator comes from an analogy to delayed-choice experiments in quantum mechanics where it appears that the observer can influence the outcome of quantum mechanical events. With every quantum particle there is an associated wave. This wave represents the probability of finding the particle at a particular point in space. Before the particle is detected there is no specific knowledge of its location—only a probability of where it might be. But, once the particle has been detected, its exact location is known. In this sense, the act of observation is said by some to give reality to the particle....
>
> In other words, the universe creates man, but man through his observations of the universe brings the universe into reality (Ross 134).

Imagine that! Humans are the creators of the universe! How pathetic can you get? This theory has a more sinister side than most of the adherents realize. It brings into scientific acceptance one of the more fundamental elements of occult doctrine. According to this new hypothesis, the cosmic universe is, then, in this sense biocentric and ultimately an organic entity in itself. Today, "learned men of science" who once repudiated such talk as mystical and speculative are beginning to accept such a worldview.

> *The properties of matter and the course of cosmic evolution are now seen to be intimately related to the structure of the living being and to its activities; they become, therefore, far more important in biology than has previously been suspected.* For the whole evolutionary process, both cosmic and organic, is one, and the biologist may now rightly regard the Universe in its very essence as biocentric (emphasis added) *(L.J. Henderson quoted in Barrow and Tipler 146).*

The idea that the universe is biocentric is so much more appealing than a stark, lifeless, purposeless, meaningless, chaotic, materialistic machine-like reality. Henderson uses the term *biocentric* when, in fact, it is *anthropocentric*. It is humankind at the center of the universe if humans are the authors of it all.

Henderson avoids it because evolutionists have for centuries been castigating Christians and Jews, accusing them of being narcissistically anthropocentric because they believe that God created the universe for humans. But, in fact, Christians and Jews are not anthropocentric but rather deocentric. They believe that God is the center of reality and it is God who chose to make it so. Their opinion counts as nothing in this matter.

We are now approaching the dawning of another fundamental shift in paradigms in postmodern man. Those who have for so long been frustrated at the sterility of a mechanistic worldview are reaching out for something else. They are seeking a mystical component to their failed, sterile Darwinist worldview while attempting to remain fast within their naturalistic framework.

They cannot deny their intrinsic transcendent need, but they refuse to give up the naturalistic paradigm that gives them the freedom to create the moral framework of their own choosing. We are poised to take an even larger leap across the great divide into the irrational. Pierre Tielhard de Chardin has been one of the first and most influential prophets of this coming new age.

De Chardin conceptualized a tangential energy that is subject to the second law of thermodynamics and a radial energy that is regarded as a sort of psychic energy not subject to the second law of thermodynamics. He posited this to circumvent the obvious problem for the evolutionist; that is, the second law of thermodynamics is in contradiction to the evolutionary postulate that life evolves in ever increasing complexity.

This radial energy, he states, is subject to a universal law that runs contrary to the second law of thermodynamics and becomes more concentrated and more available with time. It is an energy that is present in all forms of matter in a rudimentary way. I find it quite ironic that the reductionists who once opposed the vitalists are now distorting the spiritual realm into a profaned form.

According to this pantheistic/occult worldview, that vital force is not limited to living things. The entire cosmos is possessed with a sort of vital force that is responsible to drive the evolution of life in an upward mode. But listen carefully, my friend. This is simply and explicitly nothing less than the occult doctrine of Akasha, Anima Mundi (the world soul), the Great Breath, the Architect, and the Paramatman all dressed up and masqueraded in scientific jargon. These are, in fact, all synonyms for Satan.

Here is a new twist on the vital force theory that fits squarely into occult theology. In this theory, the vital force resides not only in living things but also in inanimate matter. The universe is therefore not meaningless; it is now alive and filled with a "force." They have simply dressed the closed universe with a ghost in order to assuage their transcendental angst.

It is amazing to see those who were once ardent reductionists and staunch empiricists become cosmic vitalists. It is clear that the vast majority of evolutionary scientists seem to only be objective within the confines of the framework of their naturalistic presupposition—a closed universe. It is their primary metaphysical doctrine, and all science must conform to it. They are beginning to recognize that the very presupposition of naturalism limits their objectivity by categorically denying the possibility of any intervention outside of their naturalistic system from the very onset.

This negation of the supernatural was rationalized on the premise that humans cannot test or scientifically examine the supernatural realm. And yet, in complete contradiction to this premise, they accept as scientific (1) the anthropic cosmological principle, (2) the mystical view of the cosmos as an organism, and (3) the supposed existence of parallel universes.

It seems that their opposition does not really come from the notion of the untestability of the unknown but rather from their antipathy toward the existence of a supreme God. They can stomach the supernatural idea of cosmic vitalism because it does not rob them of their autonomy in moral choices.

It is logical that if the litmus test for the scientific process is limited to the realm of objects and processes that can be physically tested and directly observed, then much of reality would be overlooked. Moreover, even the concept of the existence of dark matter and dark energy must be discarded. In all fairness, to be consistent with this logic, evolutionists should abandon any attempt to explain the origin of the universe, for it too defies testing and scientific examination by the mere fact that it happened when they were not there.

All we are left with is the present existence, and therefore, we must extrapolate from the present facts. But in a naturalistic framework, what assurance do evolutionists have that their experience can be grounded in reality? And what universal law do they draw from that automatically considers the supernatural an illegitimate consideration? It is nothing more than a subjective choice predicated on their predisposed bias.

True science thrives on our ability to provide a reasonable and consistent explanation for experimental data—called hypothesis. But when data cannot be directly experienced, we must extrapolate from the known to the unobservable. But we must never limit any possible answers until they are ruled out by reason and not personal bias.

Part of the uniformitarian hypothesis is correct and helpful. We test theories by implementing experiments, and we assume that the results of those experiments are repeatable and constant universally. That, however, does not necessitate denying intelligence as the primal force that brought reality into existence. If the evidence we find today points to intelligence as the only possible logical and rational alternative, then what part of science prohibits that?

Therefore, if we are to attempt to understand our genesis, we must, through reason, build from the known a framework that remains consistent with empirical data. We must also be willing to objectively examine all possible solutions. All hypotheses that henceforth fail to remain consistent with observable data must be summarily discarded, no matter how much we like or dislike the hypothesis and no matter how popular the hypothesis is in our specific culture. That is the meaning of scientific integrity.

The postmodern disenchantment with the naturalistic worldview is driving many toward the acceptance of the supernatural, but their desire for moral autonomy limits the supernatural to a nebulous force and ignores God. Little do they understand that they are accepting an occult view that will have a significant impact on our future global society.

Our morality should not dictate our theology or our worldview. It should rather be the other way around. Reason and observed reality should determine our worldview, which in turn should determine our morality.

We must not deny the examination of all possible avenues in spite of our personal preferences. True scientific integrity demands that the model chosen to represent the observable facts must be discarded objectively when the empirical data do not correlate with the hypothesis. The tenacious refusal to do so must be viewed as unscientific and irrational. Such recalcitrant thinking is obviously emotionally influenced by an unwillingness to consider a scientific conclusion that does not square with a personal preconceived bias. That is the definition of subjective dogma and closed-minded bigotry. It is the epitome of self-imposed ignorance.

REFERENCES

Axe, Douglas. 2016. *Undeniable*. New York: Harper One.

Barrow, John D., and Frank J. Tippler. 1986. *The Anthropic Cosmological Principle*. Oxford: Oxford University Press.

Behe, Michael. 1996. *Darwin's Black Box*. New York: The Free Press.

Bendewald, Jim, with Frank Sherwin. 2004. *Evolution Shot Full of Holes*. Madison, WI: Evidence Press.

Bertalanffy, Ludwig Von. 1967. *Robots, Men, and Minds: Psychology in the Modern World*. New York: G. Braziller.

Brock, Thomas. 1979. *Biology of Microorganisms*, 3rd ed. Upper Saddle River, NJ: Prentice Hall.

Brooks, Jim. 1985. *Origins of Life*. Herts, England: Lion Books.

Coppedge, James F. 1993. *Evolution: Possible or Impossible*. Grand Rapids, MI: Zondervan.

Crick, Francis. 1981. *Life Itself, Its Origin and Nature*. New York: Simon & Shuster.

Darwin, Charles. 1859. *The Origin of Species by Means of Natural Selection, or the Preservation of Favored Races in the Struggle for Life*, 1st ed. London: John Murray.

Dawkins, Richard. 2009. *The Greatest Show on Earth*. New York: Free Press.

Dobzhansky, Theodosius. "Discussion of G. Schram's Paper." *In The Origins of Prebiological Systems and Their Molecular Matrices*, edited by Sidney Fox, 309–15. New York: Academic, 1965.

Dybvig, K., and L. L. Voelker. "Molecular Biology of Microplasmas." *Annual Review of Microbiology* 50 (October 1996): 25–57. https://doi.org/10.1146/annurev.micro.50.1.25.

Fox, Sidney W., ed. 1965. *The Origins of Prebiological Systems and of Their Molecular Matrices.* New York: Academic Press.

Greene, Brian. 2000. *The Elegant Universe.* New York: W.W. Norton & Company.

Guillen, Michael. 2015. *Amazing Truths.* Grand Rapids, MI: Zondervan.

Haeckel, Ernst. 1892. *The History of Creation, Volume 1.* New York: D. Appleton & Co.

Hawking, Stephen. 1988. *A Brief History of Time.* New York: Bantam Books.

Hull, D. E. "Thermodynamics and Kinetics of Spontaneous Generation." *Nature* 186, (May 1960).

Johnston, Ian. "Dogs Can Understand Human Speech, Scientists Discover." *Independent News.* (August 2016). http://www.independent.co.uk/news/science/dogs-can-understand-human-speech-scientists-say-a7216481.html.

Kendrew, J. C., G. Bodo, H. M. Dintzis, R. G. Parrish, H. Wyckhoff, and D. C. Phillips. "A Three-Dimensional Model of the Myoglobin Molecule Obtained by X-Ray Analysis." *Nature 181* (March 1958): 662–666.

Kenyon, Dean and Gary Steinman. 1969. *Biochemical Predestination.* New York: McGraw-Hill.

Kleene, Stephen Cole. 1967. *Mathematical Logic.* New York: John Wiley & Sons.

Meyer, Stephen C. 2009. *Signature in the Cell.* New York: Harper Collins.

Miller, Kenneth R. 1999. *Finding Darwin's God.* New York: Harper Perennial.

Morowitz, Harold J. 1968. *Energy Flow in Biology: Biological Organization as a Problem in Thermal Physics.* New York: New York Academic Press.

Newbigin, Leslie. 1986. Foolis*hness to the Greeks: The Gospel and Western Culture.* Grand Rapids, MI: Eerdman's Publishing Company.

Norman, Jeremy. "John Kendrew Reports the First Solution of the Three-Dimensional Molecular Structure of a Protein." *Historyof Information.com.* http://www.historyofinformation.com/expanded. php?id=3015.

Oparin, A.I. 1968. *Genesis and Evolutionary Development of Life.* New York: Academic Press.

Osborne, Hannah. "Brain Architecture: Scientists Discover 11 Dimensional Structures That Could Help Us Understand How the Brain Works." *Newsweek.* (June 2017). http://www.newsweek.com/ brain-structure-hidden-architecture-multiverse-dimensions-how-brain-works-624300.

Patiño, Henry. 2015. *Machine or Man.* Areli Media.

Patiño, Henry. 2018. *Supersymmetry or Chaos.* Areli Media.

Pearcey, Nancy. 2004. *Total Truth.* Wheaton, IL: Crossway Books.

Polanyi, Michael. *"Life's Irreducible Structures." Science 160,* no. 3834 (June 1968): 1308–1312. doi: 10.1126/science.160.3834.1308.

Polanyi, Michael. "Life Transcending Physics and Chemistry." *Chemical & Engineering News 45,* no. 35 (August 1967): 54–69. doi: 10.1021/cen-v045n035.p054.

Ponnamperuma, Cyril. "Chemical Evolution and the Origin of Life." *Nature* 201 (January 1964): 337–340.

Reimann, Michael W., Max Nolte, Martina Scolamiero, et al. "Cliques of Neurons Bound into Cavities Provide a Missing Link between Structure and Function." *Frontiers in Computational Neuroscience.* (June 2017). https://doi.org/10.3389/fncom.2017.00048.

Ross, Hugh. 1989. *The Fingerprint of God.* Orange, CA: Promise Publishing.

Sagan, Carl. 1980. *Cosmos: A Personal Voyage.* Public Broadcasting Stations. Television Series. Released September 28, 1980.

Schaeffer, Francis. 1968. *The God Who is There.* Downers, IL: Intervarsity Press.

Smith, Wesley J. 2004. *Consumer's Guide to a Brave New World.* San Francisco: Encounter Books.

Sproul, R. C. 1974. *The Psychology of Atheism.* Minneapolis, MN: Bethany Fellowship.

Tarnas, Richard. 1991. *The Passion of the Western Mind.* New York: Ballantine Books.

Thaxton, Charles B., Walter L. Bradley, and Roger Olsen. 1984. *The Mystery of Life's Origin.* Dallas, TX: Lewis and Stanley.

Thorpe, W. H. 1978. *Purpose in a World of Chance: A Biologist's View.* London: Oxford University Press.

Wikipedia, s.v. "Sidney W. Fox." Accessed January 28, 2019. https://en.wikipedia.org/wiki/Sidney_W._Fox.

Wilder-Smith, A. E. 1968. *Man's Origin, Man's Destiny: A Critical Survey of the Principles of Evolution and Christianity.* Wheaton, IL: Harold Shaw Publishers.

INDEX

A

Abdus Salam 76
abiogenesis 5
adenosine 88
ADP 156
A. E. Wilder-Smith 172
A. I. Oparin 113, 114, 142, 170, 178
Akasha 305
Albert Einstein 44, 64, 66, 81, 263, 265, 286, 300, 302
amino acids 78
Anima Mundi 305
anthropic cosmological principle 303
Antonie van Leeuwenhoek 5
Apollo 11 272
Aristotle 5
ATP 86, 90
Attila Andics 23, 24
Avida 238

B

Bathybius haeckelli 79
Benjamin Franklin 264
Ben Stein 231
bi-lipid membrane 82
biomimetics 296
Birkeland currents 14
bosons 70
brain 7, 17, 26, 28, 36
Brian Greene 67, 72, 74, 76

C

Carl Sagan 3, 9, 10, 188
Carl Woese 214
Charles Darwin 7, 79, 80, 81, 131, 133, 139, 141, 142, 209, 243, 246, 247, 248, 252, 253, 255, 256, 257, 258, 259, 261, 282
Charles Thaxton 82, 122, 127, 161, 183, 187, 188, 190, 191, 219, 220, 221, 282, 283
chemical affinities 123, 194, 204, 207, 208, 210, 212, 213
Christopher Adami 238
Clausius 191
codons 65, 92, 120, 129, 139
cokes 182, 184
cosmic vitalism 306
covalent bonds 75, 146
C. S. Lewis 36
C. Titus Brown 238
cytosine 88, 205, 216, 220

D

David Goodsell 136
David Hume 46, 285, 286, 287
deamination 216
Dean Kenyon 82, 195, 196, 197, 198, 199, 200, 210, 218, 219, 282, 283
Democritus 63
deocentric valuation 57, 58
directed panspermia 274, 276, 277, 278, 279
displacement 77, 236, 238
DNA 4, 9, 14, 65, 86, 87, 88, 89
DNA code 90, 125, 169, 192, 193, 225
Dorothy Hodgkin 106
Douglas Axe 170, 171, 258, 265, 266, 276
dualism 38
dysteleology 39, 40, 50, 220, 237, 242

E

Edwin Black 20, 21, 246
electromagnetic force 14, 72, 73, 76
electron shells 42, 74
Eötvös Loránd 23
Ernst Haeckel 79, 80, 81, 131, 133, 142
eugenics 18, 19, 20, 21, 22
eukaryotes 78, 107
Ev 237
Evolution by computers 229

F

formose reaction 217, 218
Francesco Redi 6
Francis Crick 100, 119, 122, 131, 169, 273
Frank Fish 296
Fred Hoyle 210
Freidrich Wöhler 6

G

Gary Steinman 195, 196, 197, 199
gene deserts 282
gene expression system 55, 85, 97, 98, 117, 118, 127, 149, 175, 177, 204, 302
Genesis Singularity 10, 13, 49
Genghis Khan 20
George de Mestral 296
gluons 70
glycolysis 134, 135, 156
gradualist 9, 14, 96, 177, 254
gravitons 70
gravity 10, 14, 32, 33, 70, 72, 164, 298
Gregoire Nicolis 209
GTP 134, 249
guanine 88, 205, 215, 216, 217, 220

H

haemoglobin 146
Harold J. Morowitz 155, 157, 159, 160, 163
Hitler 20
Hubble Constant 9
Hubble Space Telescope 273
Hugh Ross 303
Hull 168
Human Genome Project 274
Thomas Henry Huxley 79, 80, 131, 133, 142

I

Ilya Prigogine 209, 210
immune system iv, 256, 257, 258
Impotence of RNA 221
integral membrane proteins 83
integrated specified complexity 291, 292
irreducible complexity 257

J

James F. Coppedge 155, 157, 158, 159, 160, 162
James Watson 122, 126
J. B. S. Haldane 171, 178
J. D. Bernal 106
Jeremy Norman 107
Jim Brooks 144, 147, 183
J. J. Thompson 255
John D. Barrow 66, 174, 268, 269, 304
John Dalton 63
John Kendrew 105, 106, 107
Johnston 24
Judeo-Christian cosmological model 13, 14, 15, 61
junk DNA 279, 280

K

Kant 46
K. Dybvig 81
Ken Miller 185, 186, 216, 262, 263, 281, 282
Kenneth R. Miller 261
Kurt Gödel 47

L

Lawrence J. Henderson 172, 173, 174, 304
Lazzaro Spallanzani 6
left-handed amino acids 113, 114, 152, 155, 157, 158, 159, 166, 168, 181, 293, 295
Leslie Newbigin 45, 47, 53
Levinthal's paradox 104
lipids 84, 157
L. L. Voelker 81
Louis Pasteur 6, 78, 81, 172
Ludwig von Bertalanffy 193
Lyell 264

M

Mao Tse-tung 20
Margaret Sanger 18, 19, 21
Max Perutz 106
Michael Behe 246, 257, 261
Michael Guillen 10, 12
Michael Polanyi 200, 201, 202, 203, 205
Michael Reimann 270
mitochondria 86, 134, 136, 139, 255
Monera 79
mRNA 90, 91, 92, 93, 94, 122, 127, 128, 129, 130, 131, 132, 133, 189, 192, 208, 212, 223, 224
M-Theory 68
Muhammad 20
Murray Eden 166
Murray Gell-Mann 64
mycoplasma 78, 81, 82, 155
Mycoplasma hominis H39 155
myoglobin 105, 106, 107

N

Nancy Pearcey 19
Neil Armstrong 271, 272
neshama 14
Newton 32, 43, 44, 264, 266, 273
nucleotides 65, 88, 89, 90, 111, 121, 122, 123, 207
N. W. Pirie 171

O

Ontogeny recapitulates phylogeny 81
Osborne 270

P

parallel universes 306
Paramatman 305
peptidyl transferace 93
Philip Johnson 263
phospholipid 82, 157
photons 13, 45, 70
photosynthesis 145, 257
Planned Parenthood 19
polypeptide chain 94, 95, 103, 150
Ponnamperuma 4
prebiotic soup 145, 170, 183, 184, 186, 187, 197, 214, 215, 217, 219, 220
Principia Mathematica 32, 47
prokaryotes 78, 129
protein code 4, 125
protein enzymes 91, 192, 215, 224
protein predestination 197
proteins 26, 65, 78, 82, 83, 84, 85, 86, 90, 91, 93, 94, 95, 96, 97, 98, 99, 100,
        101, 102, 103, 104, 106, 107, 108, 111, 112, 113, 114, 122, 123, 124,
        125, 126, 127, 128, 129, 130, 131, 134, 135, 136, 137, 150, 151, 152,
        155, 156, 157, 158, 159, 161, 162, 163, 164, 166, 167, 168, 171, 172,
        177, 179, 180, 181, 184, 189, 192, 193, 194, 195, 196, 197, 198, 199,
        200, 202, 207, 208, 214, 217, 219, 220, 221, 222, 223, 225, 227, 230,
        240, 250, 258, 275, 276, 280, 293, 294, 296
protocytosol 190
punctuated equilibrium 252, 257, 259

Q

quarks 45, 64, 65, 67, 68, 69, 73, 74, 75

R

R. C. Sproul 282
reducing atmosphere 145, 159, 160, 167, 178, 181, 183, 185, 186
reductionists 4, 7, 15, 17, 52, 55, 201, 305, 306
ribose 215, 217, 218

ribosomes 86, 90, 92, 95, 133, 292
Richard Dawkins 204, 229, 230, 231, 232, 233, 234, 235, 236, 237, 301
Richard Lenski 238
Richard Tarnas 46
riddle of the 20 amino acids 99, 102
right-handed amino acids 113, 181
RNA 88, 89, 90, 91, 111, 129, 214
RNA mutants 226
RNA polymerase 87, 192
RNA world 214, 215, 217, 221, 222, 225, 226, 227
Robert Hooke 5
Robert Shapiro 216
Roe v. Wade 19
Roger Olsen 283

S

Schaeffer 37, 38, 50
scientism 49, 53, 54, 118, 265, 283, 284
sequence specificity 107, 109
Sheldon Glashow 76
Sidney W. Fox 180
simple complexity 105, 109, 290
simple life 60, 172
Sir Peter Medawar 150
space trash theory 273, 274, 276
Spark discharge 186
specified complexity 9, 194, 242, 269, 289, 290, 292, 293, 295, 297, 298, 299, 300
spontaneous generation 5, 6, 78, 81, 168, 172
Stalin 20
Stanley Miller 178, 184, 216
Stephen C. Meyer 128, 150
Stephen Hawking 65
Stephen Kleene 47
Steven Weinberg 76
strong nuclear force 70, 72

T

teleology 29, 40, 49, 50, 173, 237
Theodosius Dobzhansky 193
Thomas Brock 78
Thomas Schneider 237, 238
thymine 88, 205
Tielhard de Chardin 305
Tipler 66, 268, 304
transcription 91, 96, 130, 135, 156, 192, 199, 214, 281
translation 91, 92, 95, 123, 129, 131, 133, 156, 192, 221, 223, 224
transmembrane proteins 83
traps 185, 187, 188
tRNA 92, 93, 94, 95, 103, 129, 130, 131, 132, 189, 192, 207, 212, 213, 224
tyranny of paradigms 263

U

uniformitarian hypothesis 266, 307
uracil 88, 215, 216, 217
UV 185, 191

V

vestigial organs 55, 279, 280, 282
vitalists 7, 8, 201, 305, 306
Voyager 1 110, 111

W

Walter Gilbert 214
weak nuclear force 70
Wesley Smith 22, 264
W. H. Thorpe 45, 46
William Dembski 281, 290
William Smith 264
Wistar Conference 167

X

X-ray crystallography 106, 256

9 780996 244169